Healthcare Cybersecurity

Healthcare cybersecurity, privacy, and data protection are foundational to modern healthcare operations. Healthcare organizations operate in complex environments that rely on trusted virtual and physical access by both human and nonhuman entities, as well as an extensive network of vendors, service providers, and third parties that support clinical, administrative, and technical functions. Despite these challenges, everyone needs to work together to safeguard patient information, systems, networks, devices, applications, data, and other resources.

This book offers practical guidance for individuals involved in healthcare cybersecurity, privacy, and data protection, as well as international stakeholders.

Lee Kim (JD, CISSP, CIPP/US) is an AV Preeminent-rated attorney, registered patent attorney, consultant, and expert witness. She provides strategic guidance on cybersecurity, privacy, data protection, artificial intelligence, policy, and innovation. She serves as faculty at IANS Research and is a content contributor to the SANS Institute. She also previously served as a team leader and analyst in the U.S. Department of Homeland Security's Analytic Exchange Program.

Healthcare Cybersecurity, Privacy, and Data Protection

Present and Future

Lee Kim

Routledge
Taylor & Francis Group
A PRODUCTIVITY PRESS BOOK

Designed cover image: Shutterstock

First published 2026
by Routledge
605 Third Avenue, New York, NY 10158

and by Routledge
4 Park Square, Milton Park, Abingdon, Oxon, OX14 4RN

Routledge is an imprint of the Taylor & Francis Group, an informa business

ISBN: 978-1-032-43276-2 (hbk)
ISBN: 978-1-032-43274-8 (pbk)
ISBN: 978-1-003-36656-0 (ebk)

DOI: 10.4324/9781003366560

Typeset in Garamond
by Apex CoVantage, LLC

Contents

Disclaimer

This publication is provided strictly on an "as is" and "where is" basis, without warranties of any kind, either express or implied, including but not limited to any implied warranties of merchantability, fitness for a particular purpose, non-infringement, or accuracy.

The content is intended for general informational and educational purposes only and does not constitute legal, regulatory, technical, compliance, or any other form of professional advice. No attorney-client, fiduciary, or professional relationship is created through the use of this publication. Readers must seek appropriate counsel from qualified professionals for advice tailored to their specific legal, technical, or operational circumstances.

The author does not warrant or represent that the content is current, accurate, complete, or applicable to any particular fact pattern. Reliance on any information contained herein is strictly at the user's own risk. The author expressly disclaims all liability for any direct, indirect, incidental, consequential, or special loss, injury, or damage of any kind arising out of or in connection with the use of this publication or its contents.

All third-party trademarks, service marks, trade names, product names, and logos referenced in this publication are the property of their respective owners. Any such use is for identification purposes only and does not imply or constitute endorsement, sponsorship, affiliation, or approval by the trademark holder.

By accessing or using this publication, the user agrees to the terms of this disclaimer in full.

About the Author

Lee Kim (JD, CISSP, CIPP/US) is an AV Preeminent-rated attorney, registered patent attorney, cybersecurity and privacy consultant, and expert witness. She advises companies on cybersecurity, data protection, AI, policy, and innovation across diverse industries, ranging from Fortune 100 companies to smaller entities. She is a faculty member at IANS Research, a content contributor to the SANS Institute, and previously served as a team leader and analyst in the U.S. Department of Homeland Security's Analytic Exchange Program. The Public–Private Analytic Exchange Program was sponsored by the Department of Homeland Security's Office of Intelligence and Analysis on behalf of the Office of the Director of National Intelligence (ODNI).

Preface

The book begins with an introduction to cybersecurity in healthcare and the critical connection between cybersecurity and patient safety. It then examines identity, access management, and authentication; the evolution and impact of malware; and major breaches that have shaped current practices. Governance is addressed in depth, including HIPAA, the HITECH Act, Recognized Security Practices, and the NIST Privacy and Cybersecurity Frameworks. Practical scenarios illustrate how these principles can be applied in healthcare settings. The discussion also addresses board-level oversight; leadership culture; and the importance of robust policies, procedures, and organizational alignment.

Later chapters provide a focused discussion on social engineering attacks and their mitigation, the essential role of information sharing, and the growing influence of artificial intelligence. The final chapter looks ahead, exploring the challenges and opportunities presented by emerging technologies, including quantum readiness, mobile device security, and cloud computing.

Chapter 1

Introduction to Cybersecurity

1.1 Glossary of Common Cybersecurity Terms

The definitions in this glossary are adapted from the NIST Computer Security Resource Center (CSRC) glossary and related NIST documents, except as noted.[1]

Access control means the process of granting or denying access to a system, application, network, device, configuration, data, or other resource based on defined permissions for individual users, groups, or resources.

Accountability means the ability to trace actions within a system, application, network, device, configuration, data, or other resource to specific individuals who can be held responsible for those actions.

Administrative safeguards mean administrative controls such as policies, procedures, and plans that: manage the selection, development, implementation, and maintenance of security measures; govern the conduct of personnel; and

include activities such as security awareness and training; workforce security; and contingency planning to protect systems, applications, networks, devices, configurations, data, or other resources.

In the context of HIPAA, this refers to the administrative actions, policies, procedures, and plans that protect electronic protected health information (ePHI) and govern the conduct of a covered entity's or business associate's workforce in maintaining that protection.[2]

Advanced persistent threat means a type of sophisticated cyber threat characterized by a long-term, coordinated campaign carried out by attackers who are highly skilled and well-resourced and who use multiple methods to achieve their goals. These attackers aim to infiltrate an organization's systems, applications, networks, devices, configurations, data, or other resources and remain undetected for extended periods, enabling continued access, data theft, or disruption of operations.

Adversary means a person, group, organization, or government that conducts or has the intent to conduct activities that are detrimental to an individual, organization, or nation.

Antivirus means software designed to detect and prevent malware infections and to remove malicious software from computers that have already been compromised.

DOI: 10.4324/9781003366560-1

ARPANET means a network developed by the Advanced Research Projects Agency—a precursor to the internet.[3]

Asset means a resource that is valuable to an organization that must be protected.

Attack surface means a set of points within a system, application, network, device, configuration, data, or other resource where an attacker may attempt to gain access, cause an effect, or exfiltrate data.

Audit means an independent review and examination of records and activities to evaluate the effectiveness of controls applied to systems, applications, networks, devices, configurations, data, or other resources and to verify compliance with established policies and procedures.

Authentication means the process of verifying the identity of a user, process, or device before granting access.

Authorization means the process of granting or denying specific requests to access or use information, services, or facilities.

Availability means that systems, applications, networks, devices, configurations, data, or other resources are accessible and usable when needed by authorized users.

Breach generally means an impermissible use or disclosure that compromises the security or privacy of confidential, protected, proprietary, or sensitive information.[4] *While not all privacy or security incidents are breaches, some incidents may rise to the level of a breach. Breach notification requirements exist under federal, state, and international privacy, cybersecurity, and data protection laws.*

Business associate means a person or entity who creates, receives, maintains, or transmits protected health information (PHI) on behalf of the covered entity or another business associate, in accordance with the HIPAA regulations.[5]

Business associate agreement (also called a *business associate contract*) means a contract that a *covered entity* must establish with a *business associate* to ensure compliance with appropriate safeguards for protected health information.[6]

Ciphertext means data in its encrypted form.

Common Vulnerabilities and Exposures (CVE) means a catalog of publicly disclosed cybersecurity vulnerabilities.

Compensating controls means the security and privacy controls implemented to provide equivalent or comparable protection for systems, applications, networks, devices, configurations, data, or other resources.

Confidentiality means the protection of systems, applications, networks, devices, configurations, data, or other resources from unauthorized disclosure or access.

Countermeasures means the protective controls or safeguards prescribed to meet the security requirements (i.e., confidentiality, integrity, and availability) of systems, applications, networks, devices, configurations, data, or other resources. Countermeasures are synonymous with *security or privacy controls.*

Covered entity means (1) health plans, (2) healthcare clearinghouses, and (3) healthcare providers that electronically transmit health information in connection with transactions for which the U.S. Department of Health and Human Services has adopted standards.[7]

Critical infrastructure means the essential services and related assets that support American society and form the foundation of the nation's economy, security, and health. In the United States, critical infrastructure sectors are defined by Presidential Policy Directive 21 (PPD-21). These sectors represent vital assets, systems, and networks essential to national security, economy, and public health and safety. Critical infrastructure sectors include the following[8]:

- Chemical Sector
- Commercial Facilities Sector
- Communications Sector
- Critical Manufacturing Sector
- Dams Sector
- Defense Industrial Base Sector
- Emergency Services Sector
- Energy Sector
- Financial Services Sector
- Food and Agriculture Sector
- Government Facilities Sector
- Healthcare and Public Health Sector
- Information Technology Sector
- Nuclear Reactors, Materials, and Waste Sector
- Transportation Systems Sector
- Water and Wastewater Systems Sector

Cyberattack means an attack that affects an organization's systems, applications, networks, devices, configurations, data, or other resources by disrupting, disabling, destroying, or controlling them or by compromising the confidentiality, integrity, or availability of sensitive, protected, proprietary, or confidential information.

Cybersecurity means the practice of protecting systems, applications, networks, devices, configurations, data, or other resources from unauthorized access, disruption, or cyberattacks.

Data loss prevention means the tools and processes used to detect and prevent the unauthorized access, transmission, or exfiltration of confidential, sensitive, protected, or proprietary data from systems, applications, networks, devices, configurations, or other resources.

Decryption means the process of converting ciphertext into plaintext using a cryptographic algorithm and key.

Deepfake means a video, image, or audio recording that appears authentic but has been created or manipulated using artificial intelligence (AI), including faces, facial expressions, and speech—giving an impression that a person said or did something that did not occur.[9]

Defense-in-depth means the use of multiple countermeasures applied in layers to achieve security objectives, ensuring that if one measure fails or is bypassed, others may continue to protect systems, applications, networks, devices, configurations, data, or other resources.

Denial of service (also referred to as "DoS") means an attack that prevents legitimate users from accessing systems, applications, networks, devices, configurations, data, or other resources.[10]

Distributed denial of service (also referred to as "DDoS") means a denial of service attack that uses multiple compromised systems or devices, often part of a botnet, to overwhelm the capacity and disrupt the availability of systems, networks, applications, or devices.

Dwell time means the period between the initial compromise of a system or device and the detection of the intrusion by the organization. During this period, the attacker may move laterally within the network, gather information, escalate privileges, and position malware for further actions—such as data theft or ransomware deployment—often without being detected.

Electronic protected health information (ePHI) means protected health information in electronic form. ePHI may be created, received, transmitted, or maintained on a device, computer system, photocopier, or any other electronic medium.

Encryption means the process of changing plaintext into ciphertext using a cryptographic algorithm and key.

Encryption key means a piece of information—typically a string of bits—that is used by a cryptographic algorithm to transform plaintext into ciphertext.[11]

Endpoint means a device that resides at the edge of a network, such as a laptop, desktop, or mobile device.[12]

Entropy means a measure of the amount of uncertainty or randomness in a secret, including a password or cryptographic key.

Event means an occurrence within a system, application, network, device, configuration, data, or other resource. An event may be normal, potentially adverse, or actually adverse. Some events may be of little consequence, while others may be significant and result in an actual or potential adverse effect on systems, applications, networks, devices, configurations, data, or other resources.

Exposure means the extent to which an organization or stakeholder is subject to risk.

Exfiltration means the unauthorized transfer of data from a system, application, network, device, or other resource.

Exploit means a program or piece of code that takes advantage of a vulnerability in an application, system, device, network, or other resource—typically for malicious purposes.[13]

Failover means the capability to automatically switch when the primary system fails or terminates abnormally, typically without human intervention or warning.

Federated identity management means a process or system that enables identity and authentication information to be shared across systems, applications, networks, devices, or organizations.

Firewall means a control that monitors and filters network traffic to block unauthorized access and permit authorized inbound and outbound communication.

Foothold means a stable and persistent position established by an attacker that enables continued access to a compromised system or network without requiring repeated exploitation.[14]

Framework means a set of policies, guidelines, and best practices used to establish, implement, manage, and communicate an organization's information security risks.[15]

General phishing means a phishing attack that does not target specific individuals but is widely distributed to multiple recipients.[16]

Hacktivism means the use of hacking or cyber activities by individuals or groups to advance an ideological, social, or political cause.[17]

Hacktivist means an individual who engages in hacktivism.[18]

HIPAA means the Health Insurance Portability and Accountability Act of 1996. HIPAA is a federal statute that directs the U.S. Department of Health and Human Services to establish regulatory standards to protect the privacy and security of individually identifiable health information.

HIPAA Breach Notification Rule means an implementing regulation of HIPAA that requires covered entities and their business associates to notify affected individuals, the Secretary of Health and Human Services (HHS), and, in certain cases, the media, following a breach of unsecured protected health information (PHI). A breach is generally defined as an impermissible use or disclosure under the HIPAA Privacy Rule that compromises the security or privacy of PHI. However, there are specific exceptions to this definition.[19]

HIPAA Covered Entity (covered entity) means an individual or organization that falls into one of the following categories[20]:

- Healthcare providers: Any provider of medical or health services, or any other person or organization that furnishes, bills, or is paid for healthcare in the normal course of business.
- Health plans: Entities that provide or pay the cost of medical care, including health insurance companies, HMOs, company health plans, and government programs that pay for healthcare, such as Medicare, Medicaid, and military and veterans' health programs.
- Healthcare clearinghouses: Entities that process nonstandard health information they receive from another entity into a standard format, or vice versa.

HIPAA Business Associate (business associate) means a person or entity that performs certain functions or activities on behalf of, or provides services to, a covered entity that involve the use or disclosure of protected health information (PHI). This includes functions or activities such as claims processing, data analysis, utilization review, and billing. Services provided by business associates may include legal, actuarial, accounting, consulting, data aggregation, management, administrative, accreditation, or financial services. Members of the covered entity's workforce are not considered business associates.[21]

HIPAA Organized health care arrangement (organized health care arrangement) means any of the following, as set forth in 45 C.F.R. §160.03:

- A clinically integrated care setting in which individuals typically receive healthcare from more than one healthcare provider.
- An organized system of healthcare in which more than one covered entity participates, and in which the participating covered entities either hold themselves out to the public as participating in a joint arrangement and participate in joint activities that include at least one of the following activities: utilization review, quality assessment and improvement activities, and payment activities.
- Certain group health plans, health insurance issuers, or HMOs.

HIPAA Security Rule (45 C.F.R. Part 160 and Subparts A and C of Part 164) means the national standards that have been established to protect individuals' electronic protected health information (ePHI) that is created, received, used, or maintained by a covered entity or business associate. The HIPAA Security Rule requires the implementation of administrative, physical, and technical safeguards to ensure the confidentiality, integrity, and availability of ePHI.[22]

HIPAA Privacy Rule (45 C.F.R. Part 160 and Subparts A and E of Part 164) means the national standards that have been established to govern the use and disclosure of individuals' protected health information (PHI). The HIPAA Privacy Rule applies to covered entities and business associates.

Identification means the process of establishing a claimed identity of a user, system, application, network, device, or other resource, usually as a prerequisite for granting access. Additionally, identity verification may occur before identification to confirm that the identity as claimed is legitimate. Once an identity is established, authentication verifies that the entity accessing the resource is the same one as the claimed identity.

Incident means an occurrence that actually or potentially jeopardizes the confidentiality, integrity, or availability of a system, application, network, device, configuration, data, or other resource, or the information it creates, processes, receives, transmits, or maintains, or that constitutes a violation or imminent threat of violation of an organization's security policies or procedures.

Incident response means the process of incident handling. Incident handling includes the detection and analysis of an incident (e.g., determining whether an incident occurred and prioritizing its handling), as well as containing, eradicating, and recovering from the incident, followed by post-incident activities such as gathering lessons learned.[23]

Insider threat means a threat that arises when an individual with trusted virtual or physical access (or knowledge) intentionally or unintentionally harms or has the potential to harm an organization's security, assets, or operations. This includes actions such as espionage, terrorism, unauthorized disclosure of sensitive information, or compromising organizational resources. An individual who acts unintentionally is called a negligent insider. An example of a negligent insider is a person who ignores security awareness training or the security policies of an organization—or who accidentally exposes confidential, protected, proprietary, or sensitive information to others—but does not intend to cause harm to an organization. An individual who acts intentionally is called a malicious insider, and the motivations may include personal gain, revenge, or aiding an external party.[24]

Integrity means that information is protected from unauthorized modification, destruction, or loss to ensure it remains accurate and complete. When the integrity of information is compromised, it has been modified, destroyed, or corrupted without authorization.

Internet of Things (IoT) means wireless-enabled devices, sensors, actuators, microelectromechanical systems (MEMS), and related technologies—other than traditional computers, mobile devices, or tablets—that connect and exchange information via the internet or other networks.

Intrusion Detection means the process of monitoring the events occurring within systems, applications, networks, or devices and analyzing them for signs of possible incidents.

Intrusion Detection System means a system that monitors network traffic, system activity, logs, or other events to detect signs of malicious or unauthorized activity.

Intrusion Prevention means the process of monitoring the events occurring within systems, applications, networks, or devices, analyzing them for signs of possible incidents, and attempting to stop or mitigate detected threats.

Intrusion Prevention System means a system that can detect an intrusive activity and attempt to stop it, ideally before it reaches its target.

Legacy systems means systems that no longer have any ongoing support from the hardware and software vendor(s) that provided these solutions.[25]

Living off the land means the abuse or misuse of native tools and processes within systems, applications, networks, or devices—especially living off the land binaries (LOLBins)—to blend in with normal activity and operate discreetly, reducing the likelihood of detection or blocking. Cyber threat actors effectively use LOTL techniques across multiple environments, including on-premises, cloud, hybrid, Windows, Linux, and macOS platforms, because these native tools are already deployed and eliminate the need to develop and deploy custom tools.[26]

Malicious insider means an individual such as an employee, former employee, executive, contractor, business associate, or business partner, who has or had authorized access to systems, applications, networks, devices, configurations, data, or other resources and who intentionally exceeds or misuses that access to compromise the confidentiality, integrity, or availability of the organization's information or resources.[27]

Malware means malicious software or code that is covertly placed onto a computer or electronic device with the intent to compromise the confidentiality, integrity, or availability of systems, applications, networks, devices, configurations, data, or other resources. Common types of malware include viruses, worms, malicious mobile code, Trojan horses, rootkits, spyware, and some forms of adware.

Metrics means measures used to track progress, inform decision-making, and evaluate performance relative to defined objectives or targets.

Media sanitization means the process of rendering data stored on media unrecoverable by any means.

Nation-state actors means cyber threat actors sponsored or supported by a national government. These threat actors are typically motivated by political, economic, technical, or military objectives and may engage in industrial espionage or other cyber operations. They are often highly sophisticated and well-resourced.[28] In the United States, the primary nation-state actors have been identified by the Office of the Director of National Intelligence (ODNI) as Russia, China, Iran, and North Korea. These groups are capable of conducting sophisticated, targeted attacks. Their objectives may shift over time and may include espionage, data theft, ransomware operations, and financial crimes to support state interests. Nation-state actors also frequently target personally identifiable information (PII) for intelligence collection, espionage, or blackmail; steal intellectual property (IP); and engage in destructive activities[29] against specific organizations (e.g., ransomware or wiper malware) as retaliation for international sanctions or geopolitical actions.[30]

Negligent insider (also called an *unintentional* insider) means an individual—such as an employee, former employee, contractor, business associate, or business partner—who has or had authorized access to an organization's systems, applications, networks, devices, configurations, data, or other resources, and who, through action or inaction and without malicious intent, causes harm or increases the likelihood of future harm to the confidentiality, integrity, or availability of those resources.[31]

Network means an arrangement of interconnected systems and devices that communicate and exchange data through wired or wireless connections.

Non-repudiation means a security principle that ensures that an individual or entity cannot deny having performed a specific action such as sending a message, approving a transaction, or signing a document. Non-repudiation may be achieved through verifiable evidence of the action such as the use of cryptographic methods, digital signatures, or audit trails.

Non-state actor means any cyber threat actor—whether an individual or entity—that is not sponsored or supported by a national government.[32]

Operational technology means systems and devices that manage or interact with the physical environment. These systems and devices detect or cause direct change through the monitoring and/or control of devices, processes, and events. Examples include industrial control systems, building automation systems, physical access control systems, physical environment monitoring and measurement systems.

Patch means a software component that, when installed, directly modifies the existing components or code to address security bugs, resolve performance or operational issues, or improve functionality.

Personally identifiable information (PII) means information that can be used to identify or determine an individual's identity—such as name, social security number, and biometric data—either alone or when combined with other information that is linked or linkable to a specific individual.

Phishing means a social engineering tactic that is used to persuade individuals to provide sensitive information and/or take action through seemingly trustworthy communications.[33] Phishing may take various forms, such as email (email phishing), social media (social phishing), phishing websites, voice calls (voice phishing), text messages (smishing), and quishing (QR code phishing).

Physical safeguards mean physical controls, policies, and procedures that protect a system, application, network, device, configuration, data, or other resources from natural or manmade hazards and unauthorized intrusion. In the context of HIPAA, this refers to the protection of PHI and ePHI.[34]

Plaintext means information that is not encrypted.

Privilege escalation means obtaining a higher privilege level than is normally permitted by exploiting a weakness or vulnerability.

Protected health information (PHI) means information that is created, transmitted, received, or maintained by a covered entity or a business associate, including demographic information, which relates to the past, present, or future physical or mental health or condition of an individual; the provision of healthcare to an individual; or the past, present, or future payment for the provision of healthcare to an individual, together with certain identifiers that may identify the individual.

Push bombing (also called *MFA fatigue*) means an incident in which a cyber threat actor bombards a user with mobile application push notifications until the user either approves an authentication request by accident or due to fatigue from repeated or persistent prompts.[35]

Ransomware means a type of malware that denies or restricts access to a system, application, network, device, configuration, data, or other resource and demands payment of ransom.[36]

Ransomworm means a type of ransomware that autonomously propagates across systems, networks, and devices in a worm-like manner.[37] An example of a ransomworm is WannaCry. A ransomworm is also called a ransomware worm.

Replay attack means an attack that involves the capture of transmitted authentication or access control information and its subsequent retransmission with the intent of gaining unauthorized access or performing an unauthorized action.

Replay resistance means protection against the capture of transmitted authentication or access control information and its subsequent retransmission with the intent of gaining unauthorized access or performing an unauthorized action.

Resilience means the ability to prepare for, withstand, and recover after an incident.

Risk means a measure of the extent to which an entity is exposed to a potential threat or actual adverse event.

Risk analysis means the process of assessing the nature of risk and determining the level of risk.

Risk appetite means the level of risk an organization is willing to accept based on its resources and capabilities.

Risk assessment means the process of identifying risks to a system, application, network, device, configuration, data, or other resources.

Risk identification means the process of identifying and describing risks that could affect or impact a system, application, network, device, configuration, data, or other resources.

Risk landscape means the evolving set of risks that may affect an organization and its systems, applications, networks, devices, configurations, data, or other resources.[38]

Risk management means the process of managing risks to a system, application, network, device, configuration, data, or other resources, as well as to organizational assets, individuals, or other organizations. It includes (1) identifying risks, (2) conducting the risk assessment, (3) implementing a risk mitigation strategy, and (4) continuously monitoring and managing those risks.

Risk management strategy means a strategy that defines how an organization intends to identify, assess, respond to, monitor, and manage risks to its systems, applications, networks, devices, configurations, data, or other resources.

Risk mitigation means prioritizing, evaluating, and implementing the appropriate controls or countermeasures to reduce risks identified from the risk management process.

Risk profile means a prioritized summary of the most significant risks identified and evaluated through the risk assessment process.

Risk register means a repository of risk information that documents identified risks, their likelihood, potential impact, ownership, and the mitigation or response strategies and is maintained over time to reflect the current status of those risks.

Scareware means software or a component that is designed to trick users into thinking that their computer, laptop, or device is infected with malware or harmed. The user may be asked to provide payment information, download unnecessary software or malware, or take other actions based on false warnings.[39]

Safeguards means measures, such as controls and countermeasures, that are intended to mitigate vulnerabilities in a system, application, network, device, configuration, data, or other resources. Safeguards may be physical, technical, or administrative in nature.

Shadow AI means the use of AI services, software, tools, browsers, add-ons, extensions, or devices that are not approved, managed, or governed by an organization's IT department.[40]

Security awareness means activities or programs intended to educate users; reinforce good security practices; and promote behaviors that protect systems, applications, networks, devices, configurations, data, or other resources.

Security incident means an *incident*.

Separation of duty (SOD) means the principle that no single user should have sufficient privileges to perform actions independently of others.

Shadow IT means the use of IT services, software, tools, browsers, add-ons, extensions, or devices that are not approved, managed, or governed by an organization's IT department.[41]

Social engineering means the manipulation or deception of individuals to persuade them to disclose confidential, protected, proprietary, or sensitive information; grant unauthorized access; or perform actions that may compromise systems, applications, networks, devices, configurations, data, or other resources.

SP means Special Publication, a series of publications issued by NIST that provide information on research, guidelines, and best practices in computer security and information technology. For U.S. government agencies and federal contractors, these publications establish minimum mandatory standards; for other organizations, they serve as best practices.

Spear-phishing means a targeted phishing attack.[42]

Supply chain means the interconnected network of physical, digital, and organizational resources involved in producing, managing, and delivering goods and services from the origin to the customer. In the cybersecurity context, the supply chain includes technologies, vendors, and information systems whose interdependencies can create potential vulnerabilities. U.S. Department of Homeland Security, *U.S. Maritime Trade and Port Cybersecurity: Shoring Up Maritime Cybersecurity—Enhancing Cybersecurity and Resilience*, https://www.dhs.gov/sites/default/files/2024-09/2024aepphasellusmaritimetradeandportcybersecurity.pdf.

Synthetic media means media generated or modified using AI, intended to appear realistic or immersive in nature.[43]

Technical safeguard means technical controls that protect confidential, protected, proprietary, or sensitive information. In the context of HIPAA, this refers to the technical controls used to protect electronic protected health information (ePHI) and control access to it, including access, audit, integrity, authentication, and transmission controls.[44]

Threat means anything with the potential to cause harm to confidential, protected, proprietary, or sensitive information or to a system, application, network, device, configuration, data, or other resources by exploiting vulnerabilities or weaknesses.

Threat actor means an individual or group that causes, or has the potential to cause, harm to a system, application, network, device, configuration, data, or other resource, whether intentionally or unintentionally.

Threat intelligence means vetted threat information that may support decision-making and defensive actions and measures, including tactical and strategic purposes.

Threat vector means the method or pathway an attacker uses to exploit a vulnerability or weakness or gain unauthorized access to confidential, protected, proprietary, or sensitive information or to a system, application, network, device, configuration, data, or other resource.[45]

Token means a physical or logical object that a user possesses or controls, such as a cryptographic key, hardware token, smart card, or authenticator app, used to support authentication.

Trojan horse means a type of malware that appears to perform a legitimate function but secretly performs malicious actions, often by disguising itself as a component of a trusted program or process.

Virus means a type of malware that embeds in or attaches to a legitimate component such as a program, file, process, boot sector, or firmware. A virus becomes active when the infected component runs or is otherwise triggered. Unlike a worm, a virus cannot propagate on its own. A virus may also conceal itself through techniques such as rootkits or firmware infection.

Vulnerability means a weakness or flaw in a system, application, network, device, configuration or in the physical, technical, or administrative safeguards that protect confidential, protected, proprietary, or sensitive information or a system, application, network, device, configuration, data, or other resource that may be exploited by a threat actor.

Whaling means a targeted phishing attack that is aimed at wealthy, powerful, or prominent individuals, including C-suite executives such as chief financial officers (CFO), chief executive officers (CEO), and politicians.[46]

Worm means a type of malware that self-replicates and propagates through networks, systems, or devices without requiring a host program or user interaction.

1.2 What Is Healthcare Cybersecurity?

Healthcare cybersecurity refers to the strategies, safeguards, and processes that are used to protect information, applications, devices, systems, and technology infrastructure from unauthorized access, use, disclosure, damage, or disruption.

"Healthcare" broadly refers to the healthcare and public health (HPH) sector. HPH sector stakeholders include healthcare facilities, research centers, suppliers, and manufacturers.[47] These stakeholders represent the following subsectors: direct patient care, health information technology, health plans and payers, mass fatality management services, medical materials, laboratories, blood banks, pharmaceutical companies, and public health programs. The U.S. Department of Health and Human Services has a central role in oversight and support of the HPH sector. HHS helps to ensure that these subsectors work together effectively to promote public health, care delivery, and emergency response.[48]

1.2.1 HPH Subsectors: Components That Form the Entire Healthcare Ecosystem

The subsectors within the healthcare ecosystem operate in unison to deliver the products and services essential to the provision of care. At the heart of this collaboration is the shared goal of benefiting patients, whether through lifesaving interventions or life-sustaining resources. Each subsector plays an indispensable role in supporting the delivery of care, forming a tightly interconnected network.

Direct care providers—such as hospitals, physician practices, long-term care facilities, ambulatory surgical centers, and clinics—are responsible for patient-facing services. However, their ability to function depends on how well other HPH subsectors are functioning. These include health plans and payers, laboratories and blood banks, and pharmaceutical companies. But healthcare organizations also depend on almost all other critical infrastructure sectors in order to function properly, such as water, electrical, manufacturing, information technology, telecommunications, transportation, and others.[49]

Every HPH subsector handles patient information, intellectual property, and/or other sensitive data—essential components that form the foundation of patient care. This information is critical yet inherently vulnerable without proper safeguards. Without adequate protection, data can be altered, erased, destroyed, or commingled, jeopardizing the integrity and availability of the data. Whether an HPH subsector provides direct patient care or supports care delivery through products or services, protecting information is crucial to maintaining a well-functioning healthcare ecosystem. Due to technological advances and the increased digitization of information across the HPH subsectors, healthcare cybersecurity is now more important than ever before.

Healthcare cybersecurity focuses on the protection of the digital infrastructure and information assets that enable clinical, operational, and administrative functions. It ensures that sensitive information, critical devices, and interconnected systems stay safe from cyber threats. Robust healthcare cybersecurity is vital to protecting patient safety and patient data, while ensuring the normal, safe operations of technology, assets, and infrastructure.

1.3 Cybersecurity Goals

The primary goals of healthcare cybersecurity revolve around the CIA triad—confidentiality, integrity, and availability. Confidentiality ensures that sensitive patient information is not accessed by unauthorized individuals. Integrity ensures that healthcare data is accurate and unaltered. Availability ensures that healthcare information and systems are accessible when needed (Figure 1.1).

An attack on *confidentiality* occurs when sensitive information, applications, devices, systems, or technology infrastructure are accessed, disclosed, or exposed to an unauthorized individual, entity, or process. Examples of attacks on confidentiality include data breaches, unauthorized access to files, interception of communications, and eavesdropping.

An attack on *integrity* means that information has been altered, tampered with, or otherwise corrupted by an unauthorized individual or entity. Specifically, NIST characterizes an attack on integrity as the unauthorized insertion, deletion, or modification of data in corporate information such as emails, employee records, financial records, and customer data.[50]

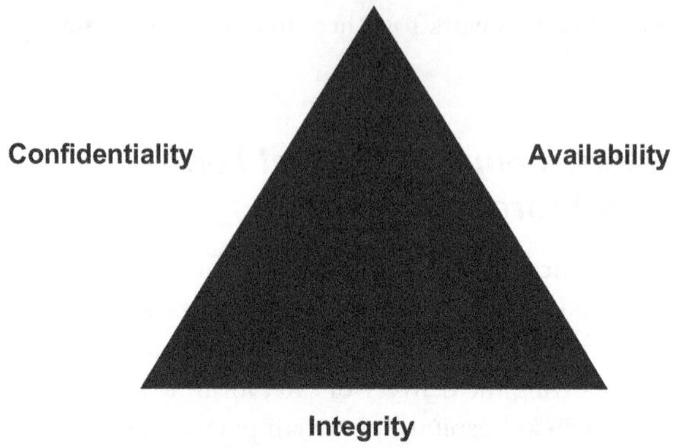

Figure 1.1 Confidentiality, integrity, and availability (CIA) triad.

An example of an attack on integrity is when a patient's medication list is altered without authorization by a cyberattacker. A clinician might unwittingly rely on incorrect data, and this may pose a risk to the patient who is under the clinician's care.

An attack on *availability* means that a network, system, device, or information has been rendered inaccessible or unavailable. An example of an attack on availability is a distributed denial-of-service attack. Yet another example is a ransomware attack, as the data held hostage is not accessible to authorized users.

A cyberattack may compromise one, two, or all three components of the *CIA triad* (confidentiality, integrity, and availability).

1.4 Cybersecurity Is Vital for Patient Safety

In the interconnected world of modern healthcare, patient safety and cybersecurity are intrinsically linked. While patient safety focuses on ensuring that individuals receive care without harm or adverse outcomes, cybersecurity protects the systems, devices, and information that are essential for healthcare delivery and the coordination of care.

Patient safety encompasses everything from infection control and accurate medication administration to timely interventions and reliable communication of information. Technology has become an indispensable tool in achieving these goals, enabling advances such as remote patient monitoring, EHRs, telemedicine, and the Internet of Medical Things (IoMT).

While improvements in technology are aimed at overcoming limitations in the current state of the art, technology is not immune to vulnerabilities, which can be introduced either unintentionally or intentionally. For instance, a backdoor—an intentional bypass of normal authentication or security controls—might be embedded in computer code to allow programmers to debug the software that they develop. However, implementing backdoors is not a security best practice due to the risk that malicious actors may access them.[51]

Backdoors can be exploited by malicious actors if discovered, granting unauthorized access to systems and data. In some cases, backdoors may be added unintentionally, such as through poorly written code or weak default configurations. Intentional backdoors, whether for debugging, surveillance, or maintenance, pose ethical and security dilemmas, as they can be weaponized if not strictly controlled. However, there have also been instances of backdoors being maliciously placed into code, which then could be exploited by bad actors (unless they are detected before this occurs).[52]

The existence of backdoor vulnerabilities underscores the need for robust security measures, including code reviews, penetration testing, and adherence to secure development practices, to minimize risks and protect against exploitation.

Cybersecurity, once considered primarily a concern of IT departments, is now a critical component of patient safety. At its core, cybersecurity ensures the confidentiality, integrity, and availability of healthcare data, systems, and devices. When these elements are compromised, the repercussions can extend far beyond operational disruptions—they can endanger the lives of patients. At least one study has documented the correlation between an increase in patient mortality and ransomware attacks.[53]

The integrity of patient data is vital to accurate diagnosis, treatment, and continuity of care. EHRs, for example, provide a centralized repository of patient information that clinicians rely on for making informed decisions. If cyberattacks compromise these records—by altering, erasing, or corrupting data—the consequences can be catastrophic. A minor alteration in a patient's allergy information or medication history could lead to a life-threatening medical error. For example, a patient can have a severe allergic reaction to a medication that may lead to serious illness, harm, or death. If this information is not available, for whatever reason, there can be a significant risk to the patient's life and well-being.

1.4.1 Medical Devices and Patient Safety

Medical devices, including pacemakers, insulin pumps, ventilators, and imaging machines, are increasingly connected to healthcare networks. While this connectivity enhances their functionality and allows for real-time monitoring, it also makes them vulnerable to cyber threats. A successful cyberattack on a medical device can have direct, physical consequences for patients, particularly when the medical device is connected to the organization's network. This is especially true if a patient is directly connected to a medical device.[54]

For instance, a compromised insulin pump could administer incorrect dosages, causing hypoglycemia or hyperglycemia. Similarly, a hacked pacemaker could disrupt its rhythm-regulating function, endangering the patient's life. The threat is not theoretical—researchers and hackers have demonstrated the feasibility of exploiting vulnerabilities in medical devices, underscoring the urgent need for robust cybersecurity measures.[55]

1.5 Cybersecurity Is a Shared Responsibility

Cybersecurity is not a one-size-fits-all discipline. Each role within a healthcare organization encounters unique risks, responsibilities, and access to information. For this reason, cybersecurity best practices must be tailored to the specific functions and duties of individuals across the organization. Training that is both role-specific and relevant to daily workflows helps bridge the gap between technical safeguards and human behavior, enabling a more resilient cybersecurity posture across all departments.

Human resources (HR) personnel are responsible for managing highly sensitive personal data, including employee records, disciplinary actions, and payroll information. Because of this, HR teams are common targets for phishing attacks and social engineering tactics that aim to exploit trust or gain unauthorized access to internal systems. HR staff must be trained in data protection laws and regulations such as HIPAA and the European Union General Data Protection Regulation (GDPR) and must understand the importance of securing personally identifiable information through encryption and access controls. Training should also address the risks associated with recruitment platforms, as attackers may attempt to use fake job applications or compromised resumes to deliver malware. HR personnel should understand how to securely onboard and offboard employees, including prompt deactivation of access credentials, and must be capable of reporting and responding to suspected data breaches.

Legal teams operate at the intersection of regulatory compliance, sensitive data, and privileged communication. Their access to contracts, litigation records, and corporate strategies makes them a high-value target for cyber espionage, ransomware, and insider threats. Legal staff must be trained in secure communication practices, including the use of encrypted email and secure document-sharing platforms. Training should also cover document handling procedures that prevent unauthorized disclosures and insider misuse. In the event of a breach, legal teams are essential to preserving digital evidence and fulfilling breach notification requirements. Legal teams need to stay informed about applicable privacy, cybersecurity, and data protection laws such as the California Consumer Privacy Act of 2018 (CCPA), Sarbanes-Oxley Act of 2002 (SOX), and others, to ensure the organization remains compliant.

IT and cybersecurity teams bear primary responsibility for implementing, maintaining, and monitoring the technical aspects of security. These teams need to routinely test and update incident response, disaster recovery, and business continuity playbooks, plans, policies, and procedures; conduct forensic investigations when breaches occur; and lead vulnerability management efforts, including patching, penetration testing, and system hardening. Additionally, application development (AppDev) teams need to adopt secure development practices and integrate development, security, and operations (DevSecOps) methodologies and tools. Cybersecurity teams, working with the vendor management office, need to evaluate third-party risk to ensure that vendors and partners meet the organization's security standards.

Executive leadership, including the C-suite, faces a different set of cybersecurity challenges. Executives are often the targets of spear-phishing and whaling attacks because of their access to strategic data and high-level authorizations. As leaders, they must understand the broader implications of cybersecurity risk, including financial, operational, and reputational consequences. Training for executives should focus on recognizing targeted threats, enforcing secure mobile and remote access policies, and maintaining awareness of cybersecurity insurance coverage. Executives are also critical during incident response efforts, where they are responsible for decision-making, crisis communication, and sustaining a security-conscious organizational culture.

Finance and accounting teams manage systems that are frequently targeted in fraud schemes, including business email compromise and ransomware. They are custodians of banking credentials, financial records, and payment processing systems. Training for these departments should emphasize fraud detection techniques, secure handling of financial information, and procedures for verifying payment instructions through secondary channels. Staff should also be familiar with regulatory requirements such as Payment Card Industry Data Security Standard (PCI DSS) for credit card data and anti-money laundering protocols. In the event of a financial data compromise, finance teams must understand how to report and respond appropriately to the incident.

The general workforce—comprising clinical staff, administrative personnel, and other support roles—also plays a vital part in organizational cybersecurity. Every employee is a potential entry point for cyber threats, making broad-based training essential. All staff should understand basic password hygiene, how to recognize phishing emails and suspicious links, and how to secure devices in line with organizational policies. Employees must also be trained in data classification and secure file handling procedures. The goal is to foster a baseline level of security awareness and to empower employees to act as the first line of defense.

To deliver effective cybersecurity training, organizations should design role-specific modules that address the scenarios and threats most relevant to each group. Interactive simulations, such as phishing tests and incident walkthroughs, can improve engagement and retention. Training content must be updated regularly to address new and emerging threats and legal, regulatory, and contractual changes. Measuring employee performance through assessments and monitoring progress over time can help identify areas requiring reinforcement.

By integrating cybersecurity responsibilities into the existing roles individuals already have, organizations can cultivate a security-minded culture. When training is aligned with day-to-day operations, it reinforces accountability and equips each employee with the knowledge and skills necessary to protect both the organization and the patients it serves.

1.6 Resources

The following are resources that may be useful for healthcare privacy, cybersecurity, and data protection professionals and others who wish to learn more about healthcare cybersecurity, regardless of their level of experience and knowledge. This is not an exhaustive list, but it provides a curated list of informative references:

1.6.1 Health Sector Cybersecurity Coordination Center—U.S. Department of Health and Human Services (HHS HC3)

The U.S. Department of Health and Human Services Health Sector Cybersecurity Coordination Center (HHS HC3) issues sector-specific threat intelligence, alerts, and advisories tailored to the HPH sector. It plays a key role in tracking ongoing campaigns and emerging cyber threats. The HHS HC3 resource center provides threat bulletins, briefs, and other informative resources. U.S. Department of Health and Human Services. *Health Sector Cybersecurity Coordination Center (HC3).* https://www.hhs.gov/about/agencies/asa/ocio/hc3/index.html.

1.6.2 HIPAA for Professionals

This guidance from HHS sets forth the key regulatory components of HIPAA, including the Privacy Rule, Security Rule, the Breach Notification Rule, and the Enforcement Rule. HHS. *HIPAA for Professionals.* https://www.hhs.gov/hipaa/for-professionals/index.html.

1.6.3 405(d) Program—Health Industry Cybersecurity Practices (HICP)

The HICP is the foundational guidance developed through the HHS 405(d) Program and the Health Sector Coordinating Council (HSCC). HICP outlines practical, threat-based recommendations for healthcare organizations of all sizes, focusing on common threats such as phishing, ransomware, data loss, and attacks on medical devices. HHS 405(d) Program. *Health Industry Cybersecurity Practices.* https://405d.hhs.gov/cornerstone/hicp.

See also HHS 405(d) Program. *Health Industry Cybersecurity Practices: Managing Threats and Protecting Patients.* https://405d.hhs.gov/Documents/HICP-Main-508.pdf.

See also HHS 405(d) Program. *Technical Volume 1—Cybersecurity Practices for Small Healthcare Organizations.* https://405d.hhs.gov/Documents/tech-vol1-508.pdf.

See also HHS 405(d) Program. *Technical Volume 2—Cybersecurity Practices for Medium and Large Health Care Organizations.* https://405d.hhs.gov/Documents/tech-vol2-508.pdf.

See also HHS 405(d) Program. *Resource Library*. https://405d.hhs.gov/resources/publications.

1.6.4 NIST Special Publications—800 Series

The NIST Special Publications 800 series provides essential standards and guidelines. Two examples of NIST Special Publications from the 800 Series are the following:

- NIST SP 800–66 Revision 2 offers mappings of the HIPAA Security Rule's *standards* and *implementation specifications* to NIST Cybersecurity Framework Subcategories and NIST SP 800–53 Revision 5 security controls.
  - NIST. *NIST SP 800–66 Rev. 2: Implementing the Health Insurance Portability and Accountability Act (HIPAA) Security Rule: A Cybersecurity Resource Guide*. https://csrc.nist.gov/pubs/sp/800/66/r2/final.
- NIST Special Publication 800–53 Revision 5 provides a structured catalog of security and privacy controls that organizations can use to assess risk and select appropriate safeguards for their information systems.[56]

1.6.5 NIST Special Publications—1800 Series

The NIST SP 1800 series includes cybersecurity practice guides developed by the National Cybersecurity Center of Excellence (NCCoE). These are practical reference architectures based on real-world use cases and include healthcare-specific implementations. Example guides include securing telehealth platforms, protecting EHRs, and managing clinical device cybersecurity. The full library of guides can be found at https://www.nccoe.nist.gov/library. The NCCoE also maintains a healthcare-specific portal at https://www.nccoe.nist.gov/healthcare.

1.6.6 HPH Sector Cybersecurity Framework Implementation Guide

The HPH Sector Cybersecurity Framework Implementation Guide (Version 2, March 2023), published by the HHS Office of the Assistant Secretary for Preparedness and Response (HHS ASPR), provides tailored guidance to help HPH sector organizations implement the NIST Cybersecurity Framework (CSF) effectively.

HHS Office of the Assistant Secretary for Preparedness and Response (HHS ASPR). *HPH Sector Cybersecurity Framework Implementation Guide*. https://aspr.hhs.gov/cip/hph-cybersecurity-framework-implementation-guide/Pages/default.aspx.

1.6.7 Healthcare and Public Health Sector Cybersecurity Performance Goals (CPGs)

The HPH Sector Cybersecurity Performance Goals (CPGs), developed by the Department of HHS in collaboration with the Cybersecurity and Infrastructure Security Agency (CISA), provide voluntary cybersecurity practices that healthcare organizations can prioritize to strengthen their cyber preparedness and resilience. These goals are intended to help the sector respond to the evolving cyber threat landscape and protect both patient safety and health information. The HPH CPGs are informed by existing federal guidance and industry-recognized frameworks, including the Healthcare Industry Cybersecurity Practices (HICP), the NIST CSF, the Healthcare and Public Health Sector Cybersecurity Framework Implementation Guide, and the National Cybersecurity

Strategy. HHS. *Healthcare and Public Health Sector Cybersecurity Performance Goals (HPH CPGs).* https://hhscyber.hhs.gov/performance-goals.html.

1.6.8 ASPR RISC 2.0 Toolkit

The Administration for Strategic Preparedness and Response is a division within HHS (HHS ASPR), which is responsible for leading the nation's medical and public health preparedness, response, and recovery efforts for disasters and emergencies. HHS ASPR monitors the threat landscape and works to ensure that the healthcare system is ready to respond to a wide range of incidents, whether natural or manmade.[57]

Risk Identification and Site Criticality (RISC) 2.0 Toolkit is an objective, data-driven, all-hazards risk assessment that can be used by public and private organizations within the HPH Sector to inform emergency preparedness planning, risk management activities, and resource investments. The RISC 2.0 Toolkit provides owners and operators in the HPH Sector with nationally recognized standards-based evaluation criteria for self-assessment in an easy-to-follow, guided format. The RISC 2.0 Toolkit provides healthcare organizations of all types and sizes with a web-based, objective, data-driven, all-hazards risk assessment.

HHS ASPR. *Risk Identification and Site Criticality (RISC) 2.0 Toolkit.* https://aspr.hhs.gov/RISC/Pages/default.aspx.

According to the U.S. Department of HHS, the RISC 2.0 Toolkit contains three self-assessment modules to do the following[58]:

- Identify external threats and internal hazards specific to their site by using objective national-level data
- Assess the vulnerability of their site based on industry standards and guidance
- Evaluate the criticality of and consequences to their site in the event of an incident

Additionally, as stated by HHS ASPR:

> The RISC Toolkit compares multiple facilities across systems, coalitions, and regions to identify dependencies and interdependencies in a consistent and repeatable method to help create a more resilient healthcare system.[59]

1.6.9 NIST Cybersecurity Framework Version 2.0

The NIST Cybersecurity Framework version 2.0 (CSF) provides a comprehensive structure for managing and communicating cybersecurity risks. The framework is organized around six core functions: Govern, Identify, Protect, Detect, Respond, and Recover. Cybersecurity supply chain risk management (C-SCRM) is addressed as a specific category within the Govern function, reflecting its strategic importance. The CSF is widely adopted across the HPH Sector and other sectors and industries. NIST. *Cybersecurity Framework.* https://www.nist.gov/cyberframework.

1.6.10 NIST National Vulnerability Database

The NIST National Vulnerability Database (NVD) provides a central resource for known software vulnerabilities using the Common Vulnerabilities and Exposures (CVE) and the Common

Vulnerability Scoring System (CVSS) scoring systems. It supports asset and patch management processes. NIST. *National Vulnerability Database (NVD).* https://nvd.nist.gov.

1.6.11 NIST Special Publications

NIST has developed guidelines, technical specifications, recommendations, and reference materials, comprising multiple subseries[60]:

- SP 800 Computer security
- SP 1800 Cybersecurity practice guides
- SP 500 Information technology

1.6.12 European Vulnerability Database

The European Vulnerability Database (EUVD) is maintained by the European Union Agency for Cybersecurity (ENISA). ENISA. *European Union Vulnerability Database (EUVD).* https://euvd.enisa.europa.eu/.

1.6.13 ISO/IEC International Standards

- ISO 14971:2019 sets forth terminology, principles, and a process for risk management of medical devices, including software as a medical device and in vitro diagnostic medical devices.[61]
- The ISO/IEC 27000 series of standards consists of internationally recognized standards for information security management systems (ISMS) and their requirements.[62]
- ISO/IEC 27001 provides guidance for establishing, implementing, maintaining, and continually improving an ISMS.[63]
- ISO/IEC 27002 is an international standard that provides guidance for organizations on establishing, implementing, and improving an ISMS focused on cybersecurity and provides best practices and control objectives related to key cybersecurity aspects, including access control, cryptography, human resource security, and incident response.[64]
- ISO 27799:2025 provides guidelines for information security standards and information security management practices, such as the selection, implementation, and management of controls within the context of the environment.[65]
- ISO/IEC 81001–1 provides the principles, concepts, terms, and definitions for health software and health IT systems, including key properties of safety, effectiveness, and security, across the full life cycle (including end-of-life).[66]
- ISO/TS 81001-2-1:2025 provides requirements and gives guidance on assurance case framework for healthcare delivery organizations (HDOs) and for health software and medical device manufacturers.[67]
- IEC 81001-5-1:2021 provides life cycle requirements for the development and maintenance of health software.[68]

1.6.14 ANSI/NEMA HN 1–2019

The Manufacturer Disclosure Statement for Medical Device Security (MDS^2) (also referred to as MDS2) is a standardized form developed to support transparency between medical device manufacturers and HDOs. It enables medical device manufacturers to communicate the cybersecurity characteristics of their devices in a standardized format and supports healthcare organizations in assessing the associated security risks as part of procurement and risk management processes.[69] MDS² forms—while voluntary—are typically made available by medical device manufacturers and may be available for download from their official websites or obtained by contacting them directly.

1.6.15 NIST Privacy Framework

The NIST Privacy Framework is designed to help organizations manage privacy risk. It aligns with the NIST CSF—as well as other NIST resources—and supports integration into enterprise risk management strategies. NIST. *Privacy Framework*. https://www.nist.gov/privacy-framework.

1.6.16 CISA

CISA provides a wide range of free tools, threat alerts, and best practices. https://www.cisa.gov/.

1.6.17 MITRE ATT&CK® Knowledge Base

The MITRE ATT&CK® knowledge base is a collection of adversary tactics and techniques based on real-world observations, providing a structured model for analyzing cybersecurity threats. MITRE Corporation. *MITRE ATT&CK® knowledge base*. https://attack.mitre.org.[70]

1.6.18 FDA Cybersecurity Resources

The U.S. Food and Drug Administration (FDA) maintains a centralized cybersecurity resource page with premarket and postmarket guidance, policy updates, and alerts related to medical device security. U.S. Food and Drug Administration. *Cybersecurity*. https://www.fda.gov/medical-devices/digital-health-center-excellence/cybersecurity.[71]

1.6.19 HPH Cyber Gateway

The HPH Cyber Gateway connects the HPH Sector with healthcare-specific cybersecurity information and resources from across HHS and other federal agencies. HHS. *HHS Cyber Gateway*. https://hhscyber.hhs.gov/.

1.6.20 International Medical Device Regulators Forum

The International Medical Device Regulators Forum (IMDRF) is a voluntary group of medical device regulators from around the world. It develops guidance documents on a range of topics, including cybersecurity for medical devices, to promote regulatory harmonization and support patient safety across jurisdictions.[72]

1.6.21 Software Bill of Materials (SBOM)

An SBOM is a detailed inventory of the components that make up a software system, including third-party libraries, open-source modules, and proprietary code. SBOMs are used for software applications as well as medical devices and other embedded technologies. In healthcare, this helps identify whether a system, device, application, or other resource includes vulnerable or outdated components.

CISA leads SBOM development and implementation efforts across government and industry. CISA. *Software Bill of Materials (SBOM).* https://www.cisa.gov/sbom.

The FDA specifically recommends that medical device manufacturers include SBOMs in their cybersecurity submissions for premarket approval. FDA. *Guidance for Industry and Food and Drug Administration Staff.* https://www.fda.gov/regulatory-information/search-fda-guidance-documents/cybersecurity-medical-devices-quality-system-considerations-and-content-premarket-submissions.

1.6.22 Postmarket Management of Cybersecurity in Medical Devices

The FDA issued the Postmarket Management of Cybersecurity in Medical Devices guidance to explain how medical device manufacturers should identify, assess, and remediate cybersecurity vulnerabilities in medical devices after they have been released to the market. FDA. *Postmarket Management of Cybersecurity in Medical Devices.* https://www.fda.gov/regulatory-information/search-fda-guidance-documents/postmarket-management-cybersecurity-medical-devices.

1.6.23 Stop Ransomware

Stop Ransomware is the U.S. government's centralized resource for ransomware prevention, response, and recovery. CISA. *Stop Ransomware.* https://www.cisa.gov/stopransomware.[73]

1.6.24 No More Ransom

The No More Ransom project is a public–private partnership among Europol, law enforcement agencies, and cybersecurity companies. It provides free ransomware decryption tools, prevention resources, and victim assistance in multiple languages.[74]

1.7 Summary—Introduction to Cybersecurity

Healthcare cybersecurity protects the systems, data, and technologies that support patient care in the HPH sector. Its importance has never been greater, as the sector faces growing threats that place patient privacy, safety, and the security of data at risk. The goals of healthcare cybersecurity extend beyond compliance, focusing on safeguarding the confidentiality, integrity, and availability of information essential for safe and effective care.

HIT is central to modern healthcare delivery, but its increasing complexity creates more opportunities for compromise. Medical devices, in particular, present unique risks, as their disruption can directly impact patient safety. Addressing these challenges requires viewing cybersecurity as a shared responsibility that involves IT and security professionals as well as clinicians, administrators, leadership, and others.

Practical guidance helps professionals and other stakeholders take meaningful steps to strengthen resilience. By applying proven practices, fostering a culture of awareness, and aligning with sector-specific frameworks, healthcare organizations can better protect patients, reduce risk, and ensure continuity of care in an increasingly digital environment.

Notes

1 National Institute of Standards and Technology (NIST). *Glossary*. NIST Computer Security Resource Center. https://csrc.nist.gov/glossary.

2 45 C.F.R. § 164.304 (2025), definition of "administrative safeguards," as set forth in the HIPAA Security Rule.

3 Britannica. *ARPANET.* https://www.britannica.com/topic/ARPANET.

4 U.S. Department of Health and Human Services (HHS). *Breach Notification Rule.* https://www.hhs.gov/hipaa/for-professionals/breach-notification/index.html.
See also 45 C.F.R. § 164.402 (2025) for the definition of "breach."

5 U.S. Department of Health and Human Services. Business Associates. https://www.hhs.gov/hipaa/for-professionals/privacy/guidance/business-associates/index.html.
See also 45 C.F.R. § 160.103 (2025) for the definition of "business associate."

6 U.S. Department of Health and Human Services. Business Associates. https://www.hhs.gov/hipaa/for-professionals/privacy/guidance/business-associates/index.html.
See also 45 C.F.R. § 164.504 (2025) for the requirements of business associate contracts (also called business associate agreements).

7 U.S. Department of Health and Human Services. *Covered Entities and Business Associates.* https://www.hhs.gov/hipaa/for-professionals/covered-entities/index.html.
See also 45 C.F.R. § 160.103 (2025) for the definition of "covered entity."

8 The White House. *Presidential Policy Directive—Critical Infrastructure Security and Resilience (PPD-21)*, February 12, 2013. https://obamawhitehouse.archives.gov/the-press-office/2013/02/12/presidential-policy-directive-critical-infrastructure-security-and-resil. See also https://www.cisa.gov/topics/critical-infrastructure-security-and-resilience/critical-infrastructure-sectors for a current list of critical infrastructure sectors.

9 U.S. Government Accountability Office (GAO). *GAO-20-379SP: Science & Tech Spotlight: Deepfakes.* https://www.gao.gov/assets/gao-20-379sp.pdf.

10 CISA. *Understanding Denial-of-Service Attacks.* https://www.cisa.gov/news-events/news/understanding-denial-service-attacks.

11 NordVPN. *Encryption Key.* https://nordvpn.com/cybersecurity/glossary/encryption-key/.

12 NIST. *NIST SP 800-128: Guide for Security-Focused Configuration Management of Information Systems.* https://nvlpubs.nist.gov/nistpubs/SpecialPublications/NIST.SP.800-128.pdf.

13 MITRE Corporation. *Tactic—TA0003: Persistence.* https://attack.mitre.org/tactics/TA0003/.

14 MITRE Corporation. *Tactic—TA0003: Persistence.* https://attack.mitre.org/tactics/TA0003/.

15 OneTrust. *Understanding IT Security Frameworks: Types and Examples.* https://www.onetrust.com/blog/security-framework-types/.

16 Public-Private Analytic Exchange Program. *Phishing—Don't be Phooled!* https://www.hsdl.org/c/view?docid=820189.

17 Federal Bureau of Investigation (FBI). *Private Industry Notification 20221104-001: Hacktivists Use of DDoS Activity Causes Minor Impacts.* https://www.ic3.gov/CSA/2022/221104.pdf.

18 HHS. *Types of Threat Actors That Threaten the Healthcare Sector.* https://www.hhs.gov/sites/default/files/types-threat-actors-threaten-healthcare.pdf.

19 HHS. *Breach Notification Rule.* https://www.hhs.gov/hipaa/for-professionals/breach-notification/index.html.

20 HHS. *Covered Entities and Business Associates.* https://www.hhs.gov/hipaa/for-professionals/covered-entities/index.html.

21 HHS. *HIPAA Guidance Materials.* https://www.hhs.gov/hipaa/for-professionals/privacy/guidance/business-associates/index.html.

22 HHS. *The Security Rule.* https://www.hhs.gov/hipaa/for-professionals/security/index.html.

23 NIST. *NIST SP 800-61 Rev. 3: Incident Response Recommendations and Considerations for Cybersecurity Risk Management.* https://nvlpubs.nist.gov/nistpubs/SpecialPublications/NIST.SP.800-61r3.pdf.

24 CISA. *Defining Insider Threats.* https://www.cisa.gov/topics/physical-security/insider-threat-mitigation/defining-insider-threats.
See also NIST. *Insider Threat.* https://csrc.nist.gov/glossary/term/insider_threat.

25 National Security Archive. *Health Care Industry Cybersecurity Task Force, Report on Improving Cybersecurity in the Health Care Industry, June 2017. Unclassified.* https://nsarchive.gwu.edu/document/15310-health-care-industry-cybersecurity-task-force.

26 CISA. *Identifying and Mitigating Living off the Land Techniques.* https://www.cisa.gov/resources-tools/resources/identifying-and-mitigating-living-land-techniques.

27 SIFMA. *Insider Threat Best Practices Guide*, 3rd ed. https://nationalinsiderthreatsig.org/itrmresources/SIFMA%20Insider%20Threat%20Best%20Practices%20Guide%202024.pdf.

28 Executive Office of the President. *Economic Report of the President, Chapter 7: Fighting Cyber Threats to the Growing Economy.* https://www.govinfo.gov/content/pkg/ERP-2018/pdf/ERP-2018-chapter7.pdf.

29 U.S. Department of Justice (DOJ). *North Korean Regime-Backed Programmer Charged With Conspiracy to Conduct Multiple Cyber Attacks and Intrusions.* https://www.justice.gov/opa/pr/north-korean-regime-backed-programmer-charged-conspiracy-conduct-multiple-cyber-attacks-and.

30 The White House. *The Cost of Malicious Cyber Activity to the U.S. Economy.* https://trumpwhitehouse.archives.gov/wp-content/uploads/2018/02/The-Cost-of-Malicious-Cyber-Activity-to-the-U.S.-Economy.pdf.

31 SIFMA. *Insider Threat Best Practices Guide*, 3rd ed. https://www.sifma.org/wp-content/uploads/2025/03/2024-SIFMA-Insider-Threat-Best-Practices-Guide-FINAL.pdf.

32 Office of the Director of National Intelligence (ODNI). *Non-State Actors Playing Greater Roles in Governance and International Affairs.* https://www.dni.gov/files/ODNI/documents/assessments/NICM-Non-State-Actors_23-01637_05-18-24_.pdf.

33 Public-Private Analytic Exchange Program. *2018 Public-Private Analytic Exchange Program: Phishing—Don't be Phooled! Vulnerabilities of Healthcare IT Systems.* https://www.hsdl.org/c/view?docid=820189.

34 45 C.F.R. § 164.304 (2025), definition of "physical safeguards," as set forth in the HIPAA Security Rule.

35 CISA. *Implementing Number Matching in MFA Applications: Fact Sheet.* https://www.cisa.gov/sites/default/files/publications/fact-sheet-implement-number-matching-in-mfa-applications-508c.pdf.

36 CISA. *Crypto Ransomware.* https://www.cisa.gov/news-events/alerts/2014/10/22/crypto-ransomware.

37 Spiceworks. *What Is a Ransomworm? History, Concerns, and Implications: Word of the Week.* https://community.spiceworks.com/topic/1995594-what-is-a-ransomworm-history-concerns-and-implications-word-of-the-week.

38 AlertMedia. *Understanding the Global Risk Landscape: Insights for 2025 and Beyond.* https://www.alertmedia.com/blog/global-risk-landscape/.

39 Argonne National Laboratory. Beware: Scareware & Ransomware. https://www.aps.anl.gov/APS-Newsletter/ITNews/01-2016/Beware-Scareware-Ransomware.

40 CreedTec. Shadow AI Risks: The Silent 2025 Crisis Draining Your Business (Urgent Fixes Inside). Medium. https://medium.com/@creed_1732/shadow-ai-risks-the-silent-2025-crisis-draining-your-business-urgent-fixes-inside-29f5ffc417e9.

41 HHS HC3. *HC3: Analyst Note—August 9, 2022, TLP: White.* https://www.hhs.gov/sites/default/files/cloud-security-analyst-note-tlpwhite.pdf.

42 Public-Private Analytic Exchange Program. *2018 Public-Private Analytic Exchange Program: Phishing—Don't be Phooled! Vulnerabilities of Healthcare IT Systems.* https://www.hsdl.org/c/view?docid=820189.

43 The Digital Speaker. *What Is Synthetic Media? The Ultimate Guide.* www.thedigitalspeaker.com/what-is-synthetic-media-ultimate-guide/.

44 45 C.F.R. § 164.304 (2025), definition of "technical safeguards," as set forth in the HIPAA Security Rule.

45 SailPoint. Threat Vector. https://www.sailpoint.com/identity-library/threat-vector.

46 Public-Private Analytic Exchange Program. *Phishing—Don't be Phooled! Vulnerabilities of Healthcare IT Systems.* https://www.hsdl.org/c/view?docid=820189.

47 U.S. Department of Homeland Security (DHS). *Healthcare and Public Health Sector-Specific Plan.* https://www.cisa.gov/sites/default/files/publications/nipp-ssp-healthcare-public-health-2015-508.pdf.

48 DHS. *Healthcare and Public Health Sector-Specific Plan.* https://www.cisa.gov/sites/default/files/publications/nipp-ssp-healthcare-public-health-2015-508.pdf.

49 CISA. *Critical Infrastructure Sectors.* https://www.cisa.gov/topics/critical-infrastructure-security-and-resilience/critical-infrastructure-sectors.

50 NIST. *Data Integrity: NIST SP 1800-26: Detecting and Responding to Ransomware and Other Destructive Events.* https://csrc.nist.gov/pubs/sp/1800/26/final.

51 TechWorm. *Android Smartphones with MediaTek Processors Open to Hacking Due to a Bug.* https://www.techworm.net/2016/01/android-smartphones-with-mediatek-processors-open-to-hacking-due-to-a-bug.html.

52 The Hacker News. *Urgent: Secret Backdoor Found in XZ Utils.* https://thehackernews.com/2024/03/urgent-secret-backdoor-found-in-xz.html.

53 SSRN. *The Need for Medical Device Cybersecurity Regulation.* https://papers.ssrn.com/sol3/papers.cfm?abstract_id=4579292.

54 Public-Private Analytic Exchange Program. *A Lifeline: Patient Safety & Cybersecurity.* https://www.govinfo.gov/app/details/GOVPUB-HS-PURL-gpo150339.

55 Sophos. *Diabetics Are Hunting Down Obsolete Insulin Pumps with a Security Flaw.* https://news.sophos.com/en-us/2019/05/01/diabetics-are-hunting-down-obsolete-insulin-pumps-with-a-security-flaw/.

56 NIST. *NIST SP 800-53 Rev. 5: Security and Privacy Controls for Information Systems and Organizations.* https://csrc.nist.gov/pubs/sp/800/53/r5/upd1/final.

57 HHS Administration for Strategic Preparedness and Response (ASPR). *Home Page.* https://aspr.hhs.gov/Pages/Home.aspx.

58 HHS ASPR. RISC Toolkit 2.0: Risk Identification and Site Criticality. https://aspr.hhs.gov/RISC/Pages/default.aspx.

59 HHS ASPR. RISC Toolkit 2.0: Risk Identification and Site Criticality. https://aspr.hhs.gov/RISC/Pages/default.aspx.

60 NIST. *Computer Security Resource Center (CSRC) Publications.* https://csrc.nist.gov/publications.

61 International Organization for Standardization (ISO). *ISO 14971—Medical Devices—Application of Risk Management to Medical Devices.* https://www.iso.org/standard/72704.html.

62 ISO. *ISO/IEC 27000 Family—Information Security Management Systems.* https://www.iso.org/standard/iso-iec-27000-family.

63 ISO. *ISO/IEC 27001—Information Security, Cybersecurity and Privacy Protection—Information Security Management Systems—Requirements.* https://www.iso.org/standard/27001.

64 ISO. *ISO/IEC 27002—Information Security, Cybersecurity and Privacy Protection—Information Security Controls.* https://www.iso.org/standard/75652.html.

65 ISO. *ISO 27799—Health Informatics—Information Security Management in Health Using ISO/IEC 27002.* https://www.iso.org/standard/84647.html.

66 ISO. *ISO 81001-1—Health Software and Health IT Systems Safety, Effectiveness and Security—Part 1: Principles and Concepts.* https://www.iso.org/standard/71538.html.

67 ISO. *ISO/TS 81001-2-1—Health Software and Health IT Systems Safety, Effectiveness and Security—Part 2-1: Coordination—Guidance and Requirements for the Use of Assurance Cases for Safety and Security.* https://www.iso.org/standard/82210.html.

68 International Electrotechnical Commission (IEC). *IEC 81001-5-1—Health Software and Health IT Systems Safety, Effectiveness and Security—Part 5-1: Security—Activities in the Product Life-Cycle.* https://www.iso.org/standard/76097.html.

69 HHS 405(d) Program. *405(d) Post—Volume IV: How MDS² Data Can Inform Smarter Medical Device Workflows.* https://405d.hhs.gov/Documents/405d-Post-March-R.pdf.

70 MITRE ATT&CK and ATT&CK are registered trademarks of The MITRE Corporation.

71 On December 29, 2022, the Consolidated Appropriations Act, 2023 ("Omnibus") was signed into law. Section 3305 of the Omnibus, "Ensuring Cybersecurity of Medical Devices," amended the Federal Food, Drug, and Cosmetic Act by adding Section 524B, "Ensuring Cybersecurity of Devices."

U.S. Congress. Consolidated Appropriations Act, 2023, Section 3305—Ensuring Cybersecurity of Medical Devices (amending FD&C Act Section 524B). Pub. L. No. 117–328, 136 Stat. 4459.

Section 3305 of the Consolidated Appropriations Act, 2023 added Section 524B to the FD&C Act, establishing new legal requirements for the cybersecurity of certain medical devices define as cyber devices. Device manufacturers are required to include a cybersecurity plan in their premarket submissions for certain cyber devices. This plan must address vulnerability identification and remediation, provision for postmarket updates and patches, and support for coordinated vulnerability disclosure (CVD) procedures. The law also directs the FDA to issue guidance that aligns with these requirements and to update it regularly to reflect evolving threats. This represents the first time that comprehensive cybersecurity requirements for certain medical devices are explicitly codified in statute under FDA jurisdiction.

U.S. Food and Drug Administration. Cybersecurity for Medical Devices: Frequently Asked Questions (FAQs). FDA. https://www.fda.gov/medical-devices/digital-health-center-excellence/cybersecurity-medical-devices-frequently-asked-questions-faqs.

72 International Medical Device Regulators Forum (IMDRF). *Official Website.* https://www.imdrf.org.

73 CISA. *Stop Ransomware.* https://www.cisa.gov/stopransomware.

74 No More Ransom. *Official Website.* https://www.nomoreransom.org/en/index.html.

Chapter 2

Overview of the Threat Landscape

2.1 Understanding the Threat Landscape

To understand how threats affect healthcare systems, it is essential to define several core terms used throughout cybersecurity: vulnerability, threat, risk, exploit, mitigation, and patching. These concepts form the basis for how healthcare organizations identify weaknesses, assess exposure, and prioritize actions to defend their systems and data.

A *vulnerability* is a weakness in software, hardware, or procedures that could be exploited by an attacker. It may arise from flaws in code, improper configurations, missing updates, or gaps in access controls. According to NIST, a vulnerability is a "[w]eakness in an information system, system security procedures, internal controls, or implementation that could be exploited or triggered by a threat source."[1]

A *threat* is anything that can exploit a vulnerability and cause harm. Threats can come from external actors—such as cybercriminals, ransomware groups, or nation-state actors—or from internal sources, including employees or contractors. As defined by NIST, a *threat* is:

> [a]ny circumstance or event with the potential to adversely impact organizational operations (including mission, functions, image, or reputation), organizational assets, or individuals through an information system via unauthorized access, destruction, disclosure, modification of information, and/or denial of service. Also, the potential for a threat-source to successfully exploit a particular information system vulnerability.[2]

Risk refers to the potential for loss or harm that arises when a threat has the opportunity to exploit a vulnerability. Risk is typically calculated based on two factors: the likelihood of exploitation and the impact that would result. The U.S. Cybersecurity and Infrastructure Security Agency (CISA) defines risk as:

DOI: 10.4324/9781003366560-2

> [a] measure of the extent to which an entity is threatened by a potential circumstance or event, and typically a function of: (i) the adverse impacts that would arise if the circumstance or event occurs; and (ii) the likelihood of occurrence.[3]

An *exploit* is the actual method or technique used to take advantage of a vulnerability.[4] This may include malicious code, scripts, or other tools that initiate unintended activity in a system to gain access, steal data, or disrupt operations.[5]

Mitigation involves decision, action, or practice that is meant to reduce the likelihood that a threat or threat scenario will succeed or to minimize the impact if it does.[6] This includes technical controls, process changes, and user training.

Patching refers to the process of updating software or firmware to correct known vulnerabilities.[7] Applying patches in a timely manner is one of the most effective defenses against exploits of known vulnerabilities. CISA maintains a "Known Exploited Vulnerabilities Catalog." The CISA Known Exploited Vulnerabilities (KEV) catalog is an authoritative resource for identifying vulnerabilities that have been actively exploited by threat actors in real-world attacks against victims.[8]

In contrast, a *proof of concept* is typically developed by security researchers to demonstrate that a vulnerability can be exploited under controlled conditions (i.e., not used "in the wild" on a real victim, but created to confirm that the exploit works). (NIST defines a *threat actor* as "[a]n individual or a group posing a threat.")[9]

2.2 Public Vulnerability Databases

2.2.1 National Vulnerability Database

The National Vulnerability Database (NVD), maintained by NIST, serves as the official U.S. repository for vulnerability information, including CVEs (Common Vulnerabilities and Exposures), severity scores, and references to cybersecurity advisories. The NVD supports *coordinated vulnerability disclosure* (CVD), a process in which researchers report vulnerabilities to vendors and the public in a structured, non-adversarial manner.[10]

2.2.2 European Vulnerability Database

The European Vulnerability Database (EUVD) is a centralized vulnerability repository developed by the European Union Agency for Cybersecurity (ENISA) (formerly known as the European Network and Information Security Agency). It was created to support greater transparency, coordination, and autonomy within the European Union (EU) in how cybersecurity vulnerabilities are managed and shared.

The EUVD brings together publicly available vulnerability information from multiple sources, including European CSIRTs, vendors, and well-established repositories such as MITRE's CVE Program and CISA's KEV Catalog. It includes technical details about vulnerabilities affecting ICT products and services, along with severity ratings, exploitation status, and mitigation guidance.

In 2024, ENISA became a CVE Numbering Authority (CNA). This means it can assign CVE identifiers (IDs)—unique identifiers used to track publicly disclosed cybersecurity vulnerabilities. These identifiers are part of the global CVE system, which is managed by MITRE. Once a CVE ID is assigned, it can be referenced consistently across security tools, reports, and advisories.[11]

2.2.3 Coordinated Vulnerability Disclosure Programs

CVD is the formal process by which a security researcher, developer, or organization responsibly reports a discovered software or hardware vulnerability to the affected vendor or maintainer before making the information public. This process allows time for the vendor to develop and release a security patch or mitigation before the vulnerability can be exploited by malicious actors.[12]

The goal of CVD is to reduce the risk to end users and the broader digital ecosystem by ensuring that vulnerabilities are addressed in a timely and controlled manner. In most cases, researchers agree to delay public disclosure until a fix is available, while vendors commit to acknowledging and addressing the report.[13]

2.3 Bug Bounty Programs

Organizations may use of incentives (e.g., financial or otherwise)—commonly referred to as "bug bounties"—to encourage external security researchers to report discovered vulnerabilities. Bug bounty programs can be tailored to the organization's needs. Some programs operate continuously, while others are conducted over a defined period of time. Bounties may be offered to the general public or limited to a curated group of participants.[14]

Bug bounty programs may focus on a wide range of systems and technologies. These include mobile applications, cloud infrastructure, application programming interfaces (APIs), third-party platforms, open-source software, internally developed applications, medical devices, and publicly accessible websites. Programs may also cover vulnerabilities introduced through system integrations, configuration changes, or software updates. The scope depends on the organization and its specific rules of engagement.

Bug bounty competitions may be organized by private entities or government agencies. These events usually take place over a set time period and allow participants to identify and report vulnerabilities under structured conditions. Private sector competitions may operate within larger programs administered by specialized platforms.[15] Government-sponsored bounties may be used to improve the security of public services, digital infrastructure, or sector-specific systems.

Examples of bug bounty competitions include capture-the-flag (CTF) events and vulnerability assessment challenges, both of which simulate real-world attack scenarios within a controlled environment. These exercises may help improve participants' technical skills and identify previously unknown vulnerabilities or weaknesses.

Individuals may participate in bug bounty programs for different reasons. Financial compensation is a common incentive. Others participate to gain hands-on experience, contribute to the field of cybersecurity, or build professional credibility. Bug bounty programs may also be part of formal learning, training, or certification efforts.

2.4 Penetration Testing

Penetration testing refers to hacking that is conducted with permission, within a defined scope, and under defined rules of engagement. It is a specialized type of assessment[16] conducted on systems, applications, networks, devices, configurations, data, and other resources to identify vulnerabilities that could be exploited by adversaries. Penetration testing may be technical, physical, or both—depending on the agreed-upon scope. It simulates realistic attack techniques to determine how vulnerabilities might be exploited. In some cases, testing includes physical intrusion attempts, such as tailgating, scaling fences, or accessing restricted areas without authorization. The findings from the penetration test are documented in the penetration tester's report. It is important to address the identified deficiencies and take appropriate corrective actions. After remediation, the organization should work with the penetration tester again and conduct a retest to confirm whether the deficiencies have been sufficiently resolved.

2.5 Traditional Focus on Avoiding Data Breaches

In the past, healthcare cybersecurity efforts focused primarily on preventing data breaches, during a time when many providers still relied on paper records and film-based imaging. Many healthcare organizations approached cybersecurity primarily through the lens of HIPAA compliance, relying on checklist-driven activities to satisfy regulatory requirements. As a result, cybersecurity programs were often shaped by compliance objectives rather than by a proactive, risk-informed strategy.

However, the digital transformation of healthcare changed this dynamic. Radiologists led this transformation in the late 1990s by implementing picture archiving and communication systems (PACS) to replace film and light boxes. By 2011, electronic health records (EHRs) were increasingly adopted, driven by the incentives of the federal Meaningful Use program. This shift paved the way for healthcare information to be processed and stored predominantly in electronic formats, relegating paper records and film to the past for many providers.

Before 2013, the largest reported breaches in healthcare were primarily due to the loss or theft of physical assets like backup tapes, servers, and laptops. Physical theft and loss were the main concerns, with the focus mainly on preventing data breaches. Ransomware attacks did exist, but they were relatively uncommon—often easy to bypass or ignore. This was in spite of the first known ransomware attack in 1989, targeting the healthcare industry, which involved the distribution of 20,000 floppy disks with the label "AIDS Information—Introductory Diskettes" to attendees of the World Health Organization's international AIDS conference.[17]

2.6 Social Engineering Attacks

Social engineering attacks remain one of the most significant threats to healthcare organizations, especially as their digital footprint grows in size, scale, and sophistication. These social engineering attacks exploit human behavior, relying on manipulation and psychological tactics to breach the most sophisticated security systems. Healthcare organizations are particularly vulnerable because they handle large amounts of sensitive data, including protected health information (PHI), personally identifiable information (PII), confidential information, proprietary information, and intellectual property.[18]

2.6.1 Understanding Social Engineering Attacks

Social engineering encompasses a range of malicious activities that rely on psychological manipulation to deceive individuals into divulging confidential information or performing actions that compromise security. These attacks may take the form of phishing, smishing, or QR code phishing attempts (quishing), impersonation scams,[19] deepfakes, or synthetic media.

2.6.1.1 General Phishing

General phishing attacks are the most common and recognizable form of social engineering. In these campaigns, attackers send mass emails, casting a wide net in the hope of tricking recipients into clicking malicious links or downloading malicious attachments. In the past, general phishing attempts were often easy to spot due to poor grammar, spelling mistakes, and specious offers. However, modern campaigns are often more polished and subtle. Inboxes are inundated with messages that appear to come from trusted sources such as banks, courier services, or healthcare providers, all intending to exploit emotions such as fear, urgency, or curiosity.

2.6.1.2 Spear-Phishing

Spear-phishing targets specific individuals or organizations, often using information tailored to the intended recipient. These attacks may leverage publicly available details such as job titles, organizational hierarchies, or social media posts to create convincing messages. For example, an attacker might pose as a vendor or colleague, crafting emails that reference ongoing projects to build trust. In healthcare, spear-phishing has been used to gain unauthorized access to EHRs or initiate fraudulent transactions.

2.6.1.3 Whaling

Whaling is a highly targeted form of phishing aimed at senior executives or high-profile individuals within an organization. These attacks often involve significant preparation, with attackers impersonating executives to request sensitive data or financial transactions. For example, an attacker may pose as a hospital's Chief Financial Officer (CFO) to authorize large payments or gain access to employee information.

2.6.2 The Psychology Behind Social Engineering

Attackers manipulate emotions and cognitive biases, often employing tactics that include the following:

- Authority
  Messages appear to come from figures of authority such as a supervisor, government agency, trusted vendor, or respected institution. Recipients are more likely to comply without question when the request comes from someone they perceive as credible.
- Urgency
  Social engineers often create a sense of time pressure, compelling recipients to act before the recipients have the time to think critically. For example, emails warning of account suspensions or system breaches prompt immediate responses, bypassing usual caution.
- Fear and greed
  Fear-based tactics, such as threats of legal action or fines, are designed to coerce recipients into action. Greed-based tactics, such as the promise of money or gift cards, can also persuade recipients to act impulsively and quickly.
- Trust and familiarity
  By impersonating known contacts or institutions, attackers lower the chances of arousing suspicion in the recipient. This might include sending emails that appear to come from trusted vendors or colleagues to gain access or obtain sensitive information.

2.6.3 Anatomy of a Social Engineering Attack

Social engineering attacks typically follow a structured approach that generally follows the following process:

- Research
  The attacker gathers information about the target organization or individual. This may involve studying social media profiles, public records, and company websites.
- Message creation
  A convincing message is developed to deceive the recipient. For instance, the attacker might pose as a vendor requiring urgent payment or an IT technician requesting login credentials.
- Engagement
  The attacker initiates contact, often through an email, phone call, or social media message. This step involves building rapport or creating a sense of urgency to elicit action from the recipient, such as sending a response, clicking on a link, or opening an attachment.
- Exploitation
  The recipient is manipulated into revealing sensitive information or performing a compromising action, such as clicking a malicious link, providing access credentials, or downloading malware. This step allows the attacker to gain access to the target system or network.
- Execution
  Using the obtained information or access to the target system or network, the attacker executes their plan to achieve specific goals, such as installing malware, stealing data, committing fraud, or disrupting operations. After achieving these objectives, the attacker may take steps to conceal their activities by deleting logs, altering system settings, or planting backdoors to enable future access.

2.6.4 Why Social Engineering Is Effective

Human behavior is often driven by desires and motivations. When we communicate, we express those desires and motivations. A person receiving a message brings a certain level of inherent trust to what is being received, often assuming that the information is genuine or beneficial. Trust and faith in others may create vulnerability.

If a message claims to offer something desirable, the recipient may be more inclined to believe it because it aligns with their desires. If a message triggers fear, the recipient may act on it to avoid something negative. In either case, humans tend to be driven by impulse and are prone to making quick decisions—especially when time is limited. This means that the recipient may act on impulse instead of pausing to think critically.

When we review a message, it is often done quickly. We usually don't have the time to scrutinize every element of the message. As a result, the recipient may respond emotionally rather than rationally, which increases the risk of the recipient falling victim to a social engineering attack.

The medium of communication does not matter. It could be a phone call, text message, email, social media message, or a direct conversation. The mechanics of deception are often the same—greed, fear, or the promise of something too good to be true. These hallmarks of deception often slip past the recipient's awareness because they operate below the threshold of detection.

2.6.5 Social Engineering: What It Is, and Why It Is So Dangerous

Social engineering attacks are a form of psychological manipulation of the recipient, especially when the recipient takes an action that would not ordinarily be done if the recipient was aware of the truth. The fraudulent nature of these scams often goes undetected due to the recipient believing that the message and the sender are trustworthy and real. Social engineering attacks can take many forms, including email phishing, social media phishing, vishing, smishing (SMS phishing), quishing (QR code phishing), and deepfake phishing (photos, images, videos, or audio).[20] The root cause of a vast majority of successful cyberattacks is a phishing email.[21] However, other forms of phishing, such as vishing, smishing, quishing, and deepfake phishing, are on the rise.[22] Individuals who fall prey to phishing attacks are typically considered to be negligent insiders. Phishing victims can include individuals who are not technologically savvy, but they may also include individuals who are IT experts.[23]

Social engineering attacks exploit human psychology to manipulate individuals into performing actions that compromise security. Attackers craft messages that exploit emotions such as fear, urgency, trust, or curiosity to increase the likelihood of compliance. These messages often mimic trusted entities such as banks, healthcare organizations, or coworkers, making them difficult to detect. For instance, an email impersonating a healthcare provider might urge recipients to verify their medical records immediately, leveraging the urgency to bypass scrutiny.[24] Social media platforms have also become fertile ground for social engineering, with attackers luring victims through fake profiles or messages promising enticing offers.

The success of social engineering attacks often relies on the victim's emotional response, causing them to act without thorough analysis. Social engineering attacks exploit human psychology. Attackers leverage cognitive biases, emotional triggers, and decision-making shortcuts to manipulate individuals into doing things they might not ordinarily do.[25] Modern phishing scams have evolved beyond poorly worded emails to immaculately worded emails that seem to be real and convincing. Modern phishing scams also employ AI techniques such as deepfakes to mimic a person's voice or likeness—someone whom the recipient may know or may have heard of and whom they may trust.[26]

Attackers often impersonate authoritative or familiar entities to gain their victims' confidence. These messages are designed to bypass critical thinking, relying on rapid, automatic responses rather than analytical, deliberate thought. Attackers also exploit key principles of persuasion, including reciprocity, authority, and scarcity, creating a sense of urgency or obligation that compels victims to act without reflection.[27]

2.6.6 Emerging Threats in Social Engineering

Attackers continually evolve their tactics, based on current events and news, as well as advances in technology. Some of these examples include the following:

1. *Thread hijacking*
   Attackers infiltrate email accounts and insert themselves into existing conversations, posing as one of the original participants. This approach leverages trust built over prior communications.

Thread hijacking example:

Fred and Bob, Chief Information Security Officers (CISOs) at two different regional hospitals, are friends and occasionally talk sports.

On a Monday morning, Fred shoots Bob an email:

Fred's email to Bob:

"Hey—are you heading to the home opener for the baseball game this Saturday?"

Bob's reply email to Fred on Monday afternoon:

"Yeah maybe. But I have to prepare to brief the board on Monday. I'll let you know. Plus, I can't believe how expensive the tickets are!"

Tuesday and Wednesday pass by—uneventfully.

Late at night on Thursday, Bob receives an email that appears as though it is from Fred that states the following:

"Hey Bob—you won't believe this. But I just got two club seats for the home opener on Saturday! Do you want to join me? My wife can't make it. Here is a screenshot of the location of the club seats." The screenshot is a graphic file that is attached to the email.

It is close to midnight when Bob receives the email. It is almost Friday and he is busy working on the presentation to the board of directors. Bob wants to clear his inbox for the morning and so he opens Fred's email and the email attachment. *Unwittingly, Bob opens the email attachment and his computer session suddenly ends.* In just a few seconds, a ransom note is displayed on his screen. "Oh great!" Bob exclaims and sheer panic sets in.

(Unfortunately, the email attachment that Bob opened was malicious. The email was not actually from Fred at all, but rather was from an attacker pretending to be Fred.)

2. *Deepfake technology*
   Advances in AI enable the creation of convincing audio, images, and videos that appear authentic. *An actual incident illustrates the seriousness of this threat.* A Hong Kong employee of a multinational financial services firm was tricked during a live video call with an individual whom he believed was the firm's chief financial officer—but this "individual" was actually a deepfake. CNN. *Finance worker pays out $25 million after video call with deepfake "chief financial officer."* https://www.cnn.com/2024/02/04/asia/deepfake-cfo-scam-hong-kong-intl-hnk.
3. *Homograph attacks*
   By using similar-looking characters in uniform resource locators (URLs) or email addresses, attackers trick recipients into clicking on malicious links or interacting with malicious domains. For instance, substituting "rn" for "m" in a domain name can easily go unnoticed.[28]

2.6.7 Homoglyph and Homograph Attacks: Exploiting Similarities in Characters or Scripts

Homoglyph[29] and homograph attacks are subtle yet highly effective tactics in the cybercriminal's toolkit. In a homograph attack, which is a specific type of homoglyph attack, the substitution targets domain names using characters from different scripts that appear identical. In both cases, attackers create content that appears legitimate at first glance but is designed to mislead and compromise security. These attacks exploit the visual similarity between characters in different character sets or scripts to deceive users into interacting with malicious links, emails, or websites. In a homoglyph attack, attackers substitute one character for another that looks similar, potentially across various contexts such as URLs, email addresses, usernames, or code.

2.6.7.1 The Mechanics of Homoglyph and Homograph Attacks

At the heart of these attacks lies the manipulation of characters or scripts that look nearly identical, whether they belong to different scripts or character sets or employ stylistic variations in typeface.

Homoglyph attacks exploit the human tendency to skim visual details, especially when under pressure or when interacting with familiar contexts like a trusted brand or service.

How does the deception work?

1. Character substitution:
   Character substitution often goes unnoticed because people usually skim a message and make a quick decision about whether it looks legitimate. Small changes—like replacing a lowercase "l" with a number "1" or using special characters—can be hard to catch unless someone is paying very close attention. However, people normally read messages fairly quickly without much discernment. Slight character substitutions often go unnoticed.

   Example 1: Attackers replace characters in URLs or email addresses with similar-looking counterparts. For instance: Substituting the letter "m" with the combination "rn" (example.com becomes exarnple.com).

   Example 2: Using the capital letter "I" in place of a lowercase "l" (paypal.com becomes paypaI.com).
2. Unicode exploitation:
   Unicode, a universal character encoding standard, enables the use of characters from numerous languages, such as Greek, Cyrillic, and others. Since some of these non-Latin characters can look similar to Latin characters, any slight differences in the appearance of text may go unnoticed.

   Example 1: The Cyrillic "*a*" (U+0430) looks identical to the Latin "a" (U+0061). An attacker could register paypal.com (using Cyrillic "p" and "a"), which looks like the well-known paypal.com domain name.

   Example 2: Using the Cyrillic letter "o" (U+043E) that looks like the Latin letter "o" (U+006F) so that "dropbox.com" looks like "dropbox.com." But the Cyrillic letter "o" looks slightly rounder and wider than the Latin letter "o." However, this would require very careful discernment that may be almost impossible to see with the naked eye.

   Example 3: Using the Greek letter "A" (U+0391) and the Greek letter "P" (U+03A1) looks like the Latin letters "A" (U+0041) and "P" (U+0050) respectively. Thus, "APPLE.COM" can look like "APPLE.COM." But the Greek letters "APP" look *nearly identical* to the Latin letters "APP" although the Greek letter "A" looks slightly narrower than the Latin letter "A."

   The risk is that—*as with any domain name*—an attacker could register a visually similar domain name that appears identical to the legitimate domain name but uses different Unicode characters. An organization can reduce this risk by proactively registering lookalike or internationalized variants of the organization's domain name as a defensive measure.
3. Internationalized domain names (IDNs):
   Domain names follow the Internationalized Domain Name (IDN) system, which allows registrars to support the registration of domain names that include characters from Latin and non-Latin scripts (e.g., Cyrillic, Greek, Arabic, and others) using the Unicode standard. However, attackers exploit this feature by creating domains that mix characters from different scripts.

   Example 1: xn--80ak6aa92e.com translates to apple.com in Unicode (via Punycode), which can be mistaken for the legitimate "apple.com" domain name.

   The characters "a," "p," and "l" in "apple.com" in this example are not Latin letters but rather Cyrillic letters that look similar to the Latin letters:

- a = Cyrillic small letter a (U+0430)
- p = Cyrillic small letter p (U+0440)
- l = Cyrillic small letter l (U+04CF)

2.6.7.2 Real-World Implications of Homoglyph and Homograph Attacks

Homoglyph and homograph attacks have proven effective in various scenarios, often bypassing traditional security measures due to their reliance on human error:

1. Phishing websites

- Attackers create websites that mimic legitimate domains to harvest login credentials, financial data, or other sensitive information.
- Example: A malicious actor might register microsoft.com (using a Cyrillic "o") to trick users into logging into a fake Microsoft account page.

2. Spoofed email addresses

- Emails from seemingly authentic senders prompt recipients to download attachments, click malicious links, or share confidential details.
- Example: An email from admìn@paypal.com (using an accented "i") might bypass a user's scrutiny.

3. Payment redirection

- Attackers impersonate vendors or partners to redirect payments to fraudulent accounts.
- Example: Invoices from payments@rnediaprorus.com could be mistaken for payments@mediaprorus.com.

2.6.8 Evolving Security Awareness Programs

Security awareness programs need to go deeper than simply spotting suspicious messages. While it is useful to know what an example of a social engineering message could look like, that knowledge alone is not enough. It used to be that unknown senders, odd subject lines, misspellings, and poor grammar were the telltale signs of a phishing message. But nowadays it is more difficult to distinguish between a social engineering (fake) message from a real message. Perfect grammar and convincing, well-written messages are more the norm than the exception to the rule. Additionally, deepfakes (of images, voices, and videos) are on the rise as well.

The following three principles explain how social engineering works, and how individuals can reduce the likelihood of being deceived:

- Individuals need to understand both the psychology of the attacker and the psychology of victims. For example, a social engineer (the attacker) may create a sense of urgency, exert authority, or offer a reward to the recipient. When successful, the social engineer creates a psychological advantage over the victim. The victim is tricked into doing something that they ordinarily would not do, such as divulging sensitive information, opening a malicious attachment, or clicking a malicious link. Having an awareness of how social engineering attacks are crafted from an attacker's perspective can help individuals be more aware of messaging that may be deceptive in nature.

- People who become targets of social engineering are often those who are deeply dedicated to their organizations and tend to be highly agreeable—that is, they are more likely to say "yes" or comply with requests. It is important for individuals to recognize their own vulnerabilities—being aware of these traits can help them stay alert and avoid being manipulated.
- Instead of reacting on instinct, individuals should take a moment to critically evaluate the messages they receive. Quick, visceral responses can increase the risk of falling prey to a social engineering attack. Slowing down and analyzing the content of the message reduce the risk of an individual being deceived.

Ultimately, teaching people how deception works—and how they personally respond to it—builds better awareness. This type of understanding does not just help with cybersecurity. It helps people think critically and respond more thoughtfully in everyday situations where trust and judgment are involved.

Social engineering can take many forms—deepfakes, phishing emails, voice phishing (vishing), SMS phishing, and more—but the underlying psychology does not change. These attacks all rely on exploiting human behavior, such as trust, urgency, or fear, to get people to act without thinking critically.

2.6.9 Human Factor as a Risk: Social Engineering and Insider Threats

Healthcare privacy and cybersecurity are a shared responsibility. Patients, providers, medical device manufacturers, laboratories, pharmacies, researchers, and other stakeholders all play a role in safeguarding healthcare information, whether it exists in electronic records, hardcopy documents, photographs, videos, or other formats. Many cyberattacks, including ransomware incidents, often originate from social engineering tactics that exploit individuals or groups. However, when individuals or groups have trusted virtual or physical access, their actions can give rise to an insider threat.

2.7 Why We Care About Ransomware

The Federal Bureau of Investigation (FBI) defines ransomware as a type of malicious software, or malware, that prevents users from accessing computer files, systems, or networks and demands ransom payment to restore access.[30] Ransomware attacks can cause costly disruptions to operations and the loss of critical information and data. The FBI emphasizes that these attacks can significantly disrupt operations and result in the loss of sensitive information. They also highlight that ransomware is frequently delivered through spear-phishing emails to end users.

When clinicians cannot access critical patient data, it may disrupt workflows, postpone procedures, and compromise patient outcomes. In emergencies, such delays can mean the difference between life and death. In at least one instance, a patient's death was reportedly caused by a delay in patient care.[31]

2.7.1 The Evolution of Ransomware

The first known ransomware attack occurred in 1989 with the AIDS Trojan, also known as the PC Cyborg Virus. Distributed via floppy disks labeled "AIDS Information—Introductory Diskettes," it demanded a $189 payment to a P.O. box in Panama for decryption. At the time, ransomware was considered more of a novelty than a serious threat.[32]

Since 2012, however, ransomware has evolved dramatically. Early strains like Reveton introduced lock-screen tactics, displaying fake law enforcement messages and demanding payment via prepaid cards.[33] Later variants such as CryptoLocker,[34] CryptoWall,[35] TeslaCrypt,[36] Locky,[37] SamSam,[38] and Petya employed advanced encryption to hold systems and data hostage. These attacks shifted the model from scareware to full-scale operational disruption, posing serious challenges for healthcare organizations.

Ransomware threatens the confidentiality, integrity, and availability of healthcare data, often crippling critical systems and, at times, directly affecting patient care. Between 2012 and 2013, Reveton demanded payments via prepaid cards (e.g., MoneyPak® prepaid cards).[39] By 2013, CryptoLocker became one of the first to demand payment in Bitcoin, marking a shift toward cryptocurrency-based extortion (Figure 2.1).[40]

Since that time, ransom—when paid as a result of a ransomware attack—is typically demanded by way of cryptocurrency payment. Bitcoin is still demanded for such ransom payments. However, Monero, Ethereum, and Litecoin are also other forms of cryptocurrency that can be demanded, depending on the attacker's preferences and/or objectives.[41]

Ransomware remains a dominant cyber threat for the healthcare and public health sector. LockBit is a top ransomware group that has targeted the healthcare and public health industry.[42] However, certain ransomware gangs, including ALPHV/BlackCat and BlackSuit (which is believed to be a rebrand or evolution of the Royal ransomware group and shares similarities in encryption methods, binary structure, and code functionality), were disrupted by the U.S.

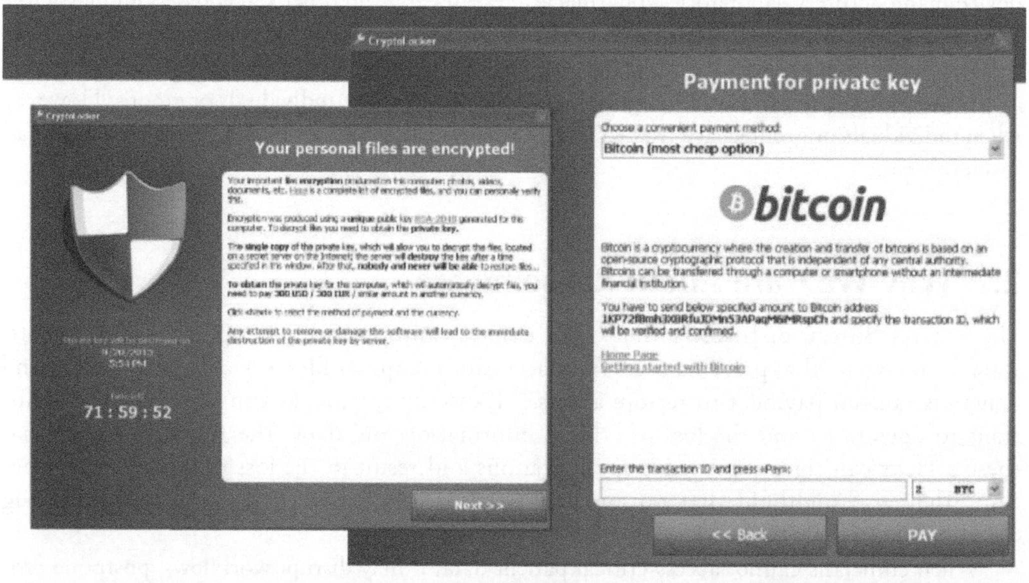

Figure 2.1 CryptoLocker ransomware ransom note associated with the GameOver Zeus botnet. FBI. *GameOver Zeus/Cryptolocker graphic*. https://www.fbi.gov/file-repository/gameover-zeus_v13_fullgraphic_web_opt2.pdf/view.

Department of Justice. (U.S. Department of Justice, Office of Public Affairs. *Justice Department Disrupts Prolific ALPHV/Blackcat Ransomware Variant.* https://www.justice.gov/archives/opa/pr/justice-department-disrupts-prolific-alphvblackcat-ransomware-variant. See also U.S. Department of Justice, Office of Public Affairs. *Justice Department Announces Coordinated Disruption Actions Against BlackSuit (Royal) Ransomware Operations.* https://www.justice.gov/opa/pr/justice-department-announces-coordinated-disruption-actions-against-blacksuit-royal.)

The discussions on BlackSuit and ALPHV/BlackCat are provided for historical context. While law enforcement actions can disrupt ransomware operations, activity often resurges as affiliates rebrand, migrate to other RaaS programs, or rebuild infrastructure. (E.g., the Chaos ransomware group may be operated by former BlackSuit members or is a rebrand of the BlackSuit group. SC Media. *New Chaos ransomware group linked to BlackSuit amid site seizures.* https://www.scworld.com/news/new-chaos-ransomware-group-linked-to-blacksuit-amid-site-seizures.)

Ransomware strains such as LockBit are currently active.[43] Many ransomware attacks occur due to a successful phishing attempt.[44]

Some ransomware operators use a *ransomware-as-a-service* (RaaS) model.[45] The ransomware operators maintain the code for the ransomware, and it is leased to affiliates. These affiliates independently execute the attacks on organizations of their choosing. Such affiliates pay a portion of the ransom proceeds from the attack. The affiliates do not need to have a high level of technical knowledge in order to execute the ransomware attack, since the tools for deploying the ransomware are provided to them.[46]

An example of RaaS is the LockBit ransomware gang, which provides affiliates with a complete set of tools and detailed instructions to launch attacks. Affiliates using RaaS platforms like LockBit can deploy ransomware to encrypt victims' data while simultaneously exfiltrating sensitive information—a tactic known as *double extortion*.[47] In double extortion, victims are pressured to pay a ransom to regain access to their data and prevent the publication of stolen information (Figure 2.2).[48]

"In order to recover your files you need to follow instructions below"

Sensitive Data
Sensitive data on your network was DOWNLOADED.
If you DON'T WANT your sensitive data to be PUBLISHED you have to act quickly.

Data includes:
- Complete network map including credentials for local and remote services.
- Private financial information including: clients data, bills, budgets, annual reports, bank statements.
- And more...

Samples are available on your User Panel.

CAUTION
DO NOT MODIFY ENCRYPTED FILES YOURSELF.
DO NOT USE THIRD PARTY SOFTWARE TO RESTORE YOUR DATA.
YOU MAY DAMAGE YOUR FILES. IT WILL RESULT IN PERMANENT DATA LOSS.

What should I do next?
1) Download and install Tor Browser from: https://torproject.org/
2) Navigate to User Panel: (Includes victim specific onion and access key for communication)

Figure 2.2 Double extortion ransom note.

Alternatively, affiliates may choose to simply exfiltrate the sensitive data and threaten to leak or publish the data unless the ransom is paid.[49] This tactic is called pure extortion. Which tactic the affiliate chooses to use depends on what it wants to do to achieve its specific goals.

Ransomware was traditionally used as a pure extortion tactic, where attackers encrypted data and demanded payment for its release. However, the emergence of Maze ransomware in late 2019 marked a major shift toward double extortion. Maze operators encrypted victims' data and also exfiltrated it, threatening to leak the information publicly if the ransom was not paid.[50] This approach introduced a powerful new pressure tactic that quickly became common among other ransomware groups, fundamentally changing the ransomware landscape.

As a general matter, to counter ransomware threats, healthcare organizations must prioritize robust cybersecurity measures. Regular backups stored offline or off-site are a critical defense against ransomware, enabling organizations to restore systems without having to pay ransom to the attackers. Network segmentation can also limit the spread of ransomware within a system, while staff training helps mitigate risks from phishing emails and other common attack vectors. Comprehensive incident response plans enable organizations to respond quickly and effectively to ransomware attacks, minimizing downtime and protecting patient safety.[51]

2.7.2 The Impact on Care Delivery: A Spotlight on Ransomware

Cyberattacks, including ransomware attacks and other types of compromise, have the potential to disrupt entire healthcare operations. The financial and reputational harm from a cyberattack can force healthcare providers to divert resources away from patient care, reducing overall capacity. In addition, the loss of patient trust following a cyberattack can have long-term implications for the relationship between providers and the communities they serve.

For example, one of the first major international cyberattacks was the May 2017 WannaCry ransomware attack. The WannaCry ransomware attack showed the devastating impact of ransomware, infecting hundreds of thousands of systems in over 150 countries within a matter of days. Victims were locked out of their systems, with a demand for Bitcoin payments to decrypt files.

The UK's National Health Service (NHS) was one of the most prominent victims, with critical systems rendered inoperable, leading to canceled surgeries, delayed treatments, and significant disruption to patient care. About one-third of NHS trusts were impacted.[52]

WannaCry exploited a vulnerability in Microsoft Windows through the EternalBlue exploit, reportedly developed by the National Security Agency (NSA) and leaked by the hacking group Shadow Brokers. This exploit targeted a vulnerability in the SMBv1 protocol, which was present across unpatched (MS17–010) systems for Windows, including Windows XP, Windows 7, and others. The danger with WannaCry is that it was a ransomware that had worm-like self-propagating capabilities that could work itself across a network without any human intervention.[53] As a result, large networked systems like hospitals, banks, and transportation systems were at great risk.

Despite a patch being available from Microsoft prior to the attack,[54] many systems remained unpatched, enabling the rapid spread of the malware. Vulnerability management is often a challenge for many healthcare organizations. While some organizations are more proactive than others in ensuring that vulnerabilities are addressed by timely patching systems, other organizations are challenged by finding the time to patch systems or having the resources to timely patch systems.

WannaCry, however, did not just affect healthcare organizations. WannaCry affected organizations worldwide, including telecommunication firms in Spain, car manufacturing facilities in France, universities in China, cinemas in South Korea, and railways and banks in Russia.[55]

2.7.3 Paying the Ransom is No Guarantee of Data Recovery—Spotlight on Ransomware

The FBI has stated that paying the ransom does not necessarily guarantee that a user will get the data back. One example of this is what happened with the WannaCry ransomware attack. The payment mechanism for ransomware victims did not adequately track who paid the ransom and who did not. As a result, it was more likely than not that ransomware victims would not receive anything in return for the payment of the ransom.[56] In fact, cybersecurity experts advised ransomware victims not to pay the ransom as there was no evidence that such victims would get their data back.[57] Accordingly, ransomware victims had to either restore their systems from reliable (uninfected) backups or rebuild systems if it was not possible to restore the data. But the WannaCry ransomware campaign was slowed down due to a security researcher finding a "kill switch" to help stop its spread.[58] Ultimately, the WannaCry campaign ceased its operations. The attack was eventually attributed to the Lazarus Group, a hacking organization linked to North Korea.[59]

Subsequently, the FBI released a practical guide on "Ransomware Prevention and Response for CISOs."[60] The FBI guidance provides a detailed framework for organizations to prepare for, respond to, and mitigate ransomware attacks. This guidance emphasizes preventive measures such as maintaining robust data backups, implementing strong access controls, patching vulnerabilities promptly, and conducting regular employee training to recognize phishing attacks. In addition, this guidance outlines response strategies, including isolating infected systems, consulting with law enforcement, and avoiding ransom payments unless absolutely necessary, as they often fail to guarantee data recovery and fund further criminal activities.

The Office for Civil Rights at the U.S. Department of Health and Human Services (HHS OCR) also released a fact sheet on ransomware and HIPAA, explaining how ransomware attacks can potentially trigger obligations under the Health Insurance Portability and Accountability Act (HIPAA).[61] This guidance outlines the obligations of covered entities (such as hospitals, physician practices, payers, and others) and business associates (entities that create, receive, transmit, or maintain PHI on behalf of a covered entity)[62] to secure electronic protected health information (ePHI) under the HIPAA Security Rule. It also provides guidance on when a ransomware incident constitutes a data breach under the HIPAA Breach Notification Rule, which requires notification to affected individuals, HHS, and, in some cases, the media. This guidance also underscores the importance of implementing safeguards such as encryption, regular risk analyses, and incident response plans to protect against ransomware while maintaining compliance with HIPAA requirements. HIPAA requirements are set forth in the HIPAA Privacy Rule, the HIPAA Security Rule, the HIPAA Breach Notification Rule, and the HIPAA Enforcement Rule.[63]

Together, HHS OCR and FBI guidance provides guidance for healthcare organizations in the HPH sector, offering both proactive measures to prevent ransomware attacks and protocols to manage incidents effectively while maintaining compliance with legal and regulatory frameworks, such as HIPAA.

2.7.4 What to Do If You Have a Ransomware Attack

When a ransomware attack occurs, the first priority is containment. Infected systems must be immediately isolated from the network to prevent the malware from spreading. Potentially exposed, at-risk systems and devices, including those that may be uninfected, should also be taken offline. At the same time, it is critical to secure backups, ensuring they are not connected to the affected network and verifying that they are free from malware before attempting restoration. Tested and verified backups play a crucial role in recovery, allowing organizations to restore systems without engaging with attackers. Further, employees and contractors also play an important role in ransomware response by reporting suspected or confirmed incidents in accordance with organizational policies. Early internal reporting through established incident response channels—*and, above all, following organizational policies, procedures, and playbooks*—can help with effective and coordinated ransomware response.

The decision to notify law enforcement ideally should be made by executive leadership in consultation with legal counsel, considering regulatory obligations and business impact. *If the incident significantly disrupts business operations, creates financial risks, or triggers regulatory reporting requirements or other significant obligations, the board of directors should be engaged.*

Once an incident is detected, the organization should activate its incident response and business continuity plans. Triage, containment, and eradication efforts must begin immediately to prevent further spread. Paying the ransom is not recommended, as it does not guarantee data recovery and may encourage further attacks. Some victims who have paid ransoms were targeted again, asked for additional payments, or never received a working decryption key. If the organization considers paying the ransom, the decision should be made with input from executive leadership and legal counsel. Engaging experienced ransomware negotiators may be helpful in handling any negotiations concerning ransom payments.

Healthcare organizations should engage cybersecurity consultants or specialized incident response firms during an active ransomware attack, to assist with containment, forensic analysis, and recovery. These experts can provide critical insights, help determine the full scope of the attack, and recommend specific security improvements to reduce future risk.[64]

The U.S. Department of the Treasury's Office of Foreign Assets Control (OFAC) has issued advisories warning that making ransom payments to sanctioned individuals, groups, or countries (such as North Korea, Iran, and Russia) may violate U.S. sanctions laws. Many ransomware groups operate in or have ties to sanctioned jurisdictions, making payments risky. Organizations considering ransom payments should conduct due diligence to avoid violating OFAC regulations. In-house counsel or retained outside counsel and law enforcement should ideally be consulted before making any ransom payments. Failure to comply with these regulations may result in significant fines and legal consequences. Given the legal, financial, and ethical implications—including potential violations of OFAC sanctions and the risk of funding criminal activity—this decision requires careful consideration.[65]

In summary, organizations should follow their policies, procedures, and playbooks and, as appropriate, consult with executive leadership, the board of directors, law enforcement, cybersecurity experts, in-house counsel and retained outside counsel, and ransomware negotiators to assess risks, explore recovery options, and ensure compliance with all applicable laws and regulations when responding to a ransomware incident.

2.8 Insider Threats

2.8.1 What Is an Insider?

An "insider" is anyone with trusted virtual or physical access to (or knowledge of) an organization's resources, including personnel, facilities, information, systems, networks, and infrastructure.[66]

Examples of people who may be considered an insider include, but are not limited to, the following[67]:

- An employee, contractor, vendor, or consultant who has been issued credentials, access badges, or remote login rights.
- A person responsible for maintaining or repairing systems, equipment, or facilities, such as a custodian, service technician, or IT support staff.
- A user provided with an organizational device, email account, or access to internal networks.
- A developer, engineer, or staff member involved in building, supporting, or maintaining proprietary systems, applications, or products.
- An individual with knowledge of sensitive internal business information, including cost models, operational workflows, client data, or intellectual property.
- A decision-maker or strategist who has access to future plans, financial data, or long-term business goals.

Examples of an insider may include, but are not limited to, the following[68]:

- Trusted employees or staff—Clinical and administrative staff who have legitimate access to patient records, billing systems, or internal communications.
- Authorized users—Anyone provided with login credentials to access the organization's network, systems, or devices, including on-site and remote workers.
- Vendors and contractors—Individuals such as IT support, custodial staff, or repair technicians with physical or digital access to healthcare facilities and systems.
- Medical equipment technicians—Personnel who install, repair, and maintain medical equipment.
- Operations staff—Personnel with knowledge of contracts, pricing structures, and vendor relationships.
- Leadership—Executives and managers who have access to organizational strategies, future plans, and key business information.

2.8.2 What Is an Insider Threat?

Insider threat is the potential for an *insider* to use their authorized access or understanding of an organization to harm that organization.[69] The access may be physical or virtual.[70]

The Cybersecurity and Infrastructure Security Agency (CISA) defines insider threat as the risk that an insider will use their authorized access, wittingly or unwittingly, to do harm to the department's mission, resources, personnel, facilities, information, equipment, networks, or systems. Actions of insider threat actors include the following[71]:

- Espionage
- Terrorism
- Unauthorized disclosure of information
- Corruption, including participation in transnational organized crime
- Sabotage
- Workplace violence
- Intentional or unintentional loss or degradation of departmental resources or capabilities

2.8.3 What Are the Types of Insider Threats?

2.8.3.1 Unintentional Threats

- Negligence—An insider of this type exposes an organization to a threat through carelessness. Negligent insiders are generally familiar with security and/or IT policies but choose to ignore them, creating risk for the organization. Examples include allowing someone to "piggyback" through a secure entrance point, misplacing or losing a portable storage device containing sensitive information, and ignoring messages to install new updates and security patches. [72]
- Accidental—An insider of this type mistakenly causes an unintended risk to an organization. Examples include mistyping an email address and accidentally sending a sensitive business document to a competitor, unknowingly or inadvertently clicking on a hyperlink, opening an attachment in a phishing email that contains a virus, or improperly disposing of sensitive documents. [73]

2.8.3.2 Intentional Threats

The intentional insider is often synonymously referenced as a "malicious insider." Intentional threats are actions taken to harm an organization for personal benefit or to act on a personal grievance. For example, many insiders are motivated to "get even" due to a perceived lack of recognition (e.g., promotion, bonuses, and desirable travel) or termination. Their actions can include leaking sensitive information, harassing associates, sabotaging equipment, perpetrating violence, or stealing proprietary data or intellectual property in the false hope of advancing their careers.[74]

2.8.3.3 Other Threats

Collusive threats—A subset of malicious insider threats is referred to as collusive threats, where one or more insiders collaborate with an external threat actor to compromise an organization[75]. These incidents frequently involve cybercriminals recruiting an insider or several insiders to enable fraud, intellectual property theft, espionage, or a combination of the three.[76]

Third-party threats—Typically, these insider threat actors may be contractors or vendors who are not formal members of an organization, but who have been granted some level of access to facilities, systems, networks, or people to complete their work. These threats may be direct or indirect threats.[77]

2.8.4 Who Is Vulnerable to the Insider Threat?

Every organization is vulnerable to insider threats, which can be malicious, negligent, or accidental. When the insider threat is malicious, insiders may work in coordination with external threat actors to compromise an organization—also known as collusive threats. Additionally, insider threat actors may include employees, contractors, vendors, or others—essentially, anyone with virtual or physical trusted access and/or with knowledge concerning the organization.

2.8.5 Dangers of Insider Threat

The danger of insider threat activity is that it can go undetected for extended periods of time and, as a result, cause a significant amount of harm to the organization.[78] While negligent and accidental insider threat activity does occur most of the time,[79] malicious insider threat activity can occur as well.

Accidental insider threat activity occurs when a person inadvertently clicks on a phishing link, opens a malicious attachment, or unwittingly discloses sensitive information to the attacker.[80]

Other times, the compromise of healthcare information or other sensitive information can be due to the malicious or negligent actions of an individual with trusted physical or virtual access to such information—also called insider threat activity.

Insiders within any organization can pose significant threats to the confidentiality and integrity of sensitive data and intellectual property. CISA defines an insider as "any person who has or had authorized access to or knowledge of an organization's resources, including personnel, facilities, information, equipment, networks, and systems."[81] Trusted access does not necessarily require physical presence or direct physical access.

The harm caused by insider threats can often be greater than that of external attacks. The U.S. Center for Development of Security Excellence (CDSE) notes that trusted insiders may engage in malicious activities such as fraud, theft, sabotage, espionage, or unauthorized disclosure. Accidental insiders may inadvertently expose sensitive information, download malware, or facilitate other cybersecurity breaches. Malicious insiders may be disgruntled employees who may wish to cause harm to the organization that they work for. No organization is immune to insider threats, making it critical to establish comprehensive insider threat mitigation programs.[82]

2.8.6 Examples of Insider Threat

- Malicious insider threat
  - A hospital employee accessed and removed electronic PHI over several months and then sold that information to people outside the organization. When federal regulators (HHS OCR) investigated, they found that the hospital allegedly had not performed a thorough risk analysis, did not have sufficient audit controls to track system use, and was not regularly reviewing access logs.[83]
- Negligent insider threat
  - A healthcare clearinghouse experienced a breach when—allegedly—ePHI was inadvertently made publicly accessible on the internet and became searchable online. The information allegedly included patient names, addresses, dates of birth, Social Security numbers, claims data, and treatment details. According to federal regulators (HHS OCR), the clearinghouse had not conducted a comprehensive risk analysis, did not adequately monitor system activity, and failed to put in place sufficient technical safeguards to prevent unauthorized public access.[84]
- Third-party insider threat
  - Some risks originate not from within the organization itself, but from trusted third parties. A prominent example of a cybersecurity supply chain attack occurred in 2013, highlighting the risk associated with third-party insider threats. In 2013, the nature of cyber threats changed significantly when a major retailer suffered a breach through a supply chain attack. Cybercriminals exploited stolen credentials from a heating, ventilation, and air conditioning (HVAC) vendor to infiltrate the retailer's systems. This marked a turning point, highlighting the importance of third-party risk management. Since then, cyber supply chain attacks have increasingly targeted healthcare organizations, often

through compromised vendor credentials. Widely adopted cybersecurity frameworks like the NIST CSF address critical topics like cybersecurity supply chain risk management (C-SCRM).[85]

2.8.7 Practical Guidance for Insider Threats

Insider threats in healthcare may originate from anyone with trusted virtual or physical access to systems, networks, devices, or data—including employees, contractors, vendors, business associates, and others—who handle, come into contact with, or possess knowledge of confidential, protected, proprietary, or sensitive information. Insider threat actors may be individuals or entities, including nonhuman accounts (e.g., service accounts), automated systems, or artificial intelligence (AI)—whether agentic or non-agentic—with authorized access. Because insiders already have virtual or physical trusted access, the risks cannot be ignored.

Healthcare organizations can reduce these risks by taking proactive measures such as, but not limited to, the following[86]:

- Create a formal insider threat program
- Consider threats to the organization from internal and external parties that have trusted access, as part of the organization's risk assessment
- Enforce separation of duties and least privilege for all workforce members
- Monitor and respond to suspicious or disruptive behavior
- Implement strict password and account management policies and practices

2.9 Summary—Threat Landscape

The HPH sector faces a complex and evolving threat landscape that targets both technology and people. Public vulnerability databases such as the NVD and the EUVD provide critical insight into known vulnerabilities, while CVD programs, bug bounty initiatives, and penetration testing help identify and remediate risks before they are exploited.

Social engineering remains one of the most persistent and dangerous threats. Attacks range from broad phishing campaigns to more targeted spear-phishing and whaling attempts. These tactics exploit human psychology through authority, urgency, fear, greed, trust, and familiarity. The anatomy of a social engineering attack helps to illustrate why these campaigns succeed. Emerging techniques, including thread hijacking, deepfake technology, and homoglyph or homograph attacks, further increase the difficulty of detection and defense.

Insider threats compound the risk. Both unintentional and intentional insiders—whether through negligence, coercion, or malicious action—can compromise systems, expose sensitive information, and disrupt operations. Real-world cases demonstrate that insiders, with their privileged access, often pose threats as significant as those from external adversaries.

Ransomware continues to have a profound impact on healthcare, disrupting care delivery, delaying treatment, and threatening patient safety. Its evolution underscores the need for preparedness and resilience. Paying the ransom offers no guarantee of data recovery, making prevention, incident response, and recovery planning essential.

Addressing these challenges requires more than technical defenses. Evolving security awareness programs, combined with governance, cultural change, and resilience—as well as appropriate privacy and security safeguards—are vital to reducing risk. Understanding the threat landscape is a critical first step toward building the resilience necessary to safeguard patients, protect data, and ensure continuity and coordination of care.

Notes

1 NIST. *Vulnerability*. https://csrc.nist.gov/glossary/term/vulnerability.

2 NIST. *Threat*. https://csrc.nist.gov/glossary/term/threat.

3 NIST. *Risk*. https://csrc.nist.gov/glossary/term/risk.

4 National Center for Biotechnology Information. *At the Nexus of Cybersecurity and Public Policy: Some Basic Concepts and Issues*. https://www.ncbi.nlm.nih.gov/books/NBK223221/.

5 Cisco. *What Is an Exploit?* https://www.cisco.com/site/us/en/learn/topics/security/what-is-an-exploit.html.

6 NIST. *Mitigation*. https://csrc.nist.gov/glossary/term/mitigation.

7 NIST. *Patching*. https://csrc.nist.gov/glossary/term/patching.

8 CISA. *Known Exploited Vulnerabilities Catalog*. https://www.cisa.gov/known-exploited-vulnerabilities.

9 NIST. *Threat Actor*. https://csrc.nist.gov/glossary/term/threat_actor.

10 National Vulnerability Database (NVD). *Homepage*. https://nvd.nist.gov.

11 European Union Agency for Cybersecurity (ENISA). *European Vulnerability Database (EUVD)*. https://euvd.enisa.europa.eu/.

See also European Union Agency for Cybersecurity (ENISA). *Another Step Forward Towards Responsible Vulnerability Disclosure in Europe*. https://www.enisa.europa.eu/news/another-step-forward-towards-responsible-vulnerability-disclosure-in-europe.

12 NIST. *Vulnerability Disclosure Guidelines*. https://csrc.nist.gov/projects/vulnerability-disclosure-guidelines.

13 CISA. *Coordinated Vulnerability Disclosure Program*. https://www.cisa.gov/resources-tools/programs/coordinated-vulnerability-disclosure-program.

14 NIST. *SP 800-53, Rev. 5: Security and Privacy Controls for Information Systems and Organizations*. https://nvlpubs.nist.gov/nistpubs/SpecialPublications/NIST.SP.800-53r5.pdf.

15 Bugcrowd. *Public Bug Bounty Program List*. https://www.bugcrowd.com/bug-bounty-list/.

16 NIST. *SP 800-53, Rev. 5: Security and Privacy Controls for Information Systems and Organizations*. https://nvlpubs.nist.gov/nistpubs/SpecialPublications/NIST.SP.800-53r5.pdf.

17 HHS. *Ransomware & Healthcare*. https://www.hhs.gov/sites/default/files/ransomware-healthcare.pdf.

18 Public-Private Analytic Exchange Program. *Phishing—Don't be Phooled! Vulnerabilities of Healthcare Systems*. https://www.hsdl.org/c/view?docid=820189.

19 FTC. *FTC Announces Impersonation Rule Goes into Effect Today*. https://www.ftc.gov/news-events/news/press-releases/2024/04/ftc-announces-impersonation-rule-goes-effect-today. See also FTC. *Celebrating the Impersonation Rule That Helps the FTC Fight Scams*. https://www.ftc.gov/business-guidance/blog/2025/04/celebrating-impersonation-rule-helps-ftc-fight-scams.

20 Public-Private Analytic Exchange Program. *Phishing—Don't be Phooled!* https://www.hsdl.org/c/view?docid=820189.

21 CISA. *Shields Up: Guidance for Families*. https://www.cisa.gov/shields-guidance-families.

22 Cyber Magazine. *Vishing, Smishing, and Quishing Are the Next Ways to Go Phishing*. https://cybermagazine.com/articles/vishing-smishing-and-quishing-are-next-ways-to-go-phishing.

23 Public-Private Analytic Exchange Program. *Phishing—Don't be Phooled!* https://www.hsdl.org/c/view?docid=820189.

24 Public-Private Analytic Exchange Program. *Phishing—Don't be Phooled!* https://www.hsdl.org/c/view?docid=820189.

25 Public-Private Analytic Exchange Program. *Phishing—Don't be Phooled!* https://www.hsdl.org/c/view?docid=820189.

26 Onfido. *The Psychology of Deepfakes: Why We Fall for Them.* https://onfido.com/blog/the-psychology-of-deepfakes-why-we-fall-for-them/.
27 Microsoft Security Blog. *The Psychology of Social Engineering: The "Soft" Side of Cybercrime.* https://www.microsoft.com/en-us/security/blog/2020/06/30/psychology-social-engineering-soft-side-cybercrime/.
28 Proceedings of the APWG Symposium on Electronic Crime Research. *Ten Years of Attacks On Companies Using Visual Impersonation of Domain Names.* https://par.nsf.gov/servlets/purl/10256904.
29 MITRE D3FEND. *Homoglyph Detection.* https://d3fend.mitre.org/technique/d3f:HomoglyphDetection/.
30 Federal Bureau of Investigation (FBI). *Ransomware.* https://www.fbi.gov/how-we-can-help-you/scams-and-safety/common-frauds-and-scams/ransomware.
31 The New York Times. *Cyber Attack Suspected in German Woman's Death.* https://www.nytimes.com/2020/09/18/world/europe/cyber-attack-germany-ransomeware-death.html.
32 Ransomware.org. *The First Ransomware Attack: Lessons Learned from History.* https://ransomware.org/blog/the-first-ransomware-attack-lessons-learned-from-history/.
33 Federal Bureau of Investigation (FBI). *New Internet Scam.* https://www.fbi.gov/news/stories/new-internet-scam.
34 Federal Bureau of Investigation (FBI). *Ransomware on the Rise.* https://www.fbi.gov/news/stories/ransomware-on-the-rise.
35 Federal Bureau of Investigation (FBI)—San Diego Field Office. *FBI Warns Public of CryptoWall Ransomware Schemes.* https://www.fbi.gov/contact-us/field-offices/sandiego/news/press-releases/fbi-warns-public-of-cryptowall-ransomware-schemes.
36 FBI Law Enforcement Bulletin. *Growing Risk of Data Sabotage: Protecting Law Enforcement Agencies.* https://leb.fbi.gov/articles/featured-articles/growing-risk-of-data-sabotage-protecting-law-enforcement-agencies.
37 Federal Bureau of Investigation (FBI). *Ransomware Prevention and Response for CISOs.* https://www.fbi.gov/file-repository/ransomware-prevention-and-response-for-cisos.pdf.
38 CISA. *Alert (AA18-337A).* https://www.cisa.gov/news-events/cybersecurity-advisories/aa18-337a.
39 Federal Bureau of Investigation (FBI). *New Internet Scam.* https://www.fbi.gov/news/stories/new-internet-scam.
MoneyPak® prepaid card is a registered trademark of Green Dot Corporation.
40 CISA. *CryptoLocker Ransomware Infections.* https://www.cisa.gov/news-events/alerts/2013/11/05/cryptolocker-ransomware-infections.
41 International Journal of Information Security, Volume 23. *Cashing Out Crypto: State of Practice in Ransom Payments.* https://link.springer.com/article/10.1007/s10207-023-00766-z.
42 U.S. Department of Health and Human Services—Health Sector Cybersecurity Coordination Center (HHS HC3). *HC3: Top 10 Most Active Ransomware Groups (TLP: CLEAR).* https://www.hhs.gov/sites/default/files/hc3-top-10-most-active-ransomware-groups-analyst-note-tlpclear-r.pdf.
43 Ransomware.live. *Ransomware Ecosystem Map.* https://www.hhs.gov/sites/default/files/hc3-top-10-most-active-ransomware-groups-analyst-note-tlpclear-r.pdf.
44 HHS. *Ransomware & Healthcare.* https://www.hhs.gov/sites/default/files/ransomware-healthcare.pdf.
45 CISA. *Advisory (AA23-353A). #StopRansomware: ALPHV Blackcat.* https://www.cisa.gov/news-events/cybersecurity-advisories/aa23-353a.
46 CISA. *Advisory (AA23-353A). #StopRansomware: ALPHV Blackcat.* https://www.cisa.gov/news-events/cybersecurity-advisories/aa23-353a.
47 CISA. *Advisory (AA23-165A). Understanding Ransomware Threat Actors: LockBit.* https://www.cisa.gov/news-events/cybersecurity-advisories/aa23-165a.
48 CISA. *Stop Ransomware Guide.* https://www.cisa.gov/stopransomware/ransomware-guide.
49 Internet Crime Complaint Center (IC3). *Joint Cybersecurity Advisory. #StopRansomware: ALPHV Blackcat.* https://www.ic3.gov/CSA/2023/231219.pdf
50 ITPro. *The Rise of Double-Extortion Ransomware.* https://www.itpro.com/security/ransomware/367624/the-rise-of-double-extortion-ransomware.
51 Cloud Security Alliance. *Safeguarding the Healthcare Industry: Effective Measures to Prevent Ransomware Attacks.* https://cloudsecurityalliance.org/blog/2023/09/25/safeguarding-the-healthcare-industry-effective-measures-to-prevent-ransomware-attacks.
52 National Audit Office (UK). *Investigation: WannaCry Cyber Attack and the NHS.* https://www.nao.org.uk/wp-content/uploads/2017/10/Investigation-WannaCry-cyber-attack-and-the-NHS.pdf.

53 CSO Online. *WannaCry Explained: A Perfect Ransomware Storm*. https://www.csoonline.com/article/563017/wannacry-explained-a-perfect-ransomware-storm.html.
54 Microsoft Learn. *Microsoft Security Bulletin MS17-010—Critical. Security Update for Microsoft Windows SMB Server (4013389)*. https://learn.microsoft.com/en-us/security-updates/SecurityBulletins/2017/ms17-010.
55 BBC News. *Ransomware cyber-attack: Who has been hardest hit?* https://www.bbc.com/news/world-39919249.
56 PC World. *Paying the WannaCry Ransom Will Probably Get You Nothing—Here's Why*. https://www.pcworld.com/article/406793/paying-the-wannacry-ransom-will-probably-get-you-nothing-heres-why.html.
57 New Scientist. *Ransomware attack hits 200,000 computers across the globe*. https://www.newscientist.com/article/2130983-ransomware-attack-hits-200000-computers-across-the-globe/.
58 WIRED. *How an Accidental "Kill Switch" Slowed Friday's Massive Ransomware Attack*. https://www.wired.com/2017/05/accidental-kill-switch-slowed-fridays-massive-ransomware-attack/.
59 DOJ. *North Korean Regime-Backed Programmer Charged in Conspiracy to Conduct Multiple Cyber Attacks and Intrusions*. https://www.justice.gov/opa/pr/north-korean-regime-backed-programmer-charged-conspiracy-conduct-multiple-cyber-attacks-and.
60 Federal Bureau of Investigation (FBI). *Ransomware Prevention and Response for CISOs*. https://www.fbi.gov/file-repository/ransomware-prevention-and-response-for-cisos.pdf.
61 HHS. *Fact Sheet: Ransomware and HIPAA*. https://www.hhs.gov/hipaa/for-professionals/security/guidance/cybersecurity/ransomware-fact-sheet/index.html.
62 HHS. *Covered Entities and Business Associates*. https://www.hhs.gov/hipaa/for-professionals/covered-entities/index.html.
63 HHS. *Health Information Privacy*. https://www.hhs.gov/hipaa/index.html. See also HHS. The HIPAA Enforcement Rule. https://www.hhs.gov/hipaa/for-professionals/special-topics/enforcement-rule/index.html.
64 Federal Bureau of Investigation (FBI). *Ransomware Prevention and Response for CISOs*. https://www.fbi.gov/file-repository/ransomware-prevention-and-response-for-cisos.pdf.
65 U.S. Department of the Treasury—Office of Foreign Assets Control (OFAC). *Sanctions Programs and Country Information*. https://ofac.treasury.gov/sanctions-programs-and-country-information.
66 CISA. *Defining Insider Threats*. https://www.cisa.gov/topics/physical-security/insider-threat-mitigation/defining-insider-threats.
67 CISA. *Defining Insider Threats*. https://www.cisa.gov/topics/physical-security/insider-threat-mitigation/defining-insider-threats.
68 CISA. *Defining Insider Threats*. https://www.cisa.gov/topics/physical-security/insider-threat-mitigation/defining-insider-threats.
69 CISA. *Defining Insider Threats*. https://www.cisa.gov/topics/physical-security/insider-threat-mitigation/defining-insider-threats.
70 CISA. *Defining Insider Threats*. https://www.cisa.gov/topics/physical-security/insider-threat-mitigation/defining-insider-threats.
71 CISA. *Insider Threat Mitigation*. https://www.cisa.gov/topics/physical-security/insider-threat-mitigation.
72 CISA. *Defining Insider Threats*. https://www.cisa.gov/topics/physical-security/insider-threat-mitigation/defining-insider-threats.
73 CISA. *Defining Insider Threats*. https://www.cisa.gov/topics/physical-security/insider-threat-mitigation/defining-insider-threats.
74 CISA. *Defining Insider Threats*. https://www.cisa.gov/topics/physical-security/insider-threat-mitigation/defining-insider-threats.
75 CISA. *Defining Insider Threats*. https://www.cisa.gov/topics/physical-security/insider-threat-mitigation/defining-insider-threats.
76 CISA. *Defining Insider Threats*. https://www.cisa.gov/topics/physical-security/insider-threat-mitigation/defining-insider-threats.
77 CISA. *Defining Insider Threats*. https://www.cisa.gov/topics/physical-security/insider-threat-mitigation/defining-insider-threats.
78 IBM. *What are Insider Threats?* https://www.ibm.com/topics/insider-threats/.
79 Eftsure. *Insider Threat Statistics: Malicious Intent or Ignorance?* https://www.eftsure.com/statistics/insider-threat-statistics/.

80 CISA. *Defining Insider Threats*. https://www.cisa.gov/topics/physical-security/insider-threat-mitigation/defining-insider-threats.
81 CISA. *Insider Threat Mitigation*. https://www.cisa.gov/topics/physical-security/insider-threat-mitigation.
82 Public-Private Analytic Exchange Program. *Protecting and Defending Hidden Treasures*. https://www.dhs.gov/sites/default/files/publications/protecting_and_defending_hidden_treasures.pdf.
83 U.S. Department of Health and Human Services—Office for Civil Rights (HHS OCR). *Voluntary Resolution Agreement Between The United States Department of Health and Human Services, Office for Civil Rights ("HHS") and Montefiore*. https://www.hhs.gov/hipaa/for-professionals/compliance-enforcement/agreements/montiefore/index.html.
84 HHS OCR. *Inmediata Health Group, LLC Resolution Agreement and Corrective Action Plan*. https://www.hhs.gov/hipaa/for-professionals/compliance-enforcement/agreements/inmediata-health-group-ra-cap/index.html.
85 NIST. *Cybersecurity Framework (CSF)*. https://www.nist.gov/cyberframework.
86 Carnegie Mellon University (CMU)—Software Engineering Institute (SEI). *Common Sense Guide to Mitigating Insider Threats, Seventh Edition*. https://www.sei.cmu.edu/library/common-sense-guide-to-mitigating-insider-threats-seventh-edition/.

Chapter 3

Identity, Authentication, and Access Management

3.1 Why Identity Is Crucial for Cybersecurity

As stated previously, the three primary goals of cybersecurity are as follows: confidentiality, integrity, and availability in the context of the "CIA" triad. These goals are essentially the "why" of cybersecurity. This is what we do to safeguard data, systems, devices, and infrastructure using physical, technical, and administrative controls. In healthcare cybersecurity, the patient is the ultimate beneficiary of robust, effective safeguards.

3.2 Practical Example of the "CIA" Triad

Let's illustrate the "CIA" triad with a hypothetical example. Imagine that you own a building and also the personal property within the building. Only certain people are allowed in that building and they can access only certain things. "CIA" stands for the fundamental notion of "this is my stuff" and "you can't touch it unless you are allowed to do so." We safeguard infrastructure, assets, and data so that only those who are authorized to access them actually can.

But who do we allow to access the infrastructure, assets, and data? And how do we allocate this access? This depends on business requirements, the risks involved, and contractual and other applicable legal and regulatory considerations. One way to think about this concept—within the context of your own organization—is by applying the IAAA paradigm: identity, authentication, authorization, and accountability.[1] Infrastructure, systems, devices, and data can be protected using the IAAA paradigm.

Let's think of this within the context of a security guard who is protecting a building. The building is an office building with various companies and floors you can go to. Depending on who you are, you can access certain offices in the building and other areas of the building. Imagine that you are entering that building and there is a security guard at the front desk.

The first question the security guard will ask is "Who are you?" The identity is established when the individual presents a valid form of identification. Identity provides the basis for controlling access,

DOI: 10.4324/9781003366560-3

ensuring that only authorized individuals or systems interact with data, assets, and infrastructure. How do we establish and verify identity? We do that through identity proofing and then identity verification.

The security guard then asks the question "Can you show me your ID?" Typically, you will be asked for a government-issued identity card (ID) such as a driver's license, state identification card, or passport. This is known as identity proofing—proving you are who you claim to be—with a government-issued ID.

The security guard will then compare your ID to your face. This is a way that the security guard answers the question, "Is this the same person as who they claim to be?" This is the process of identity verification. In other words, who you claim to be is not simply assumed on the basis of your being able to produce an ID. Rather, the security guard will verify that you are the person you claim to be by looking at you and the photo on the ID that you presented earlier.

After the identity proofing and verification, the security guard will then ask "Where are you going?" This is a question that relates to authorization. With authorization, the following questions are involved: "What are you allowed to access? Where are you allowed to go?" The security guard can perform actions like checking the visitor list for the day to see if your name is on the list and determine which areas of the building you are allowed to access.

The security guard will then call the office where you want to go and let them know that you are there to visit. This step is part of authentication, where your identity and purpose are validated in real-time. The person receiving the call will confirm whether you are expected and authorized to proceed. If they say you are cleared to visit, the security guard will allow you access to the appropriate office. At this point, you may be given directions on how to get to your destination and otherwise how to proceed.

Let's say you then proceed to the elevators to access the particular office. Video cameras monitor your movements via closed-circuit television (CCTV), allowing the security guard to ensure that you are heading to the areas you are authorized to access. The footage is recorded and stored for later playback, if needed. This process is known as accountability, ensuring compliance with the scope of your authorization and creating a video recording of activity for security and audit purposes.

The IAAA paradigm (identification, authentication, authorization, and accountability) is sometimes expanded to IAAAA, with the additional "A" representing Audit. Auditing is a crucial function in cybersecurity, ensuring that security policies and compliance requirements are being followed. However, unlike real-time security measures, auditing is typically a post-event analysis, verifying whether security controls operated as intended.

Consider a physical security example: after visitors enter a building, security personnel may later review access logs and surveillance footage to confirm that entry rules were followed and that no unauthorized activity took place. Similarly, in cybersecurity, an audit examines system logs, activity, and security measures after the fact to ensure compliance and detect potential issues.

Auditors take a systematic and independent approach to reviewing security practices. Their role is not to react to immediate threats but to:

- Verify that policies and security controls are consistently applied.
- Identify anomalies, gaps, or potential weaknesses in the system.
- Ensure compliance with regulatory and organizational requirements.
- Provide recommendations to improve security and maintain accountability.

Auditors act as a final checkpoint, ensuring that security measures are not just in place but also effective in practice. Their assessments drive continuous improvements, helping organizations refine policies and strengthen their defenses.

3.3 A Spotlight on Patient Registration: The Importance of Identity

When a patient arrives at a hospital or clinic, they begin at the registration area, where their identity is confirmed. The patient provides a government-issued identification card or another approved form of identification, and the registrar checks the name and photo on the document to ensure it matches the person standing in front of them. This step is about establishing the individual's identity—proving they are who they say they are based on the credentials they present.

After that, the registrar gathers and verifies essential details like date of birth, address, and insurance coverage. For patients who have been there before, this information is cross-checked against existing records. For new patients, it is used to set up their profile in the system.

Throughout the visit, hospital or clinic staff repeatedly confirm the patient's identity and ask the patient to verify their identity. This happens at every key moment, including during intake, before medications are administered, ahead of any procedure or diagnostic test, and when moving the patient between units or departments. These repeated checks ensure that care is delivered accurately: the right patient, the right treatment, at the right time. It also ensures the right information is associated with the right patient.

Just like in digital systems, hospitals rely on auditing too. Compliance teams review access logs, billing records, and staff activity to verify that protocols were followed and to detect anything out of the ordinary. If something does go wrong, these logs help trace the sequence of events and identify who was involved.

3.4 Authentication, Access Control, and Authorization

Authentication is the process of verifying identity to ensure that only authorized individuals or entities can access designated areas, systems, or resources. Whether accessing email, logging into a system, or approving a sensitive transaction, authentication confirms the legitimacy of the user or entity involved.

Weak authentication mechanisms increase the risk of unauthorized access, data breaches, and fraud. Therefore, the ability to authenticate identity reliably is essential to protecting digital assets. The strength of authentication depends on the quality of the factors used to verify identity. If a factor is compromised, easily guessed, or spoofed, there is less assurance that the individual or entity is who—or what—is claimed.

3.4.1 Access Management and Least Privilege

Healthcare organizations rely on *digital identity solutions* to manage who can access systems, applications, and sensitive data. Two key types of solutions that support this are *Identity and Access Management (IAM)* and *Privileged Access Management (PAM).*

- **IAM** systems manage digital identities by handling accounts, login processes, and access permissions. On their own, IAM tools do not determine who gets access to what; they provide the infrastructure. When configured to assign access based on job functions, this approach is known as *role-based access control (RBAC)*—a widely used method in healthcare environments.

- **PAM** protects privileged accounts—such as those with *root* or *administrator* access—that can make system-wide changes or access sensitive data and systems. PAM enforces tighter controls, including session monitoring, time-based access, and stronger authentication requirements.

3.4.2 What Is Least Privilege?

Least privilege means limiting each user's access to only what is needed to perform assigned job functions. For example, a staff member who needs to view lab results should not be able to change patient medications or access billing systems.

RBAC is a widely adopted access control model for enforcing the principle of least privilege within an organization. Using this model, roles are established based on defined job functions, such as nurse, technician, or administrative staff, and access rights are assigned to these roles. The advantage of using RBAC as an access control model is that it streamlines access management, reduces administrative burden, and helps to ensure that individuals are granted only what is necessary to carry out their job functions.

In healthcare organizations, job functions frequently change due to internal transfers, reductions in force, restructuring of teams, promotions, or evolving job functions. These role changes introduce significant risk if access permissions are not updated accordingly. An individual might retain access to sensitive systems or patient data that no longer aligns with their current job functions. Therefore, it is essential that access privileges are precisely scoped to what the individual needs for the specific role at that point in time. It is also necessary for both IAM and HR systems to have current, up-to-date information that accurately reflects the roles of individuals within the healthcare organization and ensure that this information remains consistent across both systems.[2]

3.4.3 Authentication Versus Authorization

Authentication and authorization are often linked, but they serve different purposes (Table 3.1):

- Authentication verifies who the user is.
- Authorization determines what the authenticated user is allowed to do.

Table 3.1 Comparison of Authentication and Authorization

Authentication	*Authorization*
Verifies the identity of the user	Determines which resources the user is permitted to access
Occurs before authorization	Takes place after successful authentication
Example: Logging in with multi-factor authentication (MFA)	Example: Access granted to an administrative dashboard
Uses credentials (e.g., username and password), biometric data (e.g., fingerprint, facial recognition), tokens (e.g., smart cards, authenticator apps), or behavioral biometrics (e.g., typing patterns)[3]	Based on roles, policies, or access control rules

3.4.4 Authentication and Authorization

Authentication always happens first. Once the system confirms a user's identity—through a password, biometric scan, passkey, or another method—authorization rules determine what that user can access. These rules are typically based on roles, group membership, or access policies configured within IAM or PAM systems.

For example, after logging in through a Single Sign-On (SSO) portal using Multi-Factor Authentication (MFA), the system may recognize the user as part of the clinical staff and allow access only to patient records and internal messaging. MFA typically requires two or more factors—such as something the user knows (a password), something the user has (a device or token), or something the user is (a biometric). However, many organizations are now shifting toward passwordless authentication, which eliminates passwords entirely and instead relies on more secure methods like passkeys, security keys, or device-based biometrics. These approaches reduce the risk of phishing, credential theft, and account compromise, offering a stronger foundation for identity verification.

3.4.5 Applying the Principle of Least Privilege: A Best Practice

When access is managed using the principle of least privilege, each user receives only what is needed to perform their job functions. This reduces unnecessary exposure and limits the impact of compromised accounts.[4]

A best practice is a proven and widely accepted method for achieving a specific goal—in this case, securing systems and data. In cybersecurity, best practices are guidelines or strategies that consistently lead to better protection, lower risk, and fewer incidents.

For example, applying the principle of least privilege is a best practice. It means giving users only the minimum level of access they need to perform their work—nothing more.

3.4.6 The State of Authentication

The increasing frequency and sophistication of cyberattacks have highlighted the weaknesses of password-based security. Passwords can be vulnerable to credential theft, phishing, and brute force attacks. Strong passwords may be compromised through data breaches or social engineering. Authentication, the process of verifying the identity of a user, process, or device—often as a prerequisite to allowing access to resources in an information system—has traditionally relied on passwords as the primary method of verification.[5] However, the growing limitations of this approach are driving the adoption of more secure alternatives.

3.4.7 The Shift Away from Passwords

Passwords remain one of the most common ways to authenticate users, but they come with significant risks and limitations. Weak, reused, or stolen passwords are among the most common methods attackers use to gain unauthorized access to systems. If a single set of credentials is exposed, attackers can attempt to use it across multiple accounts in a technique known as *credential stuffing*.

Strong passwords can be guessed, phished, or exposed through a data breach. Furthermore, long and complex passwords, though more secure, are often difficult to remember, leading individuals to rely on insecure patterns or to record them in unsafe ways. These persistent challenges have fueled a growing shift toward passwordless authentication, which seeks to verify identity through more secure and convenient methods that do not rely on traditional passwords.

3.4.8 Spotlight on Credential Stuffing: Password Attacks

Credential stuffing is a type of cyberattack in which adversaries use stolen username and password combinations, often obtained from large-scale data breaches, to gain unauthorized access to accounts on other websites or services. Unlike *brute force attacks*, which attempt to guess passwords through repeated automated attempts, credential stuffing uses legitimate credentials that have already been exposed, giving it a higher success rate.[6]

The attack typically unfolds in several phases. First, attackers acquire massive lists of compromised usernames and passwords, frequently purchased from underground marketplaces or retrieved from public credential dumps. These lists can contain millions of entries. Next, the stolen credentials are loaded into automated tools, known as "checkers," which attempt logins across a wide range of websites such as banking, e-commerce, healthcare portals, and social media platforms.[7]

Once access is gained, attackers may steal sensitive personal or financial data, hijack email accounts for fraudulent activity, conduct identity theft, or sell the compromised accounts on criminal marketplaces. The HPH sector, for example, is a frequent target because of the value of personal health and insurance data. In some documented cases, credential stuffing has led to the compromise of thousands of customer accounts, exposing personally identifiable information, account balances, and medical records.[8]

The economics of credential stuffing attacks also favor adversaries, since a small success rate can yield thousands of compromised accounts that can be monetized.[9]

3.4.9 Spotlight on Password Spraying: Password Attacks

Password spraying is a password attack technique that exploits the tendency of users to create simple, predictable, or commonly used passwords. Unlike brute force attacks, which attempt a large number of possible passwords against a single account, password spraying uses a small set of frequently chosen passwords and tests them across many different accounts. This method allows attackers to avoid account lockouts that might occur after repeated failed attempts on a single account.[10]

Password spraying is particularly effective because many users select passwords that meet complexity rules but are still easy to guess. Examples include passwords based on dictionary words, predictable patterns, or slight variations of terms such as "password" combined with numbers or symbols. When policies require a mix of uppercase letters, digits, and special characters, attackers can anticipate these predictable patterns and incorporate them into their attempts.[11]

To defend against password spraying, security guidelines such as NIST SP 800–63 recommend disallowing commonly used or compromised passwords, promoting longer passphrases instead of short complex words, and requiring robust MFA wherever possible. These measures reduce the likelihood that an attacker using password spraying will succeed in gaining unauthorized access.

3.4.10 Password Guidelines

To strengthen defenses against attacks such as password spraying, the latest NIST Digital Identity Guidelines (Special Publication 800–63) continue to emphasize modern best practices for password security[12]:

- **Block weak or compromised passwords**
  Authentication systems (verifiers) must screen new passwords against lists of commonly used, expected, or previously breached passwords, preventing their use at account creation or reset.
- **Encourage longer passphrases**
  Greater length and unpredictability are recommended.
- **Require multi-factor authentication (MFA)**
  MFA is mandatory for higher risk accounts and strongly recommended for all others. A second factor can reduce the effectiveness of password spraying attacks.
- **Eliminate routine password expiration**
  Regular forced password changes are discouraged unless there is evidence of compromise. Frequent changes often lead to predictable modifications that reduce overall security.
- **Use secure storage methods**
  Passwords should never be stored in plain text. Instead, they must be protected with advanced cryptographic hashing methods that add unique random data (salts) and are designed to make large-scale cracking attempts slow and difficult

3.4.11 Security Questions: The Weak Link in Password Recovery

Security questions are often used as a backup method to recover passwords, but they are not inherently secure. Common questions—such as "What is your mother's maiden name?" or "What was your first car?"—are easily guessable or can be found through public sources or social media. A security question is only effective when both the question and the answer are unique. The security question and answer should be unique to the individual and not easily guessed or found online. This helps provide more assurance that the person responding is actually the user.

3.4.12 How Identity and Authentication Work Together

Identity and authentication form the foundation of secure access. Identity refers to the unique representation of an individual within a system, while authentication is the process of verifying that an individual is who they claim to be. Together, these mechanisms ensure that only authorized individuals are permitted access to sensitive systems and data.

NIST provides detailed guidance on identity proofing and authentication requirements through Special Publication 800–63. NIST SP 800–63A discusses identity proofing and enrollment to support Identity Assurance Levels (IALs), specifying the processes and evidence necessary to verify an individual's identity. This includes requirements for remote and in-person proofing, acceptable identity evidence, and validation procedures.[13]

NIST SP 800–63B addresses authentication mechanisms that provide a balance between usability and security to support Authenticator Assurance Levels (AALs).[14] Information on replay-resistant authentication mechanisms is provided in NIST Special Publication 800-53.[15]

These assurance levels are particularly important in healthcare, where unauthorized access to patient records or clinical systems can compromise both patient privacy and safety. By following NIST guidance, healthcare organizations can establish robust identity proofing and authentication processes that align with federal standards and industry best practices.

Passwordless authentication is an emerging approach that strengthens identity security by eliminating reliance on traditional passwords, which are often susceptible to compromise. Instead of requiring users to remember and enter a password, this method employs authenticator mobile applications (authenticator apps),[16] device-based or application-based authenticators unlocked using biometric verification, or secure hardware tokens.[17] For example, in a healthcare environment, a clinician may authenticate using a biometric scan in combination with a cryptographic key stored on a secure device, such as an RFID-enabled employee badge, a smart card, or a FIDO2-compliant security key. FIDO2 is a set of phishing-resistant authentication standards jointly developed by the FIDO Alliance and the World Wide Web Consortium (W3C), combining the Web Authentication (WebAuthn) specification and the Client-to-Authenticator Protocols (CTAP) to support passwordless and multi-factor authentication using passkeys. FIDO Alliance. *User Authentication Specifications Overview.* https://fidoalliance.org/specifications/. By removing static passwords, passwordless authentication reduces the risk of credential theft, phishing, and replay attacks while improving user convenience. This aligns with NIST recommendations for stronger authentication methods that enhance both security and usability.

3.4.13 Spotlight on Digital Federated Identity

Digital federated identity is a core element of secure access in healthcare cybersecurity. This model allows a single verified identity to be used across multiple systems, platforms, and organizations, reducing the need to manage multiple credentials while strengthening both security and usability.

The Centers for Medicare & Medicaid Services (CMS) is advancing patient-centric digital healthcare through the implementation of federated identity verification. This approach aligns with NIST standards for IAL2 and AAL2, providing secure access to electronic health information for patients, providers, and caregivers. (Federated digital identity solutions refer to systems that enable individuals to securely use a single verified identity across multiple platforms and organizations, consistent with current NIST assurance levels such as IAL2 and AAL2.)[18]

By reducing reliance on static passwords and fragmented identity systems, digital federated identity can improve interoperability, lower administrative burden, and enhance the protection of patient information—and ultimately, patient safety.

3.4.14 Passwordless Authentication

Passwordless authentication refers to any method that allows users to log in without entering a password. This approach addresses the problems associated with passwords—such as reuse, weak complexity, and phishing—and shifts authentication toward more secure and user-friendly alternatives.[19]

FIDO2 is the most widely adopted standard for strong passwordless authentication.[20] It uses public-key cryptography.

Public-key cryptography is a method of securing data using a pair of keys: a public key and a private key. The public key can be shared with anyone, while the private key is kept secret and securely stored on the user's device. Public and private keys work together as a matched pair.

In the context of passwordless authentication, the online service or application stores the public key. When the user tries to log in, the service sends a challenge. The user's device uses the private key to sign that challenge, and the service verifies the signature using the public key. At no point is the private key sent or exposed (so long as the key is securely managed in a protected environment). This allows the user to prove identity without sharing any secrets.

Services like Gmail, Windows Hello, and Apple's Face ID or Touch ID with iCloud Keychain all support passwordless login using FIDO2-based passkeys. These systems use passkeys, which are cryptographic credentials stored securely on the device. The user unlocks the passkey using a local method, such as a fingerprint, facial recognition, or a device PIN. Biometrics are not the credentials themselves—they are simply used to access the passkey stored on the device. The login process is completed without ever requiring a password—when a passwordless authentication method is used.

While many passwordless authentication methods rely on FIDO2, not all services do. Some still use one-time codes sent by SMS or email, or apps that allow users to approve login attempts with a simple tap or click—whether on a phone, desktop, or other trusted device. Although more convenient than entering a password, these methods remain vulnerable to phishing and accidental approval.

Passwordless authentication methods that rely on push notifications or approval prompts can be exploited through repeated or persistent login attempts that trick or pressure the user into granting approval to access the account. This technique is known as a *push-fatigue attack* or *push bombing*. If a user approves the request, the attacker may be granted access to the user's account.[21]

3.4.15 Spotlight on Password Attacks—Multi-Factor Authentication (MFA) Bombing

MFA is a control for reducing the risk of unauthorized access by requiring users to present two or more independent factors, such as a password, an authenticator mobile application, or a biometric scan. While MFA significantly increases security compared to password-only authentication, it is not immune to exploitation. One common technique used by attackers is MFA bombing, also known as MFA fatigue.

In an MFA bombing attack, an adversary repeatedly sends authentication prompts to a user's device in an attempt to pressure, distract, or trick the user into approving one of the requests. This may involve dozens of push notifications or login prompts delivered in rapid succession. If the user unwittingly approves the fraudulent request, the attacker can gain access to the user's account.

To reduce this risk, the Cybersecurity and Infrastructure Security Agency (CISA) recommends implementing number matching in push-based MFA systems. With number matching, a code is displayed on the login screen and must be entered into the authenticator application, preventing simple "approve" responses that attackers can exploit. This approach raises user awareness of each login attempt and reduces the likelihood of accidental approval.[22]

3.4.16 Account Takeovers

In many cyberattacks, attackers do not have to break through *firewalls* or *crack encryption*. Instead, cyberattackers can gain access by taking over accounts—including user, system, and service accounts—especially those with elevated privileges. This is known as account takeover (ATO). ATO involves using stolen login credentials to impersonate a legitimate authenticated identity. These credentials might be obtained through phishing, reused passwords, or other techniques that exploit weak access controls.

Once inside, attackers can move laterally through networks, access sensitive systems, and exfiltrate data—all while appearing as authorized activity. In the Target breach of 2013, attackers gained access to Target's network by using stolen credentials from a third-party HVAC vendor. Once inside Target's network, the attackers moved laterally through the network and ultimately accessed point-of-sale (POS) systems, leading to the theft of credit and debit card data of approximately 40 million customers, along with personal information of up to 70 million individuals.[23]

In the SolarWinds attack (2020), attackers compromised the software supply chain to insert malicious code, which gave them access to customer environments where they leveraged trusted access to move laterally and access sensitive systems.[24]

One of the most effective defenses against ATO is phishing-resistant authentication. This refers to authentication mechanisms that do not rely on shared secrets like passwords, which can be intercepted, guessed, or reused. Phishing-resistant methods include solutions based on the FIDO2 standard.

Passkeys are one such example. They are cryptographic credentials stored securely on a device—such as a phone or laptop—and unlocked using biometrics or a device PIN. Because passkeys are tied to both the specific device and the legitimate website or service, they cannot be used elsewhere and cannot be stolen through phishing. This eliminates many of the risks associated with traditional passwords.

When properly implemented, phishing-resistant authentication significantly reduces the risk of ATO. This is why strong, modern identity protections are essential to securing today's healthcare environments.

These examples highlight why identity is a critical part of cybersecurity. When attackers gain control of privileged accounts, they can move laterally through systems, access sensitive information, and cause significant harm. This is why many organizations are shifting toward passwordless authentication methods, such as FIDO2, which eliminate passwords entirely and make ATO much harder. By removing shared secrets and replacing them with cryptographic credentials bound to devices, passwordless systems help curtail one of the most commonly exploited attack vectors—the theft and misuse of passwords to take over accounts.

3.4.17 Accountability: Linking Actions to Activity

A core part of identity management is accountability—knowing which individual or what entity is performing actions within a system. In cybersecurity, every action should be linked to a specific authenticated identity—that is, a unique user, system, or service account. This linkage is established through unique identification, authentication, and detailed logging and auditing. Non-repudiation strengthens accountability by ensuring that the authenticated identity cannot later deny taking an action tied to its credentials. This is achieved through measures such as digital signatures and secure audit logs that preserve evidence and prevent tampering. Together, these controls allow organizations to trace actions to the correct authenticated identity, detect suspicious behavior, respond to incidents, and maintain compliance with security and privacy requirements.

3.4.17.1 Spotting Unusual Activity

Audit logs allow organizations to track activity over time. When activity deviates from established patterns—such as logins from unusual locations, access during atypical hours, or actions inconsistent with an assigned role—monitoring tools can generate alerts. These alerts can enable early identification of potential security incidents and help ensure timely response before they escalate.

3.4.17.2 Supporting Investigations and Response

When a security incident occurs, logs tied to authenticated identities are essential. They provide a detailed record of activity—what was done, when it was done, and by whom. This information can enable incident response teams to reconstruct events, contain the impact, and implement measures to prevent recurrence. During incident response, teams examine how the incident occurred, isolate affected systems, remove malicious code or unauthorized access, restore normal operations, and apply safeguards to reduce the likelihood of similar incidents.[25]

3.4.17.3 Practical Example: Insider Threat Activity

A hospital employee logs into the electronic health record (EHR) system using valid credentials. Over several days, the employee accesses dozens of patient records unrelated to that person's role. This includes the record of a high-profile patient recently in the news. The activity is not immediately noticed.

However, the system is configured to log all activities, with each event tied to a specific authenticated identity. These logs feed into auditing tools designed to detect unusual patterns, such as access to records during off-hours or accessing large numbers of records in a short period of time. After a period of review, the activity is flagged as abnormal.

The healthcare organization's security team investigates and takes appropriate action. They confirm the access was unauthorized. Without proper auditing and accountability measures, this type of privacy violation might go undetected or be impossible to trace.

This example highlights why accountability is essential in identity management. It is not enough to assign access—organizations must track how access is used. In cybersecurity, every action must be traceable to an individual identity. This supports real-time alerts, policy enforcement, and forensic investigations. Not all threats come from the outside. In some cases, the threat comes from someone inside the organization who already has valid credentials. This is known as an insider threat. Whether intentional or accidental, it reinforces the need to log and review user activity—not just control who has access, but monitor how that access is being used.[26]

3.5 Summary—Identity, Authentication, and Access Management

Identity forms the cornerstone of healthcare cybersecurity. Effectively establishing and verifying identity help to ensure that only authorized individuals can access sensitive systems and patient information. This principle is central to the confidentiality, integrity, and availability (CIA) triad and applies from the moment of patient registration through every interaction with clinical and administrative systems.

Authentication and authorization are the foundation of identity security. Applying the principle of least privilege ensures that individuals receive only the access necessary to perform their duties, reducing the risk of compromise. Authentication and authorization work hand in hand—first verifying who an individual is, then determining what that individual is permitted to do.

Traditional password-based authentication continues to face significant challenges. Attacks such as credential stuffing, password spraying, and phishing exploit weak or reused credentials. Security questions often prove to be a weak link in password recovery. MFA strengthens defenses but can still be undermined through techniques like MFA bombing. ATOs remain a significant threat, affecting systems and devices that rely on passwords as well as traditional MFA implementations.

The shift toward passwordless authentication and federated digital identity offers stronger protections by reducing reliance on static credentials. These approaches, when combined with role-based access controls, phishing-resistant MFA, and continuous monitoring, strengthen identity assurance while improving usability.

Accountability is equally important. Linking actions to specific authenticated identities through detailed audit logs allows organizations to detect anomalous activity, support investigations, and take appropriate response measures.

Notes

1 DustyBugger. *Access Management: What Is the IAAA Framework?* https://dustybugger.com/what-is-the-iaaa-framework.
2 HR Fraternity. *How to Ensure Accuracy and Timeliness in Syncing HR and IT Information Flow.* https://hrfraternity.com/hr-excellence/how-to-ensure-accuracy-and-timeliness-in-syncing-hr-and-it-information-flow.html.
3 CDW. *Hard Tokens vs. Soft Tokens.* https://www.cdw.com/content/cdw/en/articles/security/hard-tokens-vs-soft-tokens.html.
4 U.S. Office of Information Security—Health Sector Cybersecurity Coordination Center HC3. *Privileged User Compromise.* https://hrfraternity.com/hr-excellence/how-to-ensure-accuracy-and-timeliness-in-syncing-hr-and-it-information-flow.html.
5 NIST—Computer Security Resource Center. *Authentication.* https://csrc.nist.gov/glossary/term/authentication.
6 U.S. Department of Health and Human Services—Health Sector Cybersecurity Coordination Center (HHS HC3). *Credential Stuffing.* https://www.hhs.gov/sites/default/files/credential-stuffing.pdf.
7 HHS HC3. *Credential Stuffing.* https://www.hhs.gov/sites/default/files/credential-stuffing.pdf.
8 HHS HC3. *Credential Stuffing.* https://www.hhs.gov/sites/default/files/credential-stuffing.pdf.
9 HHS HC3. *Credential Stuffing.* https://www.hhs.gov/sites/default/files/credential-stuffing.pdf.
10 U.S. Department of the Interior—Office of Inspector General. *P@s$w0rds at the U.S. Department of the Interior: Easily Cracked Passwords, Lack of Multifactor Authentication, and Other Failures Put Critical DOI Systems at Risk (Report No. 2021-ITA-005).* https://www.doioig.gov/sites/default/files/2021-migration/Final%20Inspection%20Report_DOI%20Password_Public.pdf.
11 U.S. Department of the Interior—Office of Inspector General. *P@s$w0rds at the U.S. Department of the Interior: Easily Cracked Passwords, Lack of Multifactor Authentication, and Other Failures Put Critical DOI Systems at Risk (Report No. 2021-ITA-005).* https://www.doioig.gov/sites/default/files/2021-migration/Final%20Inspection%20Report_DOI%20Password_Public.pdf.
12 NIST. *NIST SP 800-63: Digital Identity Guidelines.* https://pages.nist.gov/800-63-4/. See also NIST. SP 800-63B-4: Digital Identity Guidelines: Authentication and Lifecycle Management. https://pages.nist.gov/800-63-4/sp800-63b.html.
13 NIST. *SP 800-63A-4: Digital Identity Guidelines: Authentication and Lifecycle Management.* https://pages.nist.gov/800-63-4/sp800-63a.html.
14 NIST. *SP 800-63B-4: Digital Identity Guidelines: Authentication and Lifecycle Management.* https://pages.nist.gov/800-63-4/sp800-63b.html.
As defined by NIST, a replay attack is an attack that involves the capture of transmitted authentication or access control information and its subsequent retransmission with the intent of producing an unauthorized effect or gaining unauthorized access. NIST. *Replay Attack.* https://csrc.nist.gov/glossary/term/replay_attack.
As also defined by NIST, replay resistance means protection against the capture of transmitted authentication or access control information and its subsequent retransmission with the intent of producing an unauthorized effect or gaining unauthorized access. NIST. Computer Security Resource Center Glossary. *Replay Resistance.* https://csrc.nist.gov/glossary/term/replay_resistance.
15 NIST. *NIST SP 800-53, Rev. 5: Security and Privacy Controls for Information Systems and Organizations.* https://nvlpubs.nist.gov/nistpubs/SpecialPublications/NIST.SP.800-53r5.pdf.
16 All About Cookies. *How Authenticators Work and Why You May Need One.* https://allaboutcookies.org/what-is-an-authenticator-app.
17 Yubico. *FIDO2 Passwordless Authentication.* https://www.yubico.com/authentication-standards/fido2/.

18 Centers for Medicare & Medicaid Services (CMS). *White House Tech Leaders Commit to Create Patient-Centric Healthcare Ecosystem.* https://www.cms.gov/newsroom/press-releases/white-house-tech-leaders-commit-create-patient-centric-healthcare-ecosystem.
19 Cybersecurity and Infrastructure Security Agency (CISA). *Hybrid Identity Solutions Guidance (HISG).* https://www.cisa.gov/resources-tools/services/hybrid-identity-solutions-guidance-hisg.
20 FIDO Alliance. *Passkeys.* https://fidoalliance.org/passkeys/.
21 CISA. *Fact Sheet: Implementing Phishing-Resistant Multi-Factor Authentication (MFA).* https://www.cisa.gov/sites/default/files/publications/fact-sheet-implementing-phishing-resistant-mfa-508c.pdf.
22 CISA. *Fact Sheet: Implementing Phishing-Resistant Multi-Factor Authentication (MFA).* https://www.cisa.gov/sites/default/files/publications/fact-sheet-implementing-phishing-resistant-mfa-508c.pdf.
23 United States Senate Committee on the Judiciary. *Testimony of John Mulligan Executive Vice President and Chief Financial Officer Target before the Senate Committee on the Judiciary Hearing on "Privacy in the Digital Age: Preventing Data Breaches and Combating Cybercrime."* https://www.judiciary.senate.gov/imo/media/doc/02-04-14MulliganTestimony.pdf.
24 HHS. *SolarWinds Critical Remote Code Execution Flaws: Analyst Note, Report 202310251500.* Health Sector Cybersecurity Coordination Center (HC3). https://www.hhs.gov/sites/default/files/solar-winds-arm-vulnerabilities-analyst-note.pdf.
25 NIST. *NIST SP 800-61 Rev. 3: Incident Response Recommendations and Considerations for Cybersecurity Risk Management.* https://nvlpubs.nist.gov/nistpubs/SpecialPublications/NIST.SP.800-61r3.pdf.
26 HHS. *Insider Threats in Healthcare.* https://www.hhs.gov/sites/default/files/insider-threats-in-healthcare.pdf.

Chapter 4

The Evolution and Impact of Malware

4.1 What Is Malware?

Malware, also known as malicious software, is designed to infiltrate, harm, or disrupt systems, or to steal, alter, or deny access to data, often without the user's consent. Malware can take many forms, including viruses, worms, ransomware, trojans, and spyware, each exploiting systems in different ways.[1]

Malware development increasingly incorporates AI and machine learning (ML) to evade detection, adapt to defenses, and carry out attacks more effectively. (AI refers to the ability of computer systems to perform tasks that normally require human intelligence, such as decision-making or pattern recognition. ML, a subset of AI, involves training algorithms on data so that systems can identify patterns and improve performance over time without being explicitly programmed.) AI-enabled malware can alter its activity in real time, generate convincing phishing lures, or automatically select the most vulnerable targets, making it more difficult for traditional security tools to detect and block.[2]

Sources of malware are diverse and include malicious email attachments, compromised websites, infected software downloads, removable media, supply chain attacks, and insider threats. Malware may also spread through vulnerable medical devices, outdated operating systems, and insecure third-party vendor connections.

4.2 Spotlight on Malware—Evolution of Malware

The evolution of malware reflects broader changes in technology, criminal tactics, and global cybersecurity risk. What began in the 1990s with macro viruses embedded in word processing documents soon escalated into financially motivated campaigns and state-sponsored threats.[3] By the 2000s, malware shifted from experimental hobbyist use toward organized criminal services, with the resurgence of ransomware and the rise of Malware-as-a-Service (MaaS). (Zeus, circa 2007, was one of the first instances of MaaS, according to Europol.)[4] By the 2010s, malware became more targeted,

DOI: 10.4324/9781003366560-4

persistent, and strategic—supporting espionage, sabotage, and credential theft at a global scale.[5] The 2020s have brought a surge in attacks aimed at disrupting clinical operations, compromising medical devices, and exploiting the growing interconnection of systems through cloud services and remote care platforms. Attackers also use AI to automatically generate and modify malware, creating polymorphic variants that adapt to defenses and evade traditional detection methods.[6]

(*Polymorphic malware* is a highly evasive form of malicious software that alters its code or appearance with each new infection. By continuously changing its structure, it becomes difficult for traditional signature-based detection methods to identify. This adaptability allows it to bypass standard security controls, avoid detection by antivirus tools, and persist within systems for extended periods.[7] A *variant* refers to a modified version of an existing piece of malware that shares the same core functionality but has been altered to avoid detection or expand capabilities.)

4.3 Early Malware Proof of Concept: The Creeper Worm

The first recognized proof of concept for malware dates back to circa 1971 with the Creeper program—a self-replicating code created to demonstrate that a program could move across networked systems. It was designed to travel between computers on ARPANET, the precursor to the modern internet, displaying the message: "I'm the creeper, catch me if you can!" Despite this message, Creeper was not made with malicious intent and did not harm or disrupt systems that were infected by it. As a proof of concept, Creeper was self-replicating code—what we now refer to as a worm.[8] The worm moved across different computers on the network.[9] In response, the first antivirus program, called Reaper, was developed to remove Creeper, which also moved across systems on the ARPANET.[10]

4.4 First Malicious Virus

Elk Cloner, created circa 1982, was the first known malicious virus to spread *in the wild*, meaning it circulated outside laboratory or research settings and infected users in the general public. It was a boot sector virus targeting Apple DOS 3.3 systems. Transferred via infected floppy disks, Elk Cloner would load into memory, copy itself to other disks, and propagate quickly. It could overwrite or erase data on floppy disks. Elk Cloner is now what we call a boot sector virus—a type of malware that embeds itself in the boot sector of a disk so that it loads into memory automatically when the computer starts up. The virus also displayed the following message:

ELK CLONER:
THE PROGRAM WITH A PERSONALITY
IT WILL GET ON ALL YOUR DISKS
IT WILL INFILTRATE YOUR CHIPS
YES IT'S CLONER!
IT WILL STICK TO YOU LIKE GLUE
IT WILL MODIFY RAM TOO
SEND IN THE CLONER!

Only a limited number of computers were infected by the Elk Cloner virus.[11]

4.5 First Personal Computer Virus

The Brain virus, developed circa 1986 by two brothers in Pakistan, is widely recognized as the first virus to infect IBM personal computers globally via floppy disk. It was originally intended as a form of digital rights management—specifically, a copy protection mechanism embedded in a medical software program written for use in diagnostic and clinical contexts. The virus targeted individuals who had pirated the software by embedding a message in the boot sector to identify unauthorized copies. However, because pirated copies of the software were widely shared, the Brain virus spread beyond its intended targets and unintentionally infected computers worldwide. The virus was not designed to harm data, but rather to deter software piracy. It embedded the creators' names, phone numbers, and addresses into the infected boot sector of the floppy disk.[12]

4.6 First Internet Worm

On November 2, 1988, a self-replicating program known as the *Morris Worm* became the first widespread malware to propagate across the internet. Released from a computer at MIT, it infected approximately 6,000 systems within 24 hours—roughly one-tenth of all internet-connected computers at the time. The worm exploited multiple *vulnerabilities* in Unix systems, including flaws in the email infrastructure and the "*finger*" service used to identify network users. It spread without user interaction, rapidly consuming resources and rendering systems unresponsive.

Although the Morris Worm did not destroy data, it resulted in disruption across universities, research institutions, and government laboratories. Many systems were disconnected or wiped entirely, and some remained offline for up to a week.[13]

In direct response to the incident, the Computer Emergency Response Team Coordination Center (CERT/CC) was established at Carnegie Mellon University's Software Engineering Institute (SEI). The center was created at the request of the Defense Advanced Research Projects Agency (DARPA) to coordinate national responses to cybersecurity threats. DARPA, formerly known as ARPA, was the same federal agency responsible for the development of ARPANET. CERT/CC provides a publicly accessible database (a knowledge base) of Vulnerability Notes,[14] including summaries, technical details, remediation information, and affected vendors.[15] CERT/CC is a member of the Forum of Incident Response and Security Teams (FIRST)—a global forum of national computer security incident response teams (CSIRTs).[16]

4.7 Melissa Virus

The Melissa virus, which first appeared in March 1999, was a macro virus, meaning it was embedded within Microsoft Word documents using Visual Basic for Applications (VBA)—a scripting language designed to automate tasks in Office programs like Word and Excel. (Note, however, that macro viruses for Microsoft Word appeared as early as 1995, such as the *Concept macro virus* that infected Microsoft Word documents.[17])

The Melissa virus was not a worm and rather required user interaction in order to propagate. For infected Mac OS systems, the Melissa virus was not able to send email, unlike infected Windows systems running Microsoft Word.

The Melissa virus primarily targeted Word 97 and Word 2000 on Windows systems and relied on Outlook 97 and Outlook 98 to distribute itself. It could also execute on Macintosh systems running Word 98.[18]

When a user opened the infected document, the virus executed immediately and sent a copy of the document to the first 50 entries in the user's Microsoft Outlook address book. In doing so, it propagated rapidly through email.[19]

Macro-based malware can potentially affect any software that supports embedded macros or scripting languages, especially if those features are enabled by default or not securely managed. However, Microsoft Office products remain the most common targets due to their widespread use and support for VBA.

4.7.1 Impact of the Melissa Virus

While Melissa did not corrupt or delete data, the operational impact was severe. Email systems failed under the weight of repeated mass mailings, and in some environments, system administrators had to temporarily disable email entirely.

4.7.2 Response to Melissa Virus

In response to the Melissa virus, antivirus vendors quickly issued updated definitions, Microsoft released relevant security patches, and IT departments implemented new policies—such as disabling macros by default, deploying email filtering, and training staff not to open unexpected attachments when they appeared to come from known senders.[20]

4.8 ILOVEYOU Worm

The ILOVEYOU worm, also known as LoveBug or Loveletter, emerged in May 2000 as a Visual Basic Script (VBS)-based malware and infected millions of Windows devices worldwide. It propagated through email messages with the subject line "ILOVEYOU" and an attachment labeled "LOVE-LETTER-FOR-YOU.TXT.vbs." The use of a double file extension (.TXT.vbs) misled users into believing the file was a harmless text document, although it was, in fact, an executable script.[21] When a user opened the attachment, the worm executed immediately, taking advantage of default Windows behaviors that hid known file extensions and permitted script execution through the Windows Scripting Host (WSH).

In order to execute and propagate as designed, the ILOVEYOU worm required a vulnerable version of Microsoft Windows—including Windows 95, Windows 98, Windows NT 4.0, or Windows 2000—with Windows Script Host (WSH) installed and enabled. It also required Microsoft Outlook 97, 98, or 2000, which exposed automation features through the Outlook Object Model. These features allowed scripts to access the user's Outlook address book. The worm used this functionality to gather email addresses and automatically send infected messages to all listed contacts, without further user interaction.[22]

Specifically, upon execution, the ILOVEYOU worm searched for specific file types located on fixed or network drives and modified them based on their extensions. For example, it replaced files with the extensions .vbe, .js, .jse, .css, .wsh, .sct, and .hta with copies of itself while changing their extensions to .vbs and created new .vbs files for audio files with the extensions .mp3 and .mp2 while preserving the original audio files but marking them as hidden. Because the ILOVEYOU worm overwrote the contents of the modified files rather than deleting them, this action made file recovery difficult and often impossible.

The ILOVEYOU worm also accessed the user's Outlook address book and automatically sent infected email messages to all entries, allowing it to spread to individual users, organizations, and networks. The ILOVEYOU worm also attempted to download and execute a separate program called WIN-BUGSFIX.exe, a password-stealing Trojan that collected cached credentials from the infected system and transmitted them to an external email address.[23]

4.8.1 ILOVEYOU Worm Response

In response to the ILOVEYOU worm outbreak, antivirus vendors issued updated virus definitions to detect and remove the worm. IT departments applied these antivirus updates, implemented new mitigation strategies, such as filtering email attachments, and increased security awareness efforts. Organizations also educated users about the dangers of opening unsolicited email attachments.[24]

4.9 GpCode Ransomware

GpCode, also known as PGPCoder, was among the earliest examples of extortion ransomware—malware designed to encrypt files and demand payment for their decryption. First observed in May 2005, GpCode targeted computers running Microsoft Windows and searched for common file types such as documents, spreadsheets, images, and archives.[25] Once encrypted, the victim was presented with a ransom note demanding payment in exchange for the decryption key.

GpCode helped to pave the way for modern, financially motivated ransomware and set the stage for more advanced and damaging campaigns in the years that followed.[26] GpCode continued to appear in the wild for many years after its initial discovery.[27]

4.10 Conficker Worm

The Conficker worm, first discovered in November 2008, exploited a critical vulnerability in Microsoft Windows systems—specifically a flaw in the Server service that was documented in Microsoft Security Bulletin MS08–067.[28] The vulnerability (CVE-2008-4250) allowed remote code execution via specially crafted network messages using the Windows Remote Procedure Call (RPC) protocol. Once exploited, Conficker—since it was a worm—could install itself on a system without any user interaction and begin spreading laterally across networks.

Conficker infected millions of systems globally, including certain computers and devices that did not have the MS08–067 security patch, which Microsoft had released in October 2008—one month before the worm was identified in the wild. Hong Kong Computer Emergency Response Team Coordination Centre (HKCERT). *Global Conficker Worm Outbreak: Millions of Computers Fallen.* https://www.hkcert.org/blog/global-conficker-worm-outbreak-millions-of-computers-fallen. See also *Cybereason.com. What Is the Conficker Worm? https://www.cybereason.com/blog/what-is-the-conficker-worm.*

Healthcare environments were impacted due to the widespread use of legacy and unpatched systems. Many medical devices—including imaging modalities, infusion pumps, and patient monitoring equipment—ran on customized versions of Microsoft Windows, such as Windows XP Embedded or Windows 2000, which had been configured by device manufacturers.

The following Microsoft Windows operating systems were vulnerable to Conficker if the security update (MS08–067) was not applied[29]:

- Windows 2000
- Windows XP
- Windows Server 2003
- Windows Vista
- Windows Server 2008

Conficker gave attackers remote control over infected systems, allowing them to send commands and update the malware. The infected computers became part of a botnet—a large network of compromised machines that could be controlled by attackers and used to carry out further malicious activities, such as spreading malware or disabling security systems.

4.11 CryptoLocker

CryptoLocker was a type of ransomware that encrypted files on infected systems and demanded payment—typically in Bitcoin—in exchange for a decryption key. It was first observed in September 2013 and spread primarily through phishing emails containing malicious attachments. These attachments were commonly disguised as business-related documents, such as invoices or shipping notifications. When a recipient opened the attachment, the ransomware executed and began encrypting files using strong asymmetric encryption, making them inaccessible to the user.

CryptoLocker primarily targeted systems running Microsoft Windows, including Windows XP, Windows Vista, Windows 7, and Windows 8. Once installed, it scanned the system for commonly used file types—such as documents, spreadsheets, images, and archives—and encrypted them. Victims were then presented with a ransom message demanding payment in exchange for a private decryption key. The message typically included a countdown timer, warning that if payment was not made within the specified time, the decryption key would be permanently destroyed. The ransomware message alleged that after the destruction of the decryption key, no one would be able to recover the files.[30]

The CryptoLocker campaign was effectively disrupted in 2014 following the takedown by law enforcement of the GameOver Zeus botnet, which the ransomware relied on for command-and-control and distribution. However, the CryptoLocker campaign was widely regarded as a successful business model, providing a blueprint for ransomware extortion.[31]

4.12 WannaCry

WannaCry was a ransomware worm that emerged in May 2017 and spread rapidly by exploiting a vulnerability (MS17–010) in the Server Message Block version 1 (SMBv1) protocol found in several versions of the Microsoft Windows operating system.[32] This vulnerability, exploited by the

EternalBlue exploit, allowed attackers to execute code remotely to enable self-propagation across vulnerable systems, devices, and networks without user interaction. Although a patch for the vulnerability had been released prior to the attack in March 2017, many organizations had not applied it, leaving large numbers of systems, devices, and networks exposed.

WannaCry primarily affected systems and devices running Windows XP, Windows 7, and Windows Server 2008, especially those that had not received the critical security update addressing the SMBv1 vulnerability. The ransomware encrypted files and demanded payment in Bitcoin in exchange for a decryption key, disrupting operations across numerous sectors.[33]

The attack had widespread consequences for both public and private institutions. Healthcare, manufacturing, logistics, telecommunications, and public administration were among the industries affected. In healthcare settings in particular, the ransomware compromised access to clinical systems, delayed routine care, and forced the cancellation of scheduled services. The incident highlighted the risks of relying on unsupported or unpatched software and underscored the need for regular system updates, segmented network architectures, and formal cybersecurity response plans.

While not the first global cyberattack, WannaCry was the first ransomworm-based cyberattack to cause widespread, coordinated disruption on a global scale. Within a single day, it affected over 200,000 systems in at least 100 countries, disrupting essential services in healthcare, transportation, and manufacturing. Its rapid propagation and impact elevated ransomware from a localized threat to a critical global cybersecurity concern.[34] WannaCry marked a turning point in global awareness of ransomware as a serious threat capable of disrupting essential services across sectors, with consequences for patient safety, financial loss, and operational disruption.

4.13 NotPetya

NotPetya began in June 2017 through a compromised software update mechanism of a third-party accounting platform widely used in Ukraine.[35] Once installed on a target system, the malware used a combination of techniques—including the SMBv1 vulnerability addressed in Microsoft's MS17–010 patch, as well as credential theft and lateral movement—to spread across networks. This incident demonstrated how a single compromised software vendor could trigger widespread disruption across industries, including healthcare, even beyond the borders of the initial geographic target.[36]

4.14 Emotet

Emotet originated in 2014 as a banking Trojan and evolved into a modular malware platform capable of delivering additional malicious payloads. It primarily targeted Windows-based systems, spreading via phishing emails containing malicious attachments or links. Once executed, Emotet could download and install various modules, enabling activities such as credential theft, email harvesting, and the deployment of other malware. HHS HC3. *Emotet Malware: The Enduring and Persistent Threat to the Health Sector.* https://www.hhs.gov/sites/default/files/emotet-the-enduring-and-persistent-threat-to-the-hph-tlpclear.pdf.

Emotet posed significant threats to the HPH sector. It facilitated ransomware attacks and data breaches, disrupting operations and compromising sensitive patient information. The malware's adaptability and persistence underscored the necessity for continuous monitoring and advanced threat detection in healthcare cybersecurity strategies. Emotet was among the most prevalent malware affecting computer systems in the healthcare industry during this period.

Emotet's operations were disrupted in January 2021 through a coordinated international law enforcement effort.[37] However, its reemergence later in 2021 highlighted the ongoing challenges in combating such sophisticated threats. The malware's resurgence emphasized the importance of maintaining robust cybersecurity measures, including regular system updates, employee training on phishing awareness, and the implementation of advanced threat detection tools.[38] However, subsequent law enforcement actions have significantly reduced its activity.

4.15 Ryuk and Conti Ransomware

Ryuk[39] and Conti[40] were ransomware strains[41] linked to coordinated attacks against large organizations, including those in the Healthcare and Public Health (HPH) sector. These campaigns were most active between 2018 and 2022 and were commonly deployed after an initial infection by TrickBot, a type of malware used to gather credentials and move laterally within networks.[42]

Ryuk, which first appeared in 2018, was used in targeted attacks against high-value networks. It focused on encrypting files and demanding ransom payments, without typically exfiltrating data.[43] Ryuk operations often involved a period of dwell time[44] within the compromised network during which attackers studied the environment to maximize disruption—including in hospitals.[45]

Conti, active primarily between 2020 and 2022, represented an evolution in ransomware strategy. It operated under a ransomware-as-a-service (RaaS) model.[46] Conti combined encryption with data theft, threatening public exposure (leaks) of sensitive information to pressure victims into paying. This double extortion model proved especially damaging in healthcare environments, where operational continuity and data confidentiality are both essential.[47]

4.16 Log4Shell

The Log4Shell vulnerability, disclosed in December 2021, was a critical remote code execution flaw found in the widely used Apache Log4j logging library (CVE-2021-44228).[48] It allowed attackers to execute arbitrary code on affected systems by exploiting how Log4j handled log messages containing specially crafted JNDI[49] lookups.[50] These lookups are typically used in Java applications to retrieve information from remote directories or services. However, in this case, Log4j would automatically process user-supplied input containing a JNDI reference without proper validation. As a result, attackers could insert malicious commands into log messages that caused the system to reach out to an external server and load executable code—effectively giving the attacker control over the system without the need for authentication or direct access.

This vulnerability posed serious risks to healthcare environments, as many applications and systems relied on Log4j. Exploitation could result in system compromise, including access to sensitive health data and operational control of clinical or administrative platforms. The scope and speed of exploitation took much of the security community by surprise.

The incident highlighted several critical gaps: the lack of visibility into third-party software components, the risks posed by open-source tools, and the urgent need for both timely patching and proactive software inventory management.[51]

4.17 LockBit

LockBit is a ransomware group that operates under a RaaS model, in which the core developers provide the ransomware code and infrastructure, while independent affiliates carry out the attacks. First observed as the ABCD ransomware variant in September 2019 and rebranded as LockBit in January 2020, LockBit has been responsible for a growing number of incidents across multiple sectors, including critical infrastructure and the healthcare industry.

In healthcare settings, LockBit ransomware attacks have resulted in encrypted electronic health records, delays in patient care, and widespread operational disruption. The ransomware has been known to include features that automate system discovery and propagation within networks, increasing its speed and impact. Its use of double extortion tactics—encrypting data while simultaneously stealing it for leverage—has further raised the stakes for affected organizations.

The persistence and adaptability of LockBit illustrate the evolving nature of ransomware threats. The ransomware group's continued activity highlights the need for healthcare organizations to implement strong access controls, maintain offline and tested backups, and conduct regular employee training focused on phishing awareness and securing credentials (including passwords and authentication tokens).[52]

4.18 Hive

Hive ransomware was first observed in June 2021 and quickly became a significant threat to the HPH sector. The group operated under an affiliate-based RaaS model in which independent threat actors (affiliates) used Hive's tools and infrastructure to conduct attacks in exchange for a share of the ransom payments.[53]

Hive attacks were human-operated and relied on a combination of common techniques, including phishing emails, exploitation of remote desktop services, and the use of legitimate administrative tools to move laterally within networks. Tools such as Cobalt Strike and ADrecon were used for post-exploitation, reconnaissance, and command-and-control purposes.[54]

Hive employed a custom, closed-source ransomware strain rewritten in Go in later variants, compiled for both 32-bit and 64-bit Windows systems. Upon execution within a compromised environment, Hive launched batch scripts—such as hive.bat and shadow.bat—to disable antivirus protections, terminate volume shadow copy services, and prepare the system for file encryption. The malware specifically targeted critical services, including those related to databases (such as SQL, Oracle, and PostgreSQL), backup mechanisms (such as VSS and BMR), and Microsoft Office applications, including Microsoft Publisher. Hive's encryption routine was configured to exclude the core Windows system directory, thus preserving basic system functionality while maximizing disruption to operational data.[55]

The Hive ransomware group utilized a double extortion strategy, in which they both encrypted data and exfiltrated it. Victims were given access to a portal with login credentials and instructed to pay a ransom within a short window—typically two to six days. If no payment was made, the stolen data were threatened with public release via the group's leak site, HiveLeaks.[56]

Healthcare organizations targeted by Hive experienced severe disruptions, including canceled surgeries, diverted ambulances, and closures of urgent care centers. The Hive ransomware group was known to exfiltrate large troves of data (i.e., gigabytes of data), including medical records, financial documents, internal work files, employee information, and legal and insurance files.[57]

In January 2023, the Hive network was disrupted by a multinational law enforcement operation, which included the FBI and international partners. Authorities infiltrated Hive's infrastructure, captured decryption keys, and made them available to victims—a significant disruption to the group's operations.[58]

4.19 BlackCat/ALPHV

BlackCat, also referred to as ALPHV, is a ransomware group first observed in 2021. It operates under a RaaS model, where the core ransomware platform is developed by one group and used by affiliated actors to carry out attacks. BlackCat is written in the Rust programming language, which allows it to function across multiple environments, including Windows, Linux, VMware ESXi, and certain Linux-based network-attached storage systems.

BlackCat is known for using triple extortion tactics. This includes (1) encrypting files on the victim's systems, (2) stealing sensitive data and threatening to release it publicly, and (3) in some cases, launching distributed denial-of-service (DDoS) attacks to increase pressure on the victim to pay the ransom.[59]

4.19.1 Encryption Process

After gaining access to a network, BlackCat scans for target files such as documents, images, and databases. It then encrypts these files using strong algorithms, including symmetric ciphers such as AES and ChaCha20. Once encryption is complete, the files become inaccessible without a specific decryption key that is controlled by the attackers. The malware supports several encryption modes, which can be adjusted to evade detection or improve performance.[60]

4.19.2 Ransom Demand

Once files have been encrypted, BlackCat delivers a ransom note to the victim's system. The note provides instructions for submitting payment, usually in cryptocurrency, in exchange for the decryption key. It may also warn that exfiltrated data will be published if the ransom is not paid. In some cases, the attackers also threaten or conduct DDoS attacks as an additional pressure tactic.[61] BlackCat has affected healthcare organizations by disrupting clinical operations, delaying care delivery, and threatening patient data confidentiality. These incidents reinforce the need for healthcare entities to maintain network segmentation, apply strict access controls, implement multi-factor authentication, and regularly test system backups and recovery procedures.[62]

According to the U.S. Department of Justice, ALPHV/BlackCat operations were disrupted through a coordinated law enforcement action involving the FBI.

DOJ. *Justice Department Disrupts Prolific ALPHV/Blackcat Ransomware Variant.* https://www.justice.gov/archives/opa/pr/justice-department-disrupts-prolific-alphvblackcat-ransomware-variant.

4.20 Royal

The Royal ransomware group is a financially motivated threat actor that emerged approximately in September 2022 and has directly impacted healthcare organizations. Unlike RaaS groups, Royal does not operate an affiliate program. Instead, it functions as a closed group, carrying out its own attacks using custom tooling. Multiple technical indicators and early operational patterns suggest that the group includes former members of the Conti ransomware operations.[63]

4.20.1 Targeting and Initial Access

Royal ransomware attacks have disproportionately affected organizations in the United States, including those in the HPH sector. The group has employed multiple methods to gain initial access, including phishing emails, callback scams, and malicious advertisements that lead victims to unknowingly install trojanized software. After gaining access to the environment, the group establishes a foothold—a stable and persistent position that enables continued access to the network without requiring repeated exploitation.[64] Once the foothold has been established, Royal deploys additional tools—such as BATLOADER, QBot, Cobalt Strike, and in some cases, components associated with Black Basta—to explore internal systems and escalate privileges, meaning to obtain broader or administrative-level access beyond what was initially assigned to the compromised account. The group then moves laterally across the network, accesses additional systems, identifies sensitive data, and disables access controls in order to reduce the likelihood of detection or interruption when executing the ransomware. The final step involves deploying the ransomware payload—that is, the portion of the malware specifically responsible for encrypting files and displaying a ransom note with payment instructions and threats of data exposure.[65]

4.20.2 Malware and Encryption

In its early stages, Royal used the BlackCat ransomware group's encryptor before developing its own malware known as the Zeon encryptor. This tool is compiled in C++ and supports command-line arguments to control which files or directories to encrypt, as well as how much of each file to encrypt. Royal uses multi-threaded encryption to increase efficiency based on the number of processor cores detected on the infected system. It places a "README.TXT" ransom note in every directory that is not excluded from encryption.[66]

Before executing the encryption routine, the Royal ransomware group deletes Volume Shadow Copies—automatic backup snapshots created by the Windows operating system—using the Windows sysadmin utility. This prevents victims from recovering encrypted files using local backup mechanisms. The ransomware also excludes certain system directories, such as C:\Windows, from encryption. This ensures that the operating system remains functional, while business-critical files and services are rendered inaccessible. The final step involves deploying the ransomware payload—that is, the portion of the code responsible for encrypting files and displaying a ransom note with payment instructions and threats of publicly leaking the stolen data if the ransom is not paid.[67]

4.20.3 Data Exfiltration and Ransom Demands

Royal performs double extortion—both encrypting data and exfiltrating sensitive files for leverage. Victims who do not pay the ransom are threatened with public leaks of stolen data. Reported ransom demands have ranged from $250,000 to over $2,000,000, though amounts vary based on the specific organization that has been targeted (the victim organization).[68]

4.20.4 Relevance to Healthcare

Royal ransomware has targeted multiple healthcare-related services, including managed service providers and telecom platforms that support hospital networks and associated infrastructure. In one notable attack, a victim organization experienced an outage that disrupted unified communications and healthcare support services.

According to the U.S. Department of Justice, Blacksuit (Royal) operations were disrupted through a coordinated law enforcement action involving the FBI and international partners.

DOJ. *Justice Department Announces Coordinated Disruption Actions Against BlackSuit (Royal) Ransomware Operations.* https://www.justice.gov/opa/pr/justice-department-announces-coordinated-disruption-actions-against-blacksuit-royal.

4.21 BlackSuit Ransomware

The BlackSuit ransomware group first emerged in May 2023 and has been identified as a developing threat to the HPH sector. BlackSuit shares significant similarities with the Royal ransomware group, including overlap in encryption methods, binary structure, and code functionality. These findings suggest that BlackSuit may be the result of a splinter group, a splinter operation, or code reuse by threat actors with ties to Royal or its predecessor, Conti.

4.21.1 Targeting and Behavior

BlackSuit employs double extortion tactics, both encrypting files and exfiltrating sensitive data, with the threat of publishing stolen information if ransom demands are not met. Its operators have targeted organizations across several countries—including the United States, Canada, Brazil, and the United Kingdom—and have impacted industries such as healthcare, government, business technology, and retail.

BlackSuit was attributed to a ransomware incident affecting a US-based radiology services provider that supports nearly 1,000 hospitals and health systems across 48 states. The attack forced the organization to shut down systems and turn away patients at multiple facilities, indicating the group's potential for broad healthcare disruption.

4.21.2 Technical Characteristics

BlackSuit is capable of targeting both Windows and Linux environments, including VMware ESXi. BlackSuit uses AES encryption implemented through the OpenSSL library, along with selective encryption techniques that improve speed while reducing the likelihood of detection. Files encrypted by the ransomware are appended with the *.blacksuit* extension, and a ransom note—titled README.BlackSuit.txt—is deposited in affected directories. The note includes a unique identifier for each victim and directs them to a Tor-based negotiation site. In addition to encrypting data, BlackSuit changes desktop wallpaper and renames files, reinforcing the visibility of the attack.

Researchers noted a high degree of similarity in code structure between BlackSuit and Royal ransomware samples targeting Linux and Windows systems. These figures suggest either shared authorship or direct code reuse.

4.21.3 Distribution Methods

BlackSuit is distributed through several common malware delivery mechanisms, including the following:

- Phishing emails with malicious attachments or embedded macros
- Torrent websites
- Malicious advertisements (malvertising)
- Trojan software downloads, which install the ransomware under the guise of legitimate applications

4.21.4 Impact on Healthcare

Although BlackSuit has been linked to a limited number of confirmed attacks within the HPH sector, its code similarity to Royal—a group known to aggressively target healthcare—and its impact on a national radiology provider underscores the risk it poses. If BlackSuit is indeed operated by individuals with ties to Royal or Conti, healthcare organizations should anticipate further activity from this group. The HPH sector's dependence on high-availability systems and sensitive data makes it a persistent and high-value target for threat actors leveraging extortion-based tactics.[69]

According to the U.S. Department of Justice, Blacksuit (Royal) operations were disrupted through a coordinated law enforcement action involving the FBI.

DOJ. *Justice Department Announces Coordinated Disruption Actions Against BlackSuit (Royal) Ransomware Operations.* https://www.justice.gov/opa/pr/justice-department-announces-coordinated-disruption-actions-against-blacksuit-royal.

4.22 Black Basta

Black Basta is a ransomware group that emerged in early 2022, which used double extortion tactics—encrypting victims' data and threatening to publish stolen information via its leak site on Tor, "Basta News," if ransom demands were not met.[70]

(Tor—The Onion Router—is a privacy-focused network that helps users remain anonymous by directing their internet traffic through multiple relays managed by volunteers around the world. It requires special software, such as the Tor Browser, to access. Tor is commonly used to reach the dark web—parts of the internet that exist outside of the visible web. The visible web refers to the portion of the internet accessible through standard web browsers and indexed by search engines. The dark web serves both legitimate and illegitimate purposes: it is used by cybercriminals to operate extortion sites and leak stolen data, and it also supports free expression, secure communication, and access to information in regions with censorship or surveillance.)[71]

The tactics, techniques, and procedures (TTPs) utilized by the Black Basta ransomware group suggest ties to other sophisticated ransomware groups, particularly Conti, FIN7,[72] and BlackMatter.[73] The Black Basta ransomware group uses a variety of TTPs to gain and maintain access.

Initial access is typically obtained through phishing emails, stolen credentials, or vulnerable RDP configurations. Once inside the network, the group deploys tools such as Qakbot

(QBot), SystemBC, Mimikatz, Cobalt Strike, and rclone to move laterally, disable access controls, exfiltrate data, and execute the ransomware payload. The ransomware is capable of infecting both Windows and Linux systems and requires administrator privileges to run.[74]

Once a foothold is gained, Black Basta operators move laterally, exfiltrate sensitive data (meaning they extract information from the network and send it to attacker-controlled systems without authorization), and deploy ransomware that hinders system processes and ultimately makes desktop files unusable. The ransomware is a cross-platform variant that is executed only with administrator privileges on both Windows and Linux systems.[75]

(TTPs refer to the observed behaviors and methods that threat actors use to carry out cyberattacks, including how they gain access, move through networks, and achieve their objectives. Analysts identify and attribute these behaviors by examining factors such as shared infrastructure, similarities in communication methods, and the reuse of custom malware or evasion techniques.)

Black Basta is believed to be a rebrand or splinter group of the former Conti ransomware operation, based on shared tactics, infrastructure, and leaks linking the two groups.[76]

The Black Basta ransomware group primarily targets large organizations, including healthcare providers, laboratories, pharmaceutical firms, and health plans. In several confirmed incidents, Black Basta exfiltrated gigabytes of personally identifiable information (PII) from US-based healthcare entities, causing operational disruption and significant data exposure.

4.23 Karakurt

Karakurt is a data extortion group first observed in late 2021. Unlike traditional ransomware groups, Karakurt does not encrypt files. Instead, it focuses on stealing sensitive data—especially PII and protected health information (PHI)—and then threatening to release or auction it unless a ransom is paid. Demands have ranged from tens of thousands to over $10 million in Bitcoin, with short payment deadlines and aggressive pressure tactics.[77]

Karakurt has targeted healthcare organizations, including hospitals, dental practices, and assisted living facilities. The group is believed to have ties to the former Conti ransomware operation, either through shared personnel or business arrangements.[78]

The group typically gains access by purchasing stolen virtual private network (VPN) or Remote Desktop Protocol (RDP) credentials or by buying access through third-party intrusion broker networks. It also exploits known vulnerabilities in outdated remote access technologies—such as unpatched SSL VPN appliances and firewalls—as well as other legacy systems, including unsupported or misconfigured Windows Server instances. Phishing emails containing malicious macros have also been used to establish initial access.[79]

Once a foothold is gained, Karakurt actors typically compress stolen data—often using 7-Zip—and exfiltrate large volumes of information. In many cases, they extract entire shared network drives, with data sets exceeding one terabyte. Data is transferred using a combination of open-source applications, File Transfer Protocol (FTP) clients such as FileZilla, and cloud storage tools including rclone and Mega.nz. After exfiltration, the group delivers ransom demands through multiple channels, including text files placed on compromised systems, emails sent from within the victim's own network, and messages from external email accounts. Victims are directed to a Tor-based site, where they are given an access code to enter a private chat portal for ransom negotiations. The threat includes the public release or auction of the stolen data if payment is not made.[80]

Karakurt is also known for its extensive harassment tactics.[81] After a breach, employees, business partners, and clients of the victim organization may receive repeated emails or calls—including samples of stolen data—to increase pressure on the organization to comply. If payment is made, the group may provide screen recordings, a deletion log, or credentials for a victim to log into a storage server and delete the files themselves.[82]

4.24 Summary—The Evolution and Impact of Malware

Malware has evolved significantly over the past three decades, transforming from simple code exploiting document macros in the 1990s to a key enabler of organized cybercrime and geopolitical conflict in the present day. Early macro viruses, such as Concept, demonstrated how attackers could exploit user habits and emerging software features. By the 2000s, malware development had become professionalized, shifting from disruptive experimentation to profit-driven operations. This period marked the rise of modern ransomware, the emergence of MaaS, and the targeting of healthcare organizations, which rely heavily on uninterrupted access to patient data and clinical systems.

The 2010s saw the rise of Advanced Persistent Threats (APTs) and nation-state involvement. Malware campaigns became more targeted, persistent, and strategic. Stuxnet, deployed in 2010, signaled the arrival of malware as a tool for physical sabotage and international cyber operations. Meanwhile, financially motivated malware such as Zeus (which includes variants such as GameOver Zeus (GOZ)) and Emotet focused on credential theft and disrupting healthcare operations through ransom demands.

The HPH sector is uniquely vulnerable due to the high value of medical data, the critical nature of healthcare delivery systems, and the prevalence of legacy technologies. Attacks such as WannaCry in 2017 and Ryuk in 2020 underscored how a single vulnerability or phishing email could lead to systemic outages, delayed care, and compromised patient records.

In the modern era, malware has adapted to new technologies and environments. Techniques such as polymorphism and fileless malware allow threats to bypass traditional detection methods. The shift to cloud infrastructure has introduced new attack vectors, particularly as healthcare systems adopt cloud-based EHR platforms and telehealth solutions. Emerging concerns include the use of AI in malware and the growing risks to connected medical devices, which are increasingly targeted in efforts to disrupt clinical care or compromise patient safety.

As malware continues to evolve in sophistication and impact, healthcare organizations must adopt proactive, layered defense strategies that include timely patching, asset visibility, secure system architecture, and ongoing security awareness training.

Looking ahead, malware is expected to become increasingly autonomous, adaptive, and integrated with AI. Future strains may employ generative AI to produce polymorphic code, craft highly personalized phishing content, and dynamically evade detection in ways that exceed current defensive capabilities. The growth of RaaS and MaaS marketplaces will continue to lower barriers for less skilled attackers. Advances in quantum computing present a significant long-term risk by threatening to break the encryption. Healthcare organizations, the broader healthcare ecosystem, public and private sector entities, and other critical infrastructure stakeholders should prepare their systems and networks to be quantum-ready in order to maintain the confidentiality, integrity, and availability of confidential and sensitive data, including PHI, PII, and intellectual property.[83]

Notes

1 FTC. *Malware: How To Protect Against, Detect, and Remove It.* https://consumer.ftc.gov/articles/malware-how-protect-against-detect-and-remove-it.

2 HHS. *AI for Malware Development (Analyst Note).* https://www.hhs.gov/sites/default/files/ai-for-malware-development-analyst-note.pdf.

3 U.S. General Accounting Office (GAO). *The Melissa Computer Virus Demonstrates Urgent Need for Stronger Protection Over Systems and Sensitive Data.* April 15, 1999. https://www.govinfo.gov/content/pkg/GAOREPORTS-T-AIMD-99-146/pdf/GAOREPORTS-T-AIMD-99-146.pdf.

4 Europol. *Banking Trojans: From Stone Age to Space Era.* https://www.europol.europa.eu/cms/sites/default/files/documents/banking_trojans_from_stone_age_to_space_era.pdf.

5 HHS. *Securing Remote Access and Management Software (HC3 Alert).* https://www.hhs.gov/sites/default/files/securing-remote-access-software-alert.pdf. NotPetya and WannaCry were two prime examples of malware in the 2010s.

6 See U.S. Department of Health and Human Services—Health Sector Cybersecurity Coordination Center (HC3). *Automation & Hacking: Potential Impacts on Healthcare.* https://www.hhs.gov/sites/default/files/automation-hacking-healthcare.pdf.

7 Medium. *Polymorphic Malware—Understanding Evasive Attack Strategies.* https://medium.com/@RocketMeUpCybersecurity/polymorphic-malware-understanding-evasive-attack-strategies-6e1708780a56.

8 IBM. *The History of Malware: A Primer on the Evolution of Cyber Threats.* https://www.ibm.com/think/topics/malware-history.

9 IBM. *The History of Malware: A Primer on the Evolution of Cyber Threats.* https://www.ibm.com/think/topics/malware-history.

10 HistoryofInformation.com. *The Creeper Worm, the First Computer Virus.* https://www.historyofinformation.com/detail.php?entryid=2860.

11 IBM. *The History of Malware: A Primer on the Evolution of Cyber Threats.* https://www.ibm.com/think/topics/malware-history.

12 IBM. *The History of Malware: A Primer on the Evolution of Cyber Threats.* https://www.ibm.com/think/topics/malware-history.

13 Federal Bureau of Investigation. *The Morris Worm.* https://www.fbi.gov/history/famous-cases/morris-worm.

14 CMU SEI CERT Coordination Center (CERT/CC). *Vulnerability Notes Database.* https://www.kb.cert.org/vuls/.

15 CMU SEI. *Fostering Growth in Professional Cyber Incident Management.* https://insights.sei.cmu.edu/history-of-innovation/fostering-growth-in-professional-cyber-incident-management/.

16 Forum of Incident Response and Security Teams (FIRST). *CERT/CC (Member Page).* https://www.first.org/members/teams/cert-cc.

17 Wikidot—The Virus Encyclopedia. *Concept.* http://virus.wikidot.com/concept.

18 CERT/CC. *Frequently Asked Questions About the Melissa Virus.* https://www.sei.cmu.edu/documents/540/2000_019_001_497190.pdf.

19 CMU SEI. *1999 CERT Advisories.* https://www.sei.cmu.edu/documents/506/1999_019_001_496184.pdf.

20 FBI. *The Melissa Virus: An $80 Million Cyber Crime in 1999 Foreshadowed Modern Threats.* https://www.fbi.gov/news/stories/melissa-virus-20th-anniversary-032519.

See also Office Watch. *Word's Melissa Virus Is 20 Years Old—What's Changed?* https://office-watch.com/2019/microsoft-words-melissa-virus-is-20-years-old/.

See also CERT/CC. *Frequently Asked Questions About the Melissa Virus.* https://www.sei.cmu.edu/documents/540/2000_019_001_497190.pdf.

21 Hacker News. *I Love You Virus (Discussion Thread).* https://news.ycombinator.com/item?id=23076341.

22 GIAC. *VBS/Loveletter@MM Worm Incident.* https://www.giac.org/paper/gcih/311/vbs-loveletteratmm-worm-incident/102928.

23 CMU SEI. *2000 CERT Advisories.* https://www.sei.cmu.edu/documents/507/2000_019_001_496188.pdf.

24 U.S. Senate, Committee on Banking, Subcommittee on Financial Institutions. *Statement of Stephen R. Malphrus Staff Director for Management, Board of Governors of the Federal Reserve System. Oversight Hearing on the "I Love You" Computer Virus and Its Impact on U.S. Financial Services Industry.* https://www.hsdl.org/c/view?docid=35679.

See also U.S. Senate, Committee on Banking, Subcommittee on Financial Institutions. *Prepared Testimony of Mr. James Adams CEO iDefense. Oversight Hearing on the "I Love You" Computer Virus and Its Impact on U.S. Financial Services Industry.* https://www.hsdl.org/c/view?docid=35679.

See also CMU SEI. *2000 CERT Advisories.* https://www.sei.cmu.edu/documents/507/2000_019_001_496188.pdf.

25 Stormshield. *A Short History of Ransomware.* https://www.stormshield.com/news/a-short-history-of-ransomware/.

26 SecureList by Kaspersky. *Blackmailer: The Story of Gpcode.* https://securelist.com/blackmailer-the-story-of-gpcode/36089/.

See also No More Ransom. *Questions & Answers.* https://www.nomoreransom.org/qa/index.html.

27 SonicWall. *GPcode Ransomware Leaves Victims Stranded.* https://www.sonicwall.com/blog/gpcode-ransomware-leaves-victims-stranded.

See also HHS. *Ransomware & Healthcare.* https://www.hhs.gov/sites/default/files/ransomware-healthcare.pdf.

28 Microsoft. *Security Bulletin MS08-067: Critical. Vulnerability in Server Service Could Allow Remote Code Execution (958644).* https://learn.microsoft.com/en-us/security-updates/securitybulletins/2008/ms08-067.

29 CISA. *Conficker Worm Targets Microsoft Windows Systems.* https://www.cisa.gov/news-events/alerts/2009/03/29/conficker-worm-targets-microsoft-windows-systems.

30 CISA. *CryptoLocker Ransomware Infections.* https://www.cisa.gov/news-events/alerts/2013/11/05/cryptolocker-ransomware-infections.

31 Federal Bureau of Investigation (FBI). *GameOver Zeus Botnet Disrupted.* https://www.fbi.gov/news/stories/gameover-zeus-botnet-disrupted.

32 Microsoft. *Security Bulletin MS17-010—Critical. Security Update for Microsoft Windows SMB Server (4013389).* https://learn.microsoft.com/en-us/security-updates/securitybulletins/2017/ms17-010.

33 CISA. *Indicators Associated with WannaCry Ransomware.* https://www.cisa.gov/news-events/alerts/2017/05/12/indicators-associated-wannacry-ransomware.

34 National Audit Office (United Kingdom). *Investigation: WannaCry Cyber Attack and the NHS.* https://www.nao.org.uk/wp-content/uploads/2017/10/Investigation-WannaCry-cyber-attack-and-the-NHS.pdf

35 CISA. *Petya Ransomware.* https://www.cisa.gov/news-events/alerts/2017/07/01/petya-ransomware.

36 DOJ. *Six Russian GRU Officers Charged in Connection with Worldwide Deployment of Destructive Malware and Other Disruptive Actions in Cyberspace.* https://www.justice.gov/opa/pr/six-russian-gru-officers-charged-connection-worldwide-deployment-destructive-malware-and.

37 Europol. *World's Most Dangerous Malware EMOTET Disrupted Through Global Action.* https://www.europol.europa.eu/media-press/newsroom/news/world%E2%80%99s-most-dangerous-malware-emotet-disrupted-through-global-action.

38 HHS HC3. *Emotet: The Enduring and Persistent Threat to the HPH Sector.* https://www.hhs.gov/sites/default/files/emotet-the-enduring-and-persistent-threat-to-the-hph-tlpclear.pdf.

39 HHS HC3. *New Ryuk Ransomware Variant Poses Threat to HPH Sector.* https://www.hhs.gov/sites/default/files/new-ryuk-ransomware-variant-poses-threat-to-hph-sector.pdf.

40 HHS HC3. *Overview of Conti Ransomware.* https://www.hhs.gov/sites/default/files/analyst-note-conti-ransomware-tlp-white.pdf.

41 A *strain* is a distinct malware family or subgroup with a shared name and core purpose. A *variant* is a modified or updated version of a known strain, typically created to bypass detection or expand capabilities (e.g., evade detection; modify behavior; improve persistence; target new systems or architectures; or add new capabilities such as keylogging, lateral movement, ransomware modules, or command-and-control techniques).

42 HHS HC3. *TrickBot.* https://www.hhs.gov/sites/default/files/trickbot.pdf.

43 CERT-FR, Agence nationale de la sécurité des systèmes d'information (ANSSI). *Ryuk Ransomware.* https://www.cert.ssi.gouv.fr/uploads/CERTFR-2021-CTI-006.pdf.

44 *Dwell time* refers to the period between the initial compromise of a system by a threat actor and the moment the organization detects the intrusion. During this time, the attacker may silently explore the network, gather information, escalate privileges, and position malware for further actions—such as data theft or ransomware deployment—often without being detected.

ConnectWise. *Dwell Time Definition.* https://www.connectwise.com/cybersecurity-center/glossary/dwell-time.

45 HHS HC3. *New Ryuk Ransomware Variant Poses Threat to HPH Sector.* https://www.hhs.gov/sites/default/files/new-ryuk-ransomware-variant-poses-threat-to-hph-sector.pdf.

46 A *RaaS (ransomware-as-a-service) affiliate* is an individual or group that partners with a ransomware developer to carry out attacks using that developer's malware. Rather than creating the ransomware themselves, affiliates typically gain access to a pre-built ransomware platform through a RaaS model. In this arrangement, the developer provides the tools—such as the malware, payment infrastructure, and support—while the affiliate is responsible for delivering the ransomware to victims, often through phishing, remote access, or exploiting vulnerabilities.

Affiliates are typically compensated by receiving a portion of the ransom payments collected from victims. This division of labor lowers the barrier to entry for cybercriminals and enables large-scale ransomware campaigns to be launched by individuals who may not have advanced technical skills.

Group-IB. *All You Need to Know about Ransomware-as-a-Service (RaaS).* https://www.group-ib.com/resources/knowledge-hub/raas/.

47 HHS HC3. *Overview of Conti Ransomware.* https://www.hhs.gov/sites/default/files/analyst-note-conti-ransomware-tlp-white.pdf.

48 NIST National Vulnerability Database. *CVE-2021-44228.* https://nvd.nist.gov/vuln/detail/CVE-2021-44228.

49 JNDI (Java Naming and Directory Interface) is a built-in feature of the Java platform that allows software applications to look up and retrieve resources—such as configuration settings, remote services, or directory objects—from directories or naming systems. It serves as a kind of address book for Java applications, enabling them to connect to local, internal, or external services by name rather than by hard-coded locations.

Oracle. *Overview of JNDI.* https://docs.oracle.com/javase/tutorial/jndi/overview/index.html.

50 CISA. *Advisory AA21-356A: Mitigating Log4Shell and Other Log4j-Related Vulnerabilities.* https://www.cisa.gov/news-events/cybersecurity-advisories/aa21-356a.

51 HHS HC3. *Log4J Vulnerabilities and the Health Sector.* https://www.hhs.gov/sites/default/files/log4j-vulnerabilities-health-sector.pdf.

52 CISA. *Advisory AA23-165A: Understanding Ransomware Threat Actors: LockBit.* https://www.cisa.gov/news-events/cybersecurity-advisories/aa23-165a.

See also NIST. *SP 800-63B-4. Authenticator and Verifier Requirements.* https://www.cisa.gov/news-events/cybersecurity-advisories/aa23-165a.

See also HHS HC3. *Lockbit 3.0 Ransomware.* https://www.hhs.gov/sites/default/files/lockbit-3-analyst-note.pdf.

53 HHS HC3. *Hive Ransomware.* https://www.hhs.gov/sites/default/files/hive-ransomware-tlpwhite.pdf.

54 HHS HC3. *Hive Ransomware.* https://www.hhs.gov/sites/default/files/hive-ransomware-tlpwhite.pdf.

55 HHS HC3. *Hive Ransomware.* https://www.hhs.gov/sites/default/files/hive-ransomware-tlpwhite.pdf.

56 FBI, Cyber Division. *FBI Flash—TLP: WHITE. Indicators of Compromise Associated with Hive Ransomware.* https://www.ic3.gov/Media/News/2021/210825.pdf.

57 HHS HC3. *Hive Ransomware.* https://www.hhs.gov/sites/default/files/hive-ransomware-tlpwhite.pdf.

58 Europol. *Cybercriminals Stung as HIVE Infrastructure Shut Down.* https://www.europol.europa.eu/media-press/newsroom/news/cybercriminals-stung-hive-infrastructure-shut-down.

59 HHS HC3. *Royal & BlackCat Ransomware: The Threat to the Health Sector.* https://www.hhs.gov/sites/default/files/royal-blackcat-ransomware-tlpclear.pdf.

60 HHS HC3. *Royal & BlackCat Ransomware: The Threat to the Health Sector.* https://www.hhs.gov/sites/default/files/royal-blackcat-ransomware-tlpclear.pdf.

61 CISA. *Advisory AA23-353A: #StopRansomware: ALPHV Blackcat.* https://www.cisa.gov/news-events/cybersecurity-advisories/aa23-353a.

62 CISA. *Advisory AA23-353A: #StopRansomware: ALPHV Blackcat.* https://www.cisa.gov/news-events/cybersecurity-advisories/aa23-353a.

63 HHS HC3. *Royal & BlackCat Ransomware: The Threat to the Health Sector.* https://www.hhs.gov/sites/default/files/royal-blackcat-ransomware-tlpclear.pdf.

See also DOJ and CISA. *#StopRansomware: Royal Ransomware.* https://www.cisa.gov/sites/default/files/2023-03/aa23-061a-stopransomware-royal-ransomware_0.pdf.

64 MITRE Corporation. *Tactic—TA0003: Persistence.* https://attack.mitre.org/tactics/TA0003/.

65 HHS HC3. *Royal & BlackCat Ransomware: The Threat to the Health Sector.* https://www.hhs.gov/sites/default/files/royal-blackcat-ransomware-tlpclear.pdf.

66 HHS HC3. *Royal & BlackCat Ransomware: The Threat to the Health Sector.* https://www.hhs.gov/sites/default/files/royal-blackcat-ransomware-tlpclear.pdf.

67 HHS HC3. *Royal & BlackCat Ransomware: The Threat to the Health Sector.* https://www.hhs.gov/sites/default/files/royal-blackcat-ransomware-tlpclear.pdf.

68 HHS HC3. *Royal & BlackCat Ransomware: The Threat to the Health Sector.* https://www.hhs.gov/sites/default/files/royal-blackcat-ransomware-tlpclear.pdf.

69 HHS HC3. *Blacksuit Ransomware.* https://www.hhs.gov/sites/default/files/blacksuit-ransomware-analyst-note-tlpclear.pdf.

70 HHS HC3. *Threat Profile: Black Basta.* https://www.hhs.gov/sites/default/files/black-basta-threat-profile.pdf.

71 Tor Project. *Tor.* https://www.torproject.org/.

72 FBI. *How Cyber Crime Group FIN7 Attacked and Stole Data from Hundreds of U.S. Companies.* https://www.fbi.gov/contact-us/field-offices/seattle/news/stories/how-cyber-crime-group-fin7-attacked-and-stole-data-from-hundreds-of-us-companies.

73 CISA. *Advisory AA21-291A: BlackMatter Ransomware.* https://www.cisa.gov/news-events/cybersecurity-advisories/aa21-291a.

74 HHS HC3. *Threat Profile: Black Basta.* https://www.hhs.gov/sites/default/files/black-basta-threat-profile.pdf.

75 HHS HC3. *Threat Profile: Black Basta.* https://www.hhs.gov/sites/default/files/black-basta-threat-profile.pdf.

76 HHS HC3. *Threat Profile: Black Basta.* https://www.hhs.gov/sites/default/files/black-basta-threat-profile.pdf.

77 HHS HC3. *Karakurt Threat Profile.* https://www.hhs.gov/sites/default/files/karakurt-threat-profile-analyst-note.pdf.

78 HHS HC3. *Karakurt Threat Profile.* https://www.hhs.gov/sites/default/files/karakurt-threat-profile-analyst-note.pdf.

79 HHS HC3. *Karakurt Threat Profile.* https://www.hhs.gov/sites/default/files/karakurt-threat-profile-analyst-note.pdf.

80 HHS HC3. *Karakurt Threat Profile.* https://www.hhs.gov/sites/default/files/karakurt-threat-profile-analyst-note.pdf.

81 CourtListener. Criminal Complaint. United States District Court for the Southern District of Ohio. *United States v. Zolotarjovs a/k/a "Sforza_cesarini."* https://storage.courtlistener.com/recap/gov.uscourts.ohsd.295290/gov.uscourts.ohsd.295290.4.0.pdf.

82 HHS HC3. *Karakurt Threat Profile.* https://www.hhs.gov/sites/default/files/karakurt-threat-profile-analyst-note.pdf.

83 National Security Agency (NSA). *Post-Quantum Cryptography: CISA, NIST, and NSA Recommend How to Prepare Now.* https://www.nsa.gov/Press-Room/Press-Releases-Statements/Press-Release-View/article/3498776/post-quantum-cryptography-cisa-nist-and-nsa-recommend-how-to-prepare-now/.

Chapter 5

Major Breaches

5.1 From Major Breaches to Proactive Security

Major breaches have shaped both the regulatory landscape and the security practices of healthcare organizations. They can disrupt healthcare operations, compromise sensitive information, and create significant risks for affected organizations. Some of these incidents have triggered significant enforcement actions under the Health Insurance Portability and Accountability Act of 1996 (HIPAA). The U.S. Department of Health and Human Services (HHS) Office for Civil Rights (HHS OCR), which is responsible for the interpretation and enforcement of HIPAA, plays a central role in holding organizations accountable when breaches reveal gaps in compliance.

5.2 Spotlight on HHS OCR Enforcement

In the context of HIPAA enforcement, HHS OCR employs two primary enforcement mechanisms to address violations: resolution agreements and civil money penalties.

5.2.1 Resolution Agreements

Resolution agreements are voluntary settlements between HHS OCR and a covered entity or business associate. These agreements typically include a monetary payment and a corrective action plan (CAP) outlining specific measures the entity must implement to address identified compliance issues. A resolution agreement does not constitute an admission of liability by the entity, nor does it represent a formal finding of a HIPAA violation by HHS OCR. The monetary payment in a resolution agreement is not classified as a civil money penalty (CMP). HHS OCR uses this mechanism when it identifies potential noncompliance but resolves the matter without formal enforcement proceedings.

5.2.2 Civil Money Penalties (CMPs)

If HHS OCR determines that a covered entity or business associate has violated HIPAA and informal resolution efforts are unsuccessful, it may impose a CMP. CMPs involve a financial

DOI: 10.4324/9781003366560-5

penalty assessed after HHS OCR issues a notice of proposed determination of noncompliance. The entity is provided the opportunity for a hearing before an administrative law judge before a final determination is made.

5.3 Major Breaches

5.3.1 State of Play—Early Days

Prior to August 2014, the healthcare and public health sector had not experienced the same scale of *high-profile* cyberattacks seen in industries like finance or retail. Although breaches did occur, they were generally smaller in scope and did not generate the same level of national attention or operational disruption.

Many healthcare organizations had maintained a reactive security posture, with efforts centered on compliance and breach avoidance. The main focus was often on preventing breaches from known risks such as the theft or loss of laptops and portable devices, as well as insider threats, including unauthorized access to patient records—commonly referred to as snooping. These concerns drove practices like asset tagging, device encryption, and audit logging of user access to electronic health records (EHRs). HIPAA compliance was commonly viewed as the primary objective, rather than a baseline for a proactive security program grounded in established cybersecurity frameworks and best practices.

Please note: The year in parentheses for the following list of breaches indicates the year in which the breach notification occurred—not necessarily the occurrence of the actual breach or subsequent events.

5.3.2 Alaska Department of Health and Social Services (DHSS) (2009)

The following description is based on the findings published by HHS OCR. HHS OCR. *Resolution Agreement.* https://www.hhs.gov/sites/default/files/ocr/privacy/hipaa/enforcement/examples/alaska-agreement.pdf.

A portable USB external hard drive was stolen from the vehicle of a computer technician at the Alaska DHSS on or about October 12, 2009. DHSS submitted a breach report on October 30, 2009, in accordance with the HIPAA Breach Notification Rule. HHS OCR opened its investigation on January 8, 2010.

During the investigation, HHS OCR found that DHSS had *not* done the following: (1) completed a risk analysis, (2) implemented sufficient risk management measures, (3) completed security training for DHSS workforce members, (4) implemented device and media controls, and (5) addressed device and media encryption.

The enforcement action resulted in a $1.7 million monetary settlement and a CAP. Under the CAP, DHSS was required to develop and implement the following:

- Procedure for tracking devices containing ePHI
- Procedure for safeguarding devices containing ePHI
- Procedure for encrypting devices that contain ePHI
- Procedure for disposal and/or re-use of devices that contain ePHI
- Procedure for responding to security incidents; and
- Procedure for applying sanctions to workforce members who violate these policies and procedures.

DHSS was also required to conduct a comprehensive and accurate risk analysis, implement a corresponding risk management plan, and provide both general Security Rule training and policy-specific training on the revised or newly implemented policies and procedures to all workforce members who access ePHI. An independent monitor was designated to assess and report on DHSS's compliance progress to HHS OCR.

5.3.3 BlueCross BlueShield of Tennessee (2009)

The following description is based on the findings published by HHS OCR.

HHS OCR. *Resolution Agreement.* https://www.hhs.gov/sites/default/files/ocr/privacy/hipaa/enforcement/examples/resolution_agreement_and_cap.pdf.

In October 2009, BlueCross BlueShield of Tennessee, Inc. (BCBST), a HIPAA-covered entity, experienced a breach involving the theft of 57 encoded computer hard drives from a network data closet at one of its former facilities in Chattanooga, Tennessee. As part of a facility relocation earlier that year, BCBST had vacated most of its leased space at the Eastgate Town Center office, but continued to maintain a secured network data closet on-site. The closet was protected by biometric and keycard access, a magnetic lock, and a separate keyed door. Building security services were being provided by the property management company.[1]

BCBST received an alert on Friday, October 2, 2009, that the server at the Eastgate facility was unresponsive, but did not respond or investigate until Monday, October 5, 2009 because the unresponsive server message did not alert BCBST that there had been a theft, and the server did not appear to adversely impact operations. The theft was discovered on October 5, 2009.[2]

The hard drives in the network data closet were part of a system that recorded and stored audio and video recordings of customer service calls. The stolen hard drives contained encoded data that included the protected health information of health plan members, such as names, member ID numbers, diagnosis codes, dates of birth, and Social Security numbers. BCBST's internal investigation confirmed that the PHI of 1,023,209 individuals was stored on the hard drives. The data on the hard drives consisted of over 300,000 video recordings and over 1 million audio recordings.[3]

BCBST submitted a breach notification to HHS OCR on November 3, 2009, in accordance with the HIPAA Breach Notification Rule. HHS OCR opened its investigation on January 8, 2010.[4]

In March 2012, the matter was resolved through a $1.5 million monetary settlement and a CAP. The CAP required BCBST to update and implement revised policies and procedures, strengthen physical security controls, improve employee training, conduct risk assessments and risk management planning, and submit regular compliance reports. HHS OCR also retained authority to monitor BCBST's implementation of the CAP.[5]

This was the first enforcement action resulting from a breach report required under the HIPAA Breach Notification Rule.[6]

5.3.4 SAIC (2011)

The following description is based on public reports.

In 2011, Science Applications International Corporation (SAIC), a contractor that was supporting the Department of Defense's TRICARE program, reported the loss of backup tapes containing patient information from the military health system. The backup tapes included patient data from 1992 through September 7, 2011, for individuals seen at or whose records were maintained or processed through San Antonio-area military treatment facilities.

Air Force Medical Service. *TRICARE Data Breach.* https://www.airforcemedicine.af.mil/News/Display/Article/426356/tricare-data-breach/.

The backup tapes held information for approximately 4.9 million individuals, such as active-duty military personnel and their dependents, as well as military retirees associated with San Antonio-area military treatment facilities. The information included clinical notes, laboratory tests, and prescriptions.[7] This breach highlighted the risks associated with storing PHI and other sensitive data on.[8]

5.3.5 IBM (2011)

The following description is based on public reports.

In 2011, IBM was involved in a data loss incident that affected members of Health Net, a health insurance company. IBM, serving as an information technology vendor, notified Health Net that several server drives were unaccounted for at a California data center. The drives were later determined to contain health, financial, and *personally identifiable information*, such as social security numbers. This incident highlighted the importance of tracking and managing physical media containing sensitive information.[9]

5.3.6 GRM Information Services (2011)

The following description is based on public reports.

In December 2010, GRM Information Management Services, a records management contractor, was transporting electronic files on behalf of New York City's public hospital system. The GRM van was left unattended and unlocked while the driver made other pickups. During this time, the theft occurred. The stolen files contained protected health information and personal information for approximately 1.7 million individuals, including patients, staff, and vendors—people who were either treated or provided services to the NYC hospital system. The data included names, addresses, Social Security numbers, medical histories, and the occupational and employee health information of staff, vendors, contractors, and others. The stolen data was not readily accessible, and there was no evidence of unauthorized access or misuse at the time.[10]

5.3.7 Anchorage Community Mental Health Services, Inc. (ACMHS) (2012)

The following description is based on the findings published by HHS OCR.

HHS. *Resolution Agreement.* https://www.hhs.gov/sites/default/files/ocr/privacy/hipaa/enforcement/examples/acmhs/amchs-capsettlement.pdf.

ACMHS experienced a compromise of the security of its information technology resources resulting in a breach of unsecured electronic protected health information (ePHI) affecting 2,743 individuals. ACMHS submitted a breach report to the U.S. Department of HHS OCR on March 2, 2012.

ACMHS was required to strengthen its compliance with the HIPAA Security Rule through a series of specific actions. These included revising its existing Security Rule policies and procedures and submitting them to HHS OCR for review and approval. Upon receiving approval, ACMHS was required to officially adopt the revised policies, distribute them to all workforce members who use or disclose ePHI, and obtain signed written or electronic certifications from each individual acknowledging their understanding and agreement to comply.

ACMHS was also required to implement a general security awareness training program. The training materials were subject to HHS OCR review and approval. Once approved, ACMHS had to provide training to all existing workforce members who use or disclose ePHI within 60 days, and to all new workforce members within 30 days of their start date. Annual training and updates were required thereafter, with certification of completion and retention of training records.

Additionally, ACMHS was obligated to conduct an annual, accurate, and thorough risk assessment consistent with its internal policy and procedure on IT risk management. This included documenting the security measures in place to reduce identified risks and vulnerabilities to a reasonable and appropriate level.[11]

5.3.7.1 Lessons Learned

The following are considerations for the healthcare industry.

- Patching and system maintenance: Organizations must ensure that all IT and *operational technology* (OT) systems[12] are running supported versions of software and are regularly updated with security patches to mitigate known vulnerabilities.
- Firewall configuration and monitoring: Technical safeguards such as firewalls must be properly configured and monitored to detect and block suspicious inbound and outbound traffic.
- Risk analysis and risk management: A comprehensive, documented risk assessment is essential. It must be regularly reviewed and must inform actionable risk management strategies.
- Security training and policy implementation: Workforce members must be trained on security policies, and organizations must ensure that security procedures are understood and followed.
- Enforcement of security procedures: Security controls are only effective when implemented, enforced, and audited. Written policies must be translated into operational practice.

5.3.8 Advocate (2013)

The following description is based on the findings published by HHS OCR.

In 2013, Advocate Health and Hospitals Corporation, doing business through its subsidiary Advocate Medical Group (AMG), experienced three separate breaches. Each breach was reported to HHS OCR and led to a separate federal investigation.[13]

The first breach occurred during the early morning hours of July 15, 2013, when four desktop computers were stolen from an AMG administrative office (Touhy Support Center). The computers contained the ePHI of approximately 4,029,530 individuals, later amended to 3,994,175. Advocate submitted a breach notification to HHS OCR on August 23, 2013. On August 29, 2013, HHS OCR informed Advocate that it was opening an investigation into the HIPAA compliance issues raised by the breach.[14]

The second breach involved a business associate who provided billing services to AMG. Advocate reported to HHS OCR on September 13, 2013, that the ePHI of 2,027 patients may have been compromised when an unauthorized third party accessed the business associate's network at some point between June 30, 2013, and August 15, 2013. HHS notified Advocate on October 29, 2013, that it was opening an investigation into the second breach.[15]

The third breach occurred when an unencrypted laptop containing the ePHI of approximately 2,237 individuals was stolen from the vehicle of an AMG workforce member. Advocate submitted the breach notification to HHS on November 1, 2013. On January 8, 2014, HHS OCR informed Advocate that it was initiating an investigation into the HIPAA compliance issues related to this third incident.[16]

Following its investigations, HHS OCR determined that Advocate had failed to conduct a comprehensive risk analysis covering all of its facilities, systems, and data; had not implemented adequate physical safeguards at the Touhy Support Center, where the theft of four desktop computers occurred; and had failed to secure a proper business associate agreement with the vendor involved in the second breach. HHS OCR also concluded that Advocate failed to safeguard ePHI appropriately in both the first breach involving the stolen desktop computers and the third breach involving the stolen unencrypted laptop.[17]

In 2016, the matter was resolved through a $5.55 million monetary settlement and a CAP. The CAP required Advocate to implement major reforms, including an enterprise-wide risk analysis, development of a risk management plan, implementation of updated encryption protocols, revised policies and procedures on device and media controls,[18] business associate agreements, and an enhanced training program. Advocate was also subject to independent monitoring and periodic assessments as part of OCR's oversight process.[19]

5.3.9 Target (2013)

The following description is based on public reports and Congressional testimony.

The 2013 breach of Target Corporation, though not healthcare-related, is often cited as an early example of a supply chain compromise. Attackers gained access to Target's network through a third-party HVAC vendor, ultimately stealing payment card data from over 40 million customers. This incident highlighted the risk of indirect access via trusted external vendors and helped bring supply chain attacks into broader focus.[20] Since this breach, threat actors have exploited supply chain vulnerabilities and attempted to compromise victim organizations through their third-party vendors and suppliers.

5.4 First Widely Reported Nation-State Cyberattack on a Hospital System

5.4.1 Community Health Systems (2014)

The following description is based on public reports.

The perception that healthcare would not be targeted by cyberattackers changed significantly in August 2014, when a major healthcare system, Community Health Systems (CHS), suffered a breach attributed to a nation-state actor. This attack compromised the personal information of 4.5 million patients,[21] marking a turning point and signaling that healthcare was no longer off-limits for sophisticated adversaries.

Before the cyberattack on CHS, many hospital leaders underestimated the cybersecurity risk, believing that the healthcare industry was not an attractive target for cybercriminals or state-sponsored actors. Some organizations assumed they were safe, relying on the belief that adversaries would avoid targeting institutions dedicated to patient care. While some hospitals had robust cybersecurity programs, others lagged behind and did not have mature cybersecurity leadership or well-developed security practices.

Some cybercriminal groups and entities publicly state their refusal to target healthcare organizations.[22] However, this notion is far from universal. Still, many ransomware groups and other threat actors continue to attack healthcare entities.

5.5 Sony Pictures (2014)

The following description is based on public reports.

The 2014 cyberattack on Sony Pictures Entertainment was attributed by the U.S. government to North Korea nation-state actors. The attackers used destructive malware—specifically a form of *wiper malware*—to compromise Sony's network. The malware rendered many computers inoperable and significantly disrupted business operations. FBI. Update on Sony Investigation. https://www.fbi.gov/news/press-releases/update-on-sony-investigation. See also Data Breach Today. Sony Hack: 'Destover' Malware Identified. https://www.databreachtoday.com/sony-hack-destover-malware-identified-a-7638.

5.6 Anthem (2015)

The following description is based on the findings published by HHS OCR.

On January 29, 2015, Anthem, one of the largest health insurers in the United States, discovered a sophisticated cyberattack on its IT system. The attackers had been operating undetected for weeks, using a method known as an advanced persistent threat (APT). The compromise began with a spear-phishing email sent to at least one employee at an Anthem subsidiary, giving the attackers initial access to the network.

Between December 2, 2014, and January 27, 2015, the attackers were able to steal sensitive ePHI of nearly 79 million individuals. This included names, Social Security numbers, medical identification numbers, addresses, dates of birth, email addresses, and employment information.[23]

In terms of lessons learned, as a suggestion for the healthcare industry to consider, there is a need for employee training, accurate and thorough risk assessments, and robust detection systems to prevent unauthorized access and protect sensitive patient data, including ePHI.

5.7 UCLA (2015)

The following description is based on a press release.

In July 2015, UCLA Health announced that it had been the victim of a criminal cyberattack. The investigation revealed that attackers may have accessed parts of its computer network containing personal and medical information for as many as 4.5 million individuals. According to publicly available information, the organization could not rule out the possibility that the information may have been accessed. Therefore, it began notifying affected individuals out of an abundance of caution.[24]

Suspicious activity was first detected in October 2014, prompting a launch of an internal investigation in collaboration with the Federal Bureau of Investigation. At the time, there was no indication that sensitive data had been breached. However, by May 5, 2015, further analysis determined that attackers had gained access to portions of the network where protected health information (PHI) was stored—including names, addresses, birthdates, Social Security numbers, medical record numbers, and health plan identifiers. The unauthorized access may have begun as early as September 2014.[25]

This incident highlighted how large healthcare systems with substantial resources can be targets of a cyberattack. It emphasized the importance of early threat detection, proactive notification protocols, and continuous investment in network security. It also reinforced the need to protect sensitive data—whether or not evidence confirms it was exfiltrated—through measures such as encryption, access controls, and regular system audits.

5.8 First Widely Reported International Cyberattack

5.8.1 WannaCry (2017)

The following description is based on public reports.

The WannaCry ransomware (more specifically, a ransomworm) spread rapidly, locking users out of their systems and displaying a ransom note demanding payment in Bitcoin. For the NHS, the consequences were significant. The cyberattack caused widespread disruption across the NHS, impacting both patients and healthcare staff. Hospitals were forced to revert to manual processes, such as relying on paper records. Radiology services were disrupted, outpatient appointments, elective admissions, procedures were canceled, and emergency ambulances had to be diverted to other hospitals.

The WannaCry attack emphasized the need for constant vigilance, regular system updates, and comprehensive incident response plans. The NHS's "Lessons Learned Review of the WannaCry Ransomware Cyber Attack" identified several key areas for improvement to enhance cybersecurity resilience:

- Leadership and accountability: The need for clear leadership and accountability within the NHS to effectively manage cybersecurity risks.
- Infrastructure and system upgrades: The importance of timely updates and patches to IT systems.
- Incident response planning: The need for a comprehensive incident response plan to quickly and effectively respond to incidents.
- Staff training and awareness: The need for staff training and awareness programs to improve the level of preparedness against potential cyber threats.
- Collaboration and communication: The need for improved communication channels between the NHS and external partners to better facilitate information sharing and coordinated responses to security incidents.

NHS England *et al. Lessons learned review of the WannaCry Ransomware Cyber Attack.* https://www.england.nhs.uk/wp-content/uploads/2018/02/lessons-learned-review-wannacry-ransomware-cyber-attack-cio-review.pdf.

5.9 Second Widely Reported International Cyberattack

5.9.1 NotPetya (2017)

The following description is based on public reports.

In June 2017, the NotPetya attack began with a malicious update to a widely used Ukrainian tax accounting software, M.E.Doc, by Ukrainian businesses. The malicious update to M.E.Doc served as the initial vector for the malware's spread. While the cyberattack was ostensibly aimed at disrupting Ukrainian systems, its effects quickly spiraled out of control, spreading globally and impacting organizations well beyond the initial target.[26] The interconnected nature of global IT systems and supply chains allowed the malware to spread far beyond its intended target, severely impacting organizations around the world. This unintended worldwide proliferation of the malware illustrates how a cyberattack aimed at a specific region can have widespread and far-reaching consequences.

The cyberattack caused widespread disruption, including significant impacts on healthcare entities. Vendors providing essential services, such as medical transcription, experienced severe disruptions, which in turn affected the clinical operations of healthcare providers and clinics relying on those services. Other healthcare organizations, including those in the life sciences subsector, were also significantly affected.[27]

NotPetya highlighted the interconnectivity—and vulnerability—of healthcare supply chains. Many entities, including hospitals and others, rely on third parties for critical services.[28] When vendors are attacked, organizations that depend on them (such as hospitals, clinics, and other entities) can also be adversely affected.

Healthcare entities are uniquely reliant on nearly all other critical infrastructure sectors to support their operations, administration, and clinical care. This interdependency makes healthcare particularly vulnerable, as an adverse event affecting a supplier or vendor—such as disruptions to water supply, electrical grids, or other essential services—can directly and significantly impact the HPH sector. This interconnectedness is a critical focus of the HPH Sector-Specific Plan under the National Infrastructure Protection Plan (NIPP), highlighting the need for resilience and collaboration across supply chains.[29]

5.10 Other Cyberattacks

5.10.1 Singapore Health Services (2018)

The following description is based on public reports.

Between August 23, 2017, and July 20, 2018, Singapore Health Services (SingHealth), the country's largest public healthcare provider, became the target of a sophisticated cyberattack with over 1.5 million patient records accessed without authorization. The Singapore Prime Minister's personal health information was specifically targeted and accessed multiple times by the cyberattackers.

The attackers gained initial access to SingHealth's network, likely through phishing, and remained dormant for several months prior to lateral movement. During this time, the attackers quietly observed how things worked before they started moving around the SingHealth network (lateral movement). From May 2018, the attackers used compromised workstations and likely virtual machines to remotely connect to SingHealth servers. Initially, the attackers were unsuccessful in accessing the central database from the servers. The IT staff noticed the unauthorized logins from the servers and failed attempts at accessing the central database on June 11, 2018, as well as June 12, 13, and 26, 2018.

On July 4, 2018, an information technology (IT) administrator with IHiS (Integrated Health Information Systems Private Limited, which was responsible for administering and operating the systems, including implementing cybersecurity measures, as well as incident response and reporting) noticed suspicious queries being made on the centralized database. Security measures were put in place to prevent further queries to the centralized database. The attackers could not make any further successful queries to the database after July 4, 2018. However, this issue was not escalated to senior management until July 9, 2018—thereby delaying a coordinated response. On July 10, 2018, cybersecurity authorities were brought in to help investigate and contain the breach. By July 20, 2018, additional protections, including restricted internet access, were implemented, effectively preventing further malicious activity.

Subsequently, the government of Singapore's Committee of Inquiry (COI) issued a detailed report on what had happened and the proactive steps it had taken to ensure appropriate remediation and improve resilience against future cyber compromises. In the report, the attackers were deemed to be an APT group.[30]

APT groups are known for their ability to carry out stealthy, long-term attacks, often motivated by geopolitical or economic interests. Unlike typical cybercriminals who may seek financial gain and/or disruption of a target, APT groups tend to be highly sophisticated and often target specific data that an organization may have.

5.10.1.1 Lessons Learned

The following are considerations for the healthcare industry.

Early detection and escalation: Incidents must be escalated without delay to senior leadership and security authorities.

Phishing as an entry point: The likely initial compromise through phishing illustrates the continued importance of user awareness training and strong email security controls.

Persistence of APTs: APT groups often remain undetected for months while mapping systems and identifying valuable data. Continuous monitoring, threat hunting, and anomaly detection are essential to identify stealthy adversaries.

Importance of root cause analysis: Remediation requires halting ongoing malicious activity and also understanding how the breach occurred, including technical, organizational, and procedural weaknesses.

Critical role of governance: The delay in reporting highlights the need for clear governance structures that define who is responsible for incident reporting, escalation, and response.

Resilience and preparedness: Implementing layered security, restricting unnecessary internet access, and rehearsing incident response plans are critical to limiting the impact of determined adversaries.

5.10.2 Eastern Health (Newfoundland and Labrador, Canada) (2021)

The following description is based on public reports.

On October 30, 2021, Newfoundland's and Labrador's healthcare system was severely impacted by a ransomware attack that disrupted IT systems across the province. The attack resulted in a province-wide outage affecting hospital operations, laboratory services, appointment scheduling, and email systems. It was later confirmed that the ransomware used was from the Hive group, a known threat actor targeting the HPH sector.

Initial attacker activity began as early as October 15, 2021, when a VPN connection to the Newfoundland and Labrador Centre for Health Information (NLCHI)-managed network was initiated using compromised credentials from a legitimate account. The attacker moved laterally through the environment, escalated privileges using an administrative account, and exfiltrated both personal and health information. On October 30, 2021, Hive ransomware was deployed, leading to widespread encryption and system failure—this was the point at which the attack was detected.

The breach involved significant exposure of data. Information taken included Social Insurance Numbers, contact information, and health details from patients whose records spanned different time periods at Eastern Health, Central Health, and Labrador-Grenfell Health. In addition, data from current and former employees, including disciplinary and HR records, were also taken. According to reports, there was no evidence that the stolen data were misused.

In response, NLCHI and the regional health authorities (RHAs) activated emergency protocols, worked closely with managed service providers, and brought in third-party cybersecurity experts to contain and investigate the breach. A comprehensive system recovery effort followed, including endpoint detection and response tools, global password resets, multi-factor authentication for remote access, and forensic analysis of all affected devices. By December 2021, most core systems had been restored or rebuilt from backups.

To strengthen long-term resilience, the Breakwater initiative was launched—a joint effort by NLCHI and the RHAs[31] to improve cybersecurity maturity across the province's health infrastructure. Breakwater focused on centralized security monitoring, asset management, firewall enhancements, SIEM deployment, and mandatory cybersecurity training for healthcare personnel.[32]

5.10.2.1 Lessons Learned

The following are considerations for the healthcare industry.

- Early detection of threats is important to help ensure threat prevention and mitigation through effective monitoring and endpoint detection capabilities.
- Secure remote access should include *FIDO2-compliant* MFA or passwordless authentication *and* continuous monitoring of VPN activity.
- Strong authentication policies and procedures are required to help ensure that the claimed identities are whom they claim to be and that privileged accounts are appropriately protected.
- Coordinated response planning is essential to support rapid incident triage, containment, and eradication, as well as to help facilitate continuity of care when clinical systems are disrupted.

5.10.3 HCA Healthcare (2023)

The following description is based on public reports.

In July 2023, HCA Healthcare reported an incident involving information for approximately 11 million patients. On or around July 5, 2023, the organization discovered that a list containing limited patient data (e.g., patient name, city, state, and zip code; patient email, telephone number, date of birth, gender; and patient service date, location, and next appointment date) had been posted online by an unauthorized party.

The incident appeared to involve a theft from an external storage location exclusively used to automate formatting of emails. It was not found to have caused any disruption to the day-to-day operations.

The exposed information did not include clinical information (e.g., treatment, diagnosis, or condition), payment information (e.g. credit card or account numbers), or sensitive information (e.g., passwords, driver's license, or Social Security numbers).

HCA disabled access to the affected storage location as an immediate containment measure, notified law enforcement, and engaged outside experts to investigate. The organization also notified the affected individuals and offered complimentary credit monitoring and identity protection services.

HCA Healthcare. *HCA Healthcare Reports Data Security Incident.* https://investor.hcahealthcare.com/news/news-details/2023/HCA-Healthcare-Reports-Data-Security-Incident/default.aspx.

See also CBS News. *HCA Healthcare says hackers stole data on 11 million patients.* https://www.cbsnews.com/news/hca-healthcare-data-breach-hack-11-million-patients-affected/.

5.10.3.1 Lessons Learned

The following are considerations for the healthcare industry.

- Organizations should ensure that all systems containing patient information, including nonclinical platforms used for communications or administrative functions, are secured with strong access controls and continuous monitoring.
- Data governance programs should include inventories of where patient information resides, including external storage locations and systems used by third parties.
- Regular security reviews of systems and infrastructure—including third parties that are processing data on behalf of the organization—are necessary to verify that all systems meet the organization's security requirements.

5.10.4 Change Healthcare (2024)

The following description is based on public reports and Congressional testimony.

On February 21, 2024, Change Healthcare—a major healthcare payment processing company—identified ransomware activity on its computer systems. Upon discovery, the entity immediately shut down affected systems, disconnected access to prevent further compromise, and contacted law enforcement. Change Healthcare's internal security team and external experts investigated the intrusion and determined the scope of the incident.[33, 34]

The investigation confirmed that a cybercriminal gained unauthorized access on February 12, 2024, using compromised login credentials to enter a Citrix remote access portal. At the time of the incident, multi-factor authentication had not been enabled on the account used.[35] The attacker remained in the system for several days.[36]

As stated by the Change Healthcare HIPAA Website Substitute Notice (https://web.archive.org/web/20250116033916/https://www.changehealthcare.com/hipaa-substitute-notice.html) Notice of Data Breach (June 20, 2024; updated July 29, 2024, August 8, 2024, and January 14, 2025):

> The information involved for individuals may have included contact information (such as first and last name, address, phone number, and email), date of birth, and one or more of the following:
>
> Health insurance information (such as primary, secondary or other health plans/policies, insurance companies, member/group ID numbers, and Medicaid-Medicare-government payor ID numbers);

Health information (such as medical record numbers, providers, diagnoses, medicines, test results, images, care and treatment information); and/or
Billing and claims information (such as claim numbers, account numbers, billing codes, payments made, and balance due).

The Change Healthcare cyberattack was executed by an affiliate of the ALPHV ransomware group, also known as BlackCat. ALPHV operates under a ransomware-as-a-service (RaaS) model, in which affiliates use the group's malware and infrastructure to carry out attacks in exchange for a share of any ransom payments. In this case, the affiliate used ALPHV's tools to breach Change Healthcare's systems. Following the attack, Change Healthcare paid a ransom of $22 million in Bitcoin, according to a Congressional testimony. However, according to statements attributed to the RansomHub group, ALPHV allegedly stole the payment, failing to distribute any portion to the affiliate who conducted the attack.[37] After the fallout, a group called RansomHub emerged, claiming it was in possession of the stolen data. RansomHub issued a ransom demand. The group threatened to publicly release the exfiltrated data if a new payment was not made.[38]

5.10.4.1 Lessons Learned

The following are considerations for the healthcare industry.

- *Enforce Multi-Factor Authentication (MFA) across All Remote Access Systems.*
  - MFA should be required for all privileged accounts and for any remote access to organizational systems. This includes access to servers, endpoints, cloud services, administrative tools, and identity and access management (IAM) systems. IAM systems are used to centrally manage user identities, enforce authentication policies, and control access to internal systems, cloud platforms, and external applications.
  - MFA helps prevent unauthorized access by requiring something in addition to a password—such as a physical device or a biometric factor. However, MFA is only as strong as the factors that are used. Text messages and voice calls are considered weaker factors, as they can be intercepted or manipulated. (For example, a person's voice may be cloned using an audio deepfake.) Stronger factors include hardware security keys that follow open standards like FIDO2—a physical device, such as a Universal Serial Bus (USB) or Near Field Communication (NFC) key, that must be present and activated to complete the login process. MFA should be implemented wherever technically feasible, and especially when users access systems containing sensitive or high-value data.[39]
- *To Pay or Not to Pay a Ransom Payment (Ransomware Attacks)—a Case-Specific Question.*
  - Paying a ransom in response to a ransomware attack does not ensure that stolen data will be deleted—either from the attacker's systems or from any public leak site where it may have been posted. Nor does it guarantee that a decryption key will be provided, or that the key will actually work. In some cases, the malware may not include a functioning decryption module at all. Payment also does not prevent the attacker from leaking, selling, or reusing the data, including through other criminal groups. In some incidents, new ransom demands have been issued after the initial payment. The decision to pay is best evaluated on a case-by-case basis and involves reputational, operational, financial, legal, and other risks. Entities should carefully weigh these risks and consult legal counsel and experienced incident response firms—particularly those with expertise in digital forensics

and incident response (DFIR), system recovery, and ransom negotiation in connection with ransomware attacks.
   - If an entity has cyber liability insurance, the terms of the policy may influence how the incident must be managed. Some policies require the use of pre-approved vendors—for example, firms that specialize in ransom negotiation, digital forensics, or technical remediation efforts such as data restoration and system reconstitution. In some cases, the insurer may designate legal counsel to advise on covered matters, which may or may not align with the organization's own legal strategy. Policies may also include notice provisions, pre-authorization requirements, or exclusions that affect coverage for ransom payments, business interruption, or incident response costs. Entities should review and understand the specific terms of their cyber liability policy in advance of an incident.
- *Dealing with Third-Party Risk.*
   - Third-party vendors, suppliers, and infrastructure providers may provide critical services throughout the healthcare ecosystem. If one of these external entities is compromised, the impact can cascade across connected systems and organizations. Healthcare entities must identify their operational dependencies and ensure that third-party risk is incorporated into the organization's risk analysis process. (This is a best practice, and it is a requirement under the HIPAA Security Rule.)[40]
   - The risk, however, is not limited to vendors, suppliers, or infrastructure providers operating within the HPH sector. Many healthcare entities depend on third-party suppliers and infrastructure providers that are external to healthcare, such as electric utilities, telecommunications carriers, cloud service providers, and water systems. These third parties may not deliver healthcare-specific services, but their availability can directly affect patient care and clinical operations. Before entities develop contingency plans, they must have a clear understanding of which third parties are essential to their operations. Examples include core infrastructure, utility services, technology platforms, and other external providers that support operational continuity. Entities should plan for how they will respond if any of these third-party vendors or suppliers become unavailable or fail to deliver the required service.

5.11 Ascension (2024)

The following description is based on public reports.

In May 2024, Ascension became the target of a significant cyberattack that disrupted clinical operations across its hospitals and outpatient facilities. The cyberattacks gained a foothold in the network based on reports indicating that an employee unwittingly downloaded a malicious file (believing it to be a legitimate file). This enabled the cyberattackers to move across the network and use ransomware to encrypt files.

On May 8, 2024, Ascension detected unusual activity on its network, prompting an immediate investigation. To mitigate the threat and protect its systems, the organization disconnected portions of its network and implemented downtime protocols. These actions, while necessary, led to disruptions in the delivery of care. Ultimately, however, the EHR system was restored.[41, 42]

According to public reports, hospitals within the healthcare system allegedly experienced delays and disruptions, with some facilities allegedly forced to divert ambulances and postpone non-emergency procedures, and some clinicians allegedly reverted to manual processes—such as using paper charts.

Test results were also allegedly delayed, and certain appointments were allegedly rescheduled. According to public reports, patients were advised to bring notes on their symptoms and a list of prescription numbers or prescription bottles with them to their appointments, while the systems were down and manual processes were in place.[43]

This incident highlighted some of the unique challenges faced by healthcare organizations:

- *Complex IT ecosystems:* Large health systems rely on interconnected networks of devices, applications, and third-party vendors.
- *Resource constraints:* Many healthcare organizations operate on tight budgets, limiting their ability to invest in state-of-the-art cybersecurity tools and personnel.[44]
- *Regulatory pressures:* Compliance with regulations such as the HIPAA Privacy and Security Rules is essential, but does not necessarily equate to robust cybersecurity.
- *Patient safety risks:* Unlike many other industries, cybersecurity incidents in healthcare can directly impact human lives. Delayed treatments, miscommunications, and system failure may have adverse consequences in regard to patient safety.

5.11.1 Lessons Learned

The following are considerations for the healthcare industry.

- **Proactive threat management**: Organizations must adopt a proactive approach to cybersecurity, including regular vulnerability assessments, penetration testing, and continuous monitoring of network activity.
- **Employee training**: Human error is a common factor in cybersecurity incidents.[45] Comprehensive training programs can help staff recognize phishing attempts, avoid risky actions, and follow best practices.
- **Incident response preparedness:** A well-documented and regularly tested incident response plan is essential. Organizations must be ready to act swiftly to contain breaches and minimize their impact.
- **Investment in cybersecurity:** Allocating sufficient resources to cybersecurity is essential. This includes investing in advanced threat detection capabilities, hiring skilled professionals, and ensuring robust data backup and recovery systems.
- **Collaboration and information sharing:** Healthcare organizations can benefit from participating in industry groups such as InfraGard, HHS 405(d) program,[46] the Health Information Sharing and Analysis Center (H-ISAC), and others to stay informed about emerging threats and share best practices.
- **Third-party risk management:** The healthcare industry's reliance on managed security service providers, medical transcription services, cloud platforms, and other third-party vendors and infrastructure providers makes it susceptible to supply chain disruptions.[47] This cascading effect can act as an unintended force multiplier, where a compromise affecting a single vendor or system leads to broader operational disruptions across multiple dependent organizations.
- **Financial losses**: Healthcare organizations operate within a significantly interconnected ecosystem, relying heavily on third-party vendors for essential services like EHRs, medical

transcription, accounting, payroll, and other critical areas. When a supply chain cyberattack occurs targeting these third parties, the resulting disruptions often lead to significant financial losses, operational setbacks, and reputational harm. For healthcare entities, these impacts are especially dire, as they directly compromise their ability to deliver critical services to patients.

5.12 Additional Lessons Learned

The following description is based on public reports.

The 2024 cyberattack on Change Healthcare caused widespread delays in claims and payment processing, resulting in cash flow disruptions for providers that depend on timely reimbursement. In 2017, the NotPetya attack—though not targeting healthcare—affected organizations indirectly through shared vendors and infrastructure. Both incidents demonstrated how a compromise involving a single entity may result in financial and operational consequences across dependent systems and services.[48]

5.13 Social Engineering Attacks

5.13.1 The Role of Social Engineering

Social engineering attacks are one of the most effective methods for cyber adversaries to infiltrate the networks and systems of healthcare organizations. By exploiting human vulnerabilities, these attacks can trick individuals into providing access to sensitive systems or information.

5.13.2 Anthem (2015)

The following description is based on reports and an unsealed indictment.

In February 2015, Anthem Inc.—formerly known as WellPoint—announced a major cyberattack that exposed the personal information of approximately 78.8 million individuals.[49]

The attack started with a phishing campaign that targeted employees at an Anthem subsidiary. According to reports, the attackers sent spear-phishing emails containing links to malware. When these malicious links were clicked, a backdoor was installed on the user's system, which essentially gave the attackers remote access to Anthem's internal network. The attackers then quietly escalated their privileges, conducted reconnaissance, and lurked for months while expanding access across systems.

The attackers registered domains that closely resembled legitimate Anthem infrastructure, including we11point.com, designed to imitate "wellpoint.com." Employees were tricked into entering credentials, which were then captured and used by the attackers to authenticate into Anthem's actual systems.[50]

Once inside, attackers moved laterally across the network, looking for valuable systems and data (conducting reconnaissance). Lateral movement allows attackers to escalate privileges and maintain access while avoiding detection. They ultimately identified and extracted (i.e., stole) names, dates of birth, Social Security numbers, email addresses, medical identification numbers, addresses, and employment information. The data was compressed into encrypted archive files, transferred through Citrix ShareFile, and routed through multiple computers before being exfiltrated to infrastructure controlled by the attackers.[51]

The breach was attributed in a 2019 U.S. federal indictment to alleged members of a hacking group operating out of China. According to the indictment (Case 1:19-cr-00153-JRS-MJD), the attackers used "sophisticated techniques," including spear-phishing, credential harvesting, malware, lateral movement, and the use of command-and-control infrastructure. They also deleted evidence of their activities to evade detection. This information was unveiled in an unsealed indictment and announcement from the U.S. Department of Justice.[52]

Sakula, a remote access trojan, was widely linked to the breach, according to researchers. According to reports, Sakula was also associated with the OPM breach, and the infrastructure used in both attacks shared similarities. The malware was said to have been digitally signed using a certificate stolen from DTOPTOOLZ Co., a Korean software vendor.[53]

This incident highlights the real-world risks of social engineering and other advanced techniques. It also shows how cyberattacks on healthcare organizations can be connected to broader campaigns focused on espionage and long-term data collection.

5.13.2.1 Lessons Learned

The following are considerations for the healthcare industry.

- *Authentication.*
  - Strong authentication measures—such as FIDO2-compliant phishing-resistant MFA or robust passwordless options—along with layered defenses can help detect misuse of valid credentials. Organizations need visibility into what normal user, system, and network activity looks like—and must be able to detect when that activity deviates in subtle but meaningful ways, such as unusual login times, unauthorized access attempts, or abnormal use of administrative tools. While no single measure will stop every attack, combining technical controls with regular employee training can help reduce the risk and improve response when incidents occur.
- *Understanding Lateral Movement.*
  - After attackers gain a foothold in a network,[54] they may begin expanding their access and moving toward high-value targets. They can move laterally—gradually expanding their access, escalating privileges (known as privilege escalation), and targeting higher-value systems over time.

Lateral movement generally occurs in three phases.

- First, attackers perform internal reconnaissance. Attackers often use built-in administrative tools—such as PowerShell and command-line utilities—to avoid detection, a technique commonly referred to as "Living off the Land" (LOTL).
- Second, the attackers obtain user credentials through credential dumping and then escalate privileges. This allows attackers to impersonate legitimate users and gain broader access across the environment.
- Third, with elevated access (i.e., privilege escalation), the attackers can move across systems until they reach their targets.
- *Understanding Sophisticated Threat Actors.*
  - Sophisticated threat actors—including nation-state groups—are known to leverage LOTL and operate with stealth. By using legitimate tools and minimizing overt activity, they can remain undetected for an extended period (i.e., dwell time).[55] This may lead to an increase in the scale and severity of the compromise.

5.13.3 SingHealth (2018)

The following description is based on official public reports.

In July 2018, SingHealth—Singapore's largest public healthcare group—disclosed a major cyberattack that compromised the personal data of approximately 1.5 million patients. This included names, National Registration Identity Card (NRIC) numbers, addresses, dates of birth, gender, and race. Additionally, outpatient medication records of around 159,000 individuals were accessed. Notably, the Prime Minister's health records were specifically targeted and repeatedly queried.[56]

It was determined that the initial point of compromise occurred in August 2017, most likely through a successful phishing attack. Front-end workstations were infected with malware, which allowed the attackers to gain a foothold in the network, thus paving the path for exploration of the network through lateral movement.[57]

Over the following months, the attackers moved laterally within the environment, escalating their privileges and compromising multiple endpoints and administrator accounts, including domain controllers. They employed APT tactics, including the use of customized malware and "living off the land" techniques to avoid detection.[58]

Remedial measures were initiated promptly following the discovery of the breach. Although no further exfiltration occurred after July 4, 2018, malicious activity was observed again on July 18 and 19, including attempts to connect to command and control servers and newly discovered malware on an internal server. In response, the Cyber Security Agency (CSA) recommended the implementation of internet surfing separation to prevent further unauthorized communication with the attacker's infrastructure. This measure was put in place at 12:00 am on July 20, 2018. No further signs of malicious activity were detected thereafter.[59]

5.13.3.1 Lessons Learned

The following are considerations for the healthcare industry.

- Organizations should implement *FIDO2-compliant phishing-resistant* MFA and ensure that such requirements are consistently enforced. Robust authentication measures reduce the risk of account compromise and limit the ability of attackers to move laterally using stolen credentials. Organizations also need to continuously monitor for unauthorized access and unusual activity when valid credentials are used. Attackers often rely on legitimate access to move through systems without being noticed.
- Phishing is a common entry point, and users need to understand what to look for and how to respond. While security awareness training has value, especially for improving general vigilance, it cannot be relied on as a primary defense. Training should support—not replace—technical safeguards such as robust authentication, email filtering, and real-time threat detection.
- Organizations should ensure that vulnerabilities, misconfigurations, and policy gaps identified in audits or penetration tests are appropriately remediated and addressed.
- Robust governance structures, escalation procedures, and incident response processes are essential. Personnel must also be trained to recognize security incidents and understand how to escalate concerns promptly and effectively.

5.13.4 Ascension (2024)

The following description is based on public reports.

In May 2024, Ascension—a large healthcare system—was hit by a ransomware attack that disrupted patient care across multiple hospitals and outpatient facilities. The incident was discovered on May 8, 2024, although data exfiltration had already occurred on May 7, 2024, and May 8, 2024.[60]

The attack began when an employee was deceived into downloading a malicious file, believing it to be legitimate. That action gave the attackers access to internal systems and enabled them to deploy ransomware across the network.[61] Certain key systems were taken offline, including EHRs, internal communications, and clinical applications. Some hospitals had to revert to manual workflows and paper records, leading to delayed appointments, rescheduled procedures, and ambulance diversions in some locations.[62]

The organization later confirmed that the attackers accessed files containing certain sensitive medical and personal information, such as patients' medical records, lab tests, and insurance information, as more specifically detailed in a letter to the Maine attorney general.[63]

A related joint advisory from CISA, the FBI, and HHS was released, which outlined the tactics used by the Black Basta ransomware group.[64] The organization confirmed that a ransomware attack resulted in data theft, and public reporting attributes the attack to Black Basta.[65]

5.13.4.1 Lessons Learned

The following are considerations for the healthcare industry.

It is important to have defense-in-depth with multiple layers. On the human side, employee awareness plays a critical role. Staff should learn to recognize warning signs—such as suspicious emails, unexpected attachments, or login prompts—that do not align with normal workflows. But awareness on its own is not sufficient. Organizations also need strong technical controls. This includes phishing-resistant MFA or robust passwordless authentication to prevent credential theft. It also includes endpoint monitoring—systems that continuously observe activity on workstations and servers to detect unusual behavior.

In healthcare, patient care cannot stop when systems go offline. Organizations need downtime procedures that actually work—so staff can continue documenting, communicating, and coordinating care without relying on systems that may not be available. Recovery must also be planned. Systems need to be brought back online in a controlled way, with clear priorities and defined steps to avoid further disruption.

Social engineering is a common entry point, and staff must be trained to recognize phishing attempts and know how to respond—such as not clicking on unfamiliar links, not opening unexpected attachments, and following a basic rule: when in doubt, throw it out.[66] But training alone is not enough. Technical safeguards are just as critical. This includes limiting user access, monitoring for unusual activity, and detecting when trusted tools—such as PowerShell—are being misused, a tactic often referred to as living off the land (LOTL).

At the same time, healthcare organizations must have business continuity and clinical downtime plans that are clear, realistic, and usable. These plans must be developed with input from business leaders and clinical staff to ensure they reflect how work is actually done—not just how it is assumed to work on paper. Plans must support the continuation of clinical care and core business operations when systems are unavailable—whether through manual workflows or other fallback procedures. And they must be kept up to date, tested regularly, and adjusted as systems and processes evolve.

Healthcare organizations need to be ready to implement contingency plans when systems fail—and making sure those plans are tested in advance, not created during a crisis. That requires coordination across people, processes, and technology—all working together to protect systems, applications, networks, devices, configurations, data, and other resources—as well as the delivery, continuity, and coordination of care to patients. Cybersecurity is a lifeline for patient safety—each supports the other. Public-Private Analytic Exchange Program. *A Lifeline: Patient Safety & Cybersecurity*. https://www.govinfo.gov/app/details/GOVPUB-HS-PURL-gpo150339.

5.14 Summary—Major Breaches

Attackers continue to exploit both human behavior and technical vulnerabilities to bypass defenses and gain access to critical systems and sensitive data. The response is not one solution, but a combination: education, sustained vigilance, clear processes, and strong technical controls. This includes but is not limited to phishing-resistant MFA, robust passwordless authentication, and layered defenses built around the principle of *defense-in-depth*. These measures work together to help reduce risk, limit the impact of an intrusion, and support the continuity of patient care and safety.

5.15 Value of Information Sharing

Information sharing helps organizations improve their ability to prevent incidents, detect and identify threats, respond appropriately, recover quickly, and strengthen overall *resilience* Resilience means the ability to withstand and recover from deliberate attacks, accidents, or naturally occurring threats or incidents.[67]

Information sharing also helps to improve situational awareness and can help improve an organization's security posture. Information sharing helps organizations become aware of threats, threat actors,[68] vulnerabilities, and risks they may not have otherwise known about. This includes current threats, vulnerabilities, observed attacker behavior, and mitigation guidance. Organizations can also share best practices for mitigating vulnerabilities, implementing safeguards, and improving overall security posture.

Shared information may include threat indicators, attacker behavior, identified vulnerabilities, and remediation guidance—such as patches, updates, temporary workarounds or fixes, and configuration changes or updates. It may also include mitigation strategies, incident response protocols, and best practices for business continuity and disaster recovery. By receiving timely and relevant information, organizations can take appropriate action to reduce risk, adjust controls, and respond more effectively to incidents.

Public–private partnerships and government agencies both play key roles in cybersecurity information sharing. They support the distribution of vetted threat intelligence, vulnerability information, and mitigation guidance to relevant stakeholders. Public–private partnerships—such as InfraGard and the HHS 405(d) Program in the United States, as well as others such as the European Cybersecurity Organisation (ECSO)—facilitate information sharing with vetted stakeholders.

Government agencies—including national cybersecurity authorities and organizations such as Europol, the Cybersecurity and Infrastructure Security Agency (CISA) of the United States, and the U.S. Federal Bureau of Investigation (FBI)—support information sharing efforts by issuing threat advisories, coordinating incident response, and facilitating cross-border communication. These entities help ensure that organizations receive timely, relevant, and actionable information to support risk management and strengthen security posture. Together, these entities help ensure that stakeholders—including healthcare organizations—receive timely and relevant information. Efforts such as these help improve the security posture of individual organizations by ensuring they have access to accurate, timely, and actionable information to guide security decisions and the implementation of safeguards.

Information sharing between trusted peer organizations—within the healthcare and public health sector, and, as appropriate, across other allied sectors—is essential. The HPH sector depends on multiple critical infrastructure sectors, including communications, information technology, energy, water and wastewater systems, and financial services. Disruptions in any one of these sectors may have cascading effects on healthcare organizations.

Information sharing may also occur directly between trusted peer organizations. Entities within a region or sector may have formal agreements or standing practices to share threat and mitigation information and best practices. The information sharing may occur by way of designated portals, platforms, email lists, meetings, events, and through other means.

5.16 Further Reading

Security teams may use tools such as the Cyber Kill Chain® methodology[69] and the MITRE ATT&CK® knowledge base to understand and analyze how attackers operate. The Cyber Kill Chain® outlines the stages of a cyberattack, while the MITRE ATT&CK® knowledge base catalogs adversary tactics and techniques based on real-world observations.[70]

Additional resources on cybersecurity threats, threat actors, vulnerabilities, mitigation strategies, and best practices are available from entities such as, but not limited to, CISA,[71] the HHS Health Sector Cybersecurity Coordination Center (HHS HC3),[72] the HHS 405(d) Program,[73] the National Institute of Standards and Technology (NIST) National Vulnerability Database,[74] the National Cybersecurity Center of Excellence (NCCoE),[75] the European Union Vulnerability Database,[76] the FBI,[77] Internet Crime Complaint Center (IC3),[78] InfraGard—a public–private partnership between the FBI and members of the critical infrastructure community,[79] and the Computer Emergency Response Team Coordination Center (CERT/CC).[80]

The future of healthcare cybersecurity depends on the collective efforts of leaders, staff, and the broader ecosystem. By learning from past incidents and taking proactive steps, the HPH sector can build a more secure and resilient foundation to protect patients and maintain trust in an increasingly digital world.

Notes

1 HHS OCR. *Resolution Agreement.* https://www.hhs.gov/sites/default/files/ocr/privacy/hipaa/enforcement/examples/resolution_agreement_and_cap.pdf.
2 HHS OCR. *Resolution Agreement.* https://www.hhs.gov/sites/default/files/ocr/privacy/hipaa/enforcement/examples/resolution_agreement_and_cap.pdf.
3 HHS OCR. *Resolution Agreement.* https://www.hhs.gov/sites/default/files/ocr/privacy/hipaa/enforcement/examples/resolution_agreement_and_cap.pdf.

4 HHS OCR. *Resolution Agreement*. https://www.hhs.gov/sites/default/files/ocr/privacy/hipaa/enforcement/examples/resolution_agreement_and_cap.pdf.
5 HHS OCR. *Resolution Agreement*. https://www.hhs.gov/sites/default/files/ocr/privacy/hipaa/enforcement/examples/resolution_agreement_and_cap.pdf.
See also HHS OCR. *HHS settles HIPAA case with BCBST for $1.5 million*. https://www.hhs.gov/hipaa/for-professionals/compliance-enforcement/examples/bcbst/index.html.
6 HHS OCR. *HHS settles HIPAA case with BCBST for $1.5 million*. https://wayback.archive-it.org/3926/20150121155524/http://www.hhs.gov/news/press/2012pres/03/20120313a.html.
7 Nextgov/FCW. *SAIC: Medical Records for 4.9 Million TRICARE Beneficiaries Were Stolen*. https://www.nextgov.com/digital-government/2011/09/saic-medical-records-for-49-million-tricare-beneficiaries-were-stolen/49858/.
8 Nextgov/FCW. SAIC: *Medical Records for 4.9 Million TRICARE Beneficiaries Were Stolen*. https://www.nextgov.com/digital-government/2011/09/saic-medical-records-for-49-million-tricare-beneficiaries-were-stolen/49858/.
9 Gibbs Mura. *Health Net & IBM Privacy Breach Settlement: Insurer settles claims that it violated California's patient privacy law*. https://www.classlawgroup.com/health-net-ibm-privacy-breach.
See also California Department of Managed Health Care. *In re DMHC Enforcement Matter 11-260 SETTLEMENT AGREEMENT The Department of Managed Health Care and Health Net of California, Inc*. https://wpso.dmhc.ca.gov/enfactions/docs/2214/1602277464557.pdf.
10 NYC Health and Hospitals. *HHC Reports Theft of Personal Health Information*. https://nychealthandhospitals-appservice-east-us.azurewebsites.net/pressrelease/hhc-reports-theft-of-personal-health-information/.
11 HHS OCR. *Resolution Agreement*. https://www.hhs.gov/sites/default/files/ocr/privacy/hipaa/enforcement/examples/acmhs/amchs-capsettlement.pdf.
12 Examples of OT devices include medical devices such as those that monitor, control, or support clinical functions.
13 HHS OCR. *Resolution Agreement*. https://www.hhs.gov/sites/default/files/Advocate_racap.pdf.
14 HHS OCR. *Resolution Agreement*. https://www.hhs.gov/sites/default/files/Advocate_racap.pdf.
15 HHS OCR. *Resolution Agreement*. https://www.hhs.gov/sites/default/files/Advocate_racap.pdf.
16 HHS OCR. *Resolution Agreement*. https://www.hhs.gov/sites/default/files/Advocate_racap.pdf.
17 HHS OCR. *Resolution Agreement*. https://www.hhs.gov/sites/default/files/Advocate_racap.pdf.
18 "Advocate shall review, and to the extent necessary, revise its policies and procedures related to the use of hardware and electronic media including, but not limited to, desktop computers, laptop computers, servers, tablets, mobile phone devices, USB drives, external hard drives, DVDs and CDs that may be used to access, store, download, or transmit Advocate ePHI. The policies shall identify criteria for the use of such hardware and electronic media and procedures for obtaining authorization for the use of personal devices and media that utilize Advocate ePHI systems. The policies shall also address security responsibilities, including disposal and reuse of personal devices and media, and regular compliance monitoring."
HHS OCR. *Resolution Agreement*. https://www.hhs.gov/sites/default/files/Advocate_racap.pdf.
19 HHS OCR. *Advocate Health Care Settles Potential HIPAA Penalties for $5.55 Million*. https://www.hhs.gov/hipaa/for-professionals/compliance-enforcement/agreements/ahcn/index.html.
20 TribLive. *Sharpsburg Vendor Confirms Link to Target Data Probe*. https://archive.triblive.com/business/local-stories/sharpsburg-vendor-confirms-link-to-target-data-probe/.
21 BBC. Community Health Systems data hack hits 4.5 million. https://www.bbc.com/news/technology-28838661.
22 Infosecurity Magazine. *Darkside 2.0 Ransomware Promises Fastest Ever Encryption Speeds*. https://www.infosecurity-magazine.com/news/darkside-20-ransomware-fastest/.
23 HHS OCR. *Anthem Pays OCR $16 Million in Record HIPAA Settlement Following Largest U.S. Health Data Breach in History*. https://www.hhs.gov/hipaa/for-professionals/compliance-enforcement/agreements/anthem/index.html.

24 UCLA Health. *UCLA Health Victim of a Criminal Cyber Attack.* https://www.uclahealth.org/news/release/ucla-health-victim-of-a-criminal-cyber-attack-2472.

25 UCLA Health. *UCLA Health Victim of a Criminal Cyber Attack.* https://www.uclahealth.org/news/release/ucla-health-victim-of-a-criminal-cyber-attack-2472.

26 CISA. *Petya Ransomware.* https://www.cisa.gov/news-events/alerts/2017/07/01/petya-ransomware.

27 ISS Source—Industrial Safety and Security Source. *NotPetya Attack Costs Mount.* https://www.isssource.com/notpetya-attack-costs-mount/.

28 DHS. *Healthcare and Public Health Sector-Specific Plan.* https://www.cisa.gov/sites/default/files/publications/nipp-ssp-healthcare-public-health-2015-508.pdf.

29 DHS. *Healthcare and Public Health Sector-Specific Plan.* https://www.cisa.gov/sites/default/files/publications/nipp-ssp-healthcare-public-health-2015-508.pdf.

30 Government of Singapore. *Public Report of the Committee of Inquiry into the Cyber Attack on Singapore Health Services Private Limited's Patient Database on or Around 27 June 2018.* https://file.go.gov.sg/singhealthcoi.pdf.

31 The Newfoundland and Labrador Centre for Health Information (NLCHI) was a provincial organization responsible for managing digital health infrastructure, including the development and operation of the province's electronic health record (EHR) and health data systems. NLCHI also supported cybersecurity initiatives, data analytics, and health system planning.

As of April 1, 2023, NLCHI, along with the province's four former Regional Health Authorities (RHAs), was integrated into a single entity known as NL Health Services. This transition created a unified provincial health authority, with NL Health Services now responsible for delivering health services and overseeing digital health, cybersecurity, and data governance functions across Newfoundland and Labrador. In this structure, NLCHI's responsibilities and expertise continue within the broader organization.

Newfoundland and Labrador Centre for Health Information—Government of Newfoundland and Labrador. *2022–2023 Annual Report.* https://www.gov.nl.ca/hcs/files/NLCHIAnnualReport2022-2023.pdf.

32 Government of Newfoundland and Labrador. *Cyberattack on the Newfoundland and Labrador Health Care System.* https://www.gov.nl.ca/hcs/files/OVERVIEW-NL-Health-Cyber-Incident-March-2023.pdf.

33 U.S. Senate Committee on Finance. *Testimony of Andrew Witty Chief Executive Officer, UnitedHealth Group Before the Senate Finance Committee: "Hacking America's Health Care: Assessing the Change Healthcare Cyber Attack and What's Next."* https://www.finance.senate.gov/imo/media/doc/0501_witty_testimony.pdf.

34 Change Healthcare. *HIPAA Substitute Notice.* https://web.archive.org/web/20250116033916/https://www.changehealthcare.com/hipaa-substitute-notice.html.

See also HHS OCR. *Change Healthcare Cybersecurity Incident Frequently Asked Questions.* https://www.hhs.gov/hipaa/for-professionals/special-topics/change-healthcare-cybersecurity-incident-frequently-asked-questions/index.html.

35 Reuters. *UnitedHealth Hackers Used Stolen Login Credentials to Break In, CEO Says.* https://www.reuters.com/technology/cybersecurity/unitedhealth-hackers-took-advantage-citrix-vulnerabilty-break-ceo-says-2024-04-29/.

36 Change Healthcare. *HIPAA Substitute Notice.* https://web.archive.org/web/20250116033916/https://www.changehealthcare.com/hipaa-substitute-notice.html.

See also HHS OCR. *Change Healthcare Cybersecurity Incident Frequently Asked Questions.* https://www.hhs.gov/hipaa/for-professionals/special-topics/change-healthcare-cybersecurity-incident-frequently-asked-questions/index.html.

37 U.S. House of Representatives, Committee on Energy and Commerce. *What We Learned: Change Healthcare Cyber Attack.* https://energycommerce.house.gov/posts/what-we-learned-change-healthcare-cyber-attack.

See also Comparitech. *After paying a $22M ransom to delete it, data stolen in Change HealthCare breach resurfaces.* https://www.comparitech.com/news/after-paying-a-22m-ransom-to-delete-it-data-stolen-in-change-healthcare-breach-resurfaces/.

38 U.S. Senate, Office of Senator Elizabeth Warren. *Letter to the Cybersecurity and Infrastructure Security Agency Regarding the Change Healthcare Ransomware Attack,* April 29, 2024. https://www.warren.senate.gov/imo/media/doc/warren_cassidy_blumenthal_letter_to_cisa_on_change_healthcare_ransomware_attack.pdf.

> "On February 21, 2024, Russian-linked cybercriminal group., ALPHV Blackcat conducted a ransomware attack on Change, the largest processor of medical claims in the United States. [citation omitted] This attack, in which the cybercriminal group shut down Change platforms until it received a $22 million Bitcoin ransom payment, caused widespread and ongoing disruptions to the nation's healthcare system. [citation omitted] Seven weeks later, on April 8, 2024, a second ransomware group, RansomHub, took control of the stolen data and is demanding additional payment. And RansomHub has begun leaking sensitive patient data to up the ante. [citation omitted] These attacks highlight a dire need for stronger tools to crack down on ransomware attacks."

39 CISA. *Next Level MFA: FIDO Authentication.* https://www.cisa.gov/news-events/news/next-level-mfa-fido-authentication.

40 45 C.F.R. § 164.308 (2025).

41 Ascension. *Network Interruption Update.* https://web.archive.org/web/20250613042314/https://about.ascension.org/news/2024/05/network-interruption-update2. See also CBS News. Ascension cyberattack caused after employee accidentally downloaded malicious file. https://www.cbsnews.com/detroit/news/ascension-cyberattack-employee-malicious-file-downloaded/.

42 National Public Radio (NPR). *Cyberattack Led to Harrowing Lapses at Ascension Hospitals, Clinicians Say.* https://www.npr.org/2024/06/19/nx-s1-5010219/ascension-hospital-ransomware-attack-care-lapses.

43 Associated Press (AP). *A Cyberattack Forces a Big US Health System to Divert Ambulances and Take Records Offline.* https://apnews.com/article/728ab2a0e5afaf7c344e46a5ce5ca42c.

44 Healthcare Dive. *Most Healthcare Organizations Face Significant Financial, Operational Impact from Cyber Threats: Survey.* https://www.healthcaredive.com/news/healthcare-organizations-financial-operational-impact-cyberattack-klas-research-ey/804668/.

45 Forbes. Right-Hand Cybersecurity Focuses On Human Behavior To Mitigate Attacks. https://www.forbes.com/sites/waynerash/2023/05/23/right-hand-cybersecurity-focuses-on-human-behavior-tomitigate-attacks. See also CBS News. Ascension cyberattack caused after employee accidentally downloaded malicious file. https://www.cbsnews.com/detroit/news/ascension-cyberattack-employee-malicious-file-downloaded/.

46 HHS 405(d) Program. *Health Industry Cybersecurity Practices.* https://405d.hhs.gov/cornerstone/hicp.

47 Federal Reserve Bank of New York. *Pirates without Borders: The Propagation of Cyberattacks through Firms' Supply Chains.* https://www.newyorkfed.org/medialibrary/media/research/staff_reports/sr937.pdf.

48 Federal Reserve Bank of New York. *Pirates without Borders: The Propagation of Cyberattacks through Firms' Supply Chains.* https://www.newyorkfed.org/medialibrary/media/research/staff_reports/sr937.pdf (financial analysis of NotPetya and the economic consequences).

49 BankInfoSecurity. *New In-Depth Analysis: Anthem Breach.* https://www.bankinfosecurity.com/new-in-depth-analysis-anthem-breach-a-9627.

50 Reuters. *U.S. Employee Data Breach Tied to Chinese Intelligence: Sources.* https://www.reuters.com/article/us-usa-data-breach-idUSKBN0OZ20Z20150620/.

See also HHS. *Anthem Pays OCR $16 Million in Record HIPAA Settlement Following Largest U.S. Health Data Breach in History.* https://www.hhs.gov/hipaa/for-professionals/compliance-enforcement/agreements/anthem/index.html.

See also California Department of Insurance. *Anthem Data Breach.* https://www.insurance. ca.gov/0400-news/0100-press-releases/anthemcyberattack.cfm. See also United States of America v. Fujie Wang and John Doe No. 1:19-cr-00153-JRS-MJD (N.D. Ind. May 7, 2019) (unsealed indictment May 9, 2019). https://www.justice.gov/d9/press-releases/attachments/2019/05/09/anthem_indictment_0.pdf.

51 DOJ. United States of America v. Fujie Wang and John Doe No. 1:19-cr-00153-JRS-MJD (N.D. Ind. May 7, 2019) (unsealed indictment May 9, 2019). https://www.justice.gov/d9/press-releases/attachments/2019/05/09/anthem_indictment_0.pdf.

52 DOJ. *Member of Sophisticated China-Based Hacking Group Indicted in Series of Computer Intrusions, Including 2015 Data Breach of Health Insurer Anthem Inc. Affecting Over 78 Million People.* https://www.justice.gov/archives/opa/pr/member-sophisticated-china-based-hacking-group-indicted-series-computer-intrusions-including.
53 Federal News Network. *FBI Arrest May Be First Linked to OPM Hack.* https://federalnewsnetwork.com/workforce/2017/08/fbi-arrest-may-be-first-linked-to-opm-hack. See also Reuters. U.S. Employee Data Breach Tied to Chinese Intelligence: Sources. https://www.reuters.com/article/us-usa-data-breach-idUSKBN0OZ20Z20150620/.
54 Foothold generally occurs after initial access by the attacker.
55 Google Cloud. *M-Trends 2024: Our View from the Frontlines* (defining "dwell time"). https://cloud.google.com/blog/topics/threat-intelligence/m-trends-2024.
56 Government of Singapore. *Public Report of the Committee of Inquiry into the Cyber Attack on Singapore Health Services Private Limited's Patient Database on or Around 27 June 2018.* https://file.go.gov.sg/singhealthcoi.pdf.
57 Government of Singapore. *Public Report of the Committee of Inquiry into the Cyber Attack on Singapore Health Services Private Limited's Patient Database on or Around 27 June 2018.* https://file.go.gov.sg/singhealthcoi.pdf.
58 Government of Singapore. *Public Report of the Committee of Inquiry into the Cyber Attack on Singapore Health Services Private Limited's Patient Database on or Around 27 June 2018.* https://file.go.gov.sg/singhealthcoi.pdf.
59 Government of Singapore. *Public Report of the Committee of Inquiry into the Cyber Attack on Singapore Health Services Private Limited's Patient Database on or Around 27 June 2018.* https://file.go.gov.sg/singhealthcoi.pdf.
60 Ascension Health. *Notice of Data Breach Submitted to the Iowa Attorney General,* December 19, 2024. https://www.iowaattorneygeneral.gov/media/cms/12192024_Ascension_Health_4CFC274204C7C.pdf.
61 BankInfoSecurity. *Worker-Downloaded Malware Caused Ascension Ransomware Attack.* https://www.bankinfosecurity.com/worker-downloaded-malware-caused-ascension-ransomware-attack-a-25514.
62 AP. A Cyberattack Forces a Big US Health System to Divert Ambulances and Take Records Offline. https://apnews.com/article/728ab2a0e5afaf7c344e46a5ce5ca42c.
See also Digital Health. *Ascension Says EHR is Down Following Ransomware Attack.* https://www.digitalhealth.net/2024/05/us-firm-ascension-says-ehr-is-down-following-ransomware-attack/.
63 Reuters. *US Hospital Operator Ascension Says 5.6 Million Affected in Medical Data Breach in May.* https://www.reuters.com/technology/cybersecurity/us-hospital-operator-ascension-says-56-million-affected-medical-data-breach-may-2024-12-20/.
See also Ascension Health. *Data Breach Notification—Maine Office of the Attorney General,* December 19, 2024. https://www.maine.gov/cgi-bin/agviewerad/ret?loc=1691.
64 CISA. *#StopRansomware: Black Basta.* https://www.cisa.gov/news-events/cybersecurity-advisories/aa24-131a.
65 HIPAA Journal. *Ascension Ransomware Attack Affects 5.6 Million Patients.* https://www.hipaajournal.com/ascension-cyberattack-2024/.
66 National Cyber Security Alliance. *Protect Data and Devices.* https://www.staysafeonline.org/articles/protect-data-and-devices.
67 NIST. *Resilience.* https://csrc.nist.gov/glossary/term/resilience.
68 Cyber threat actors include individuals or groups that exploit vulnerabilities in systems or misuse trusted access to gain unauthorized access or disrupt operations. These actors may be financially motivated, ideologically driven, or state-sponsored. Tactics may include exploiting technical vulnerabilities, using social engineering, or leveraging insider access. Insider threats involve individuals—such as employees, contractors, or others—with physical or virtual access to an organization's systems, data, infrastructure, or devices. "Insiders" may have physical access to facilities or virtual access to systems, networks, or equipment. Threats may originate from outside or from within the organization. HHS HC3. *Types of Cyber Threat Actors That Threaten Healthcare.* https://www.hhs.gov/sites/default/files/types-threat-actors-threaten-healthcare.pdf.

See also CISA. *Defining Insider Threats.* https://www.cisa.gov/topics/physical-security/insider-threat-mitigation/defining-insider-threats/.

69 Lockheed Martin. *Cyber Kill Chain® framework.* https://www.lockheedmartin.com/en-us/capabilities/cyber/cyber-kill-chain.html.

70 MITRE Corporation. *MITRE ATT&CK® Framework.* https://attack.mitre.org.

71 CISA. *Home Page.* https://www.cisa.gov/.

72 HHS HC3. *A Prescription for Health Sector Cybersecurity.* https://www.hhs.gov/about/agencies/asa/ocio/hc3/index.html.

73 HHS 405(d) Program. *Health Industry Cybersecurity Practices.* https://405d.hhs.gov/cornerstone/hicp.

74 NIST. *National Vulnerability Database (NVD).* https://nvd.nist.gov/.

75 NIST. National Cybersecurity Center of Excellence. *Working Together for Cybersecurity.* https://www.nccoe.nist.gov/.

76 ENISA, *European Union Vulnerability Database (EUVD).* https://euvd.enisa.europa.eu/.

77 FBI. *What We Investigate. The Cyber Threat.* https://www.fbi.gov/investigate/cyber.

78 Internet Crime Complaint Center (IC3). *Welcome to the Internet Crime Complaint Center.* https://www.ic3.gov/.

79 InfraGard. Partnership for Protection. *Welcome to InfraGard.* https://www.infragard.org/.

80 CERT/CC. *Vulnerability Notes Database.* https://www.kb.cert.org/vuls/.

Chapter 6

Governance

6.1 Introduction to Governance

Cybersecurity is a shared responsibility across the organization. Leadership, administrative staff, technical teams, clinical personnel, and others all contribute to managing cybersecurity risk. Governance ensures that these responsibilities are clearly defined, supported, and integrated across the enterprise.

Cybersecurity governance refers to the structures, policies, and processes that guide how an organization manages cybersecurity risk. It establishes accountability, defines responsibilities, and aligns cybersecurity efforts with organizational objectives. It ensures that cybersecurity is addressed as part of enterprise risk management (ERM) and needs appropriate oversight and strategic direction. One of the frameworks used to support cybersecurity governance is the NIST Cybersecurity Framework.

Privacy is foundational to cybersecurity. While cybersecurity focuses on protecting the confidentiality, integrity, and availability of information systems and data, privacy addresses how personal information is collected, used, stored, shared, and accessed (i.e., processed). In healthcare, this includes activities such as capturing patient data during intake, storing it in electronic health records, using it for treatment or billing, and disclosing it to authorized third parties.

Privacy governance ensures that these activities are carried out lawfully, ethically, and in accordance with individual rights. It also ensures compliance with regulatory frameworks such as the HIPAA Privacy Rule. Because privacy risks arise from how information is processed, privacy must be integrated into the broader cybersecurity governance structure. This includes defining policies for appropriate data use, establishing access controls, monitoring disclosures, and ensuring that privacy risks are assessed and managed alongside technical cybersecurity risks.

6.2 HIPAA

The Health Insurance Portability and Accountability Act of 1996 (HIPAA), Public Law 104–191, was enacted to improve the efficiency and effectiveness of the healthcare system. As part of its

DOI: 10.4324/9781003366560-6

Administrative Simplification provisions, HIPAA required the U.S. Department of Health and Human Services (HHS) to adopt national standards for electronic healthcare transactions, unique identifiers, code sets, and security.[1]

Congress recognized that advances in electronic technology could pose risks to the privacy and security of health information. Congress directed HHS to develop and implement regulations to carry out the Administrative Simplification provisions of the HIPAA. These included requirements to establish national standards for the privacy and security of individually identifiable health information. In response, HHS promulgated the HIPAA Privacy Rule, the Security Rule, and the Breach Notification Rule.[2] These rules apply to specific regulated entities and establish national standards for protecting protected health information. The Privacy Rule covers health information in any form, while the Security Rule applies specifically to electronic protected health information (ePHI).[3]

HIPAA applies to covered entities, including health care providers that conduct certain electronic transactions, health plans, and health care clearinghouses. Business associates are also subject to HIPAA requirements when creating, receiving, maintaining, or transmitting protected health information (PHI) on behalf of a covered entity, or on behalf of another business associate.[4] Business associates include vendors such as billing companies, IT service providers, consultants, and others who perform functions or services involving PHI. HIPAA also applies to subcontractors of business associates if they handle PHI in the same manner. In addition, HIPAA recognizes the concept of an organized health care arrangement (OHCA), which allows legally separate covered entities engaged in joint operations to share PHI for certain purposes under a unified compliance structure. Each participant in an OHCA, however, remains independently responsible for complying with HIPAA.

The HIPAA Privacy Rule, originally published in December 2000 and revised in 2002, establishes national standards for the use and disclosure of PHI. It also grants individuals specific rights, including the right to access and amend their medical records. Most covered entities were required to comply with the Privacy Rule by April 14, 2003, while small health plans had until April 14, 2004.

The HIPAA Security Rule, published in February 2003, establishes requirements for safeguarding ePHI. It includes administrative, physical, and technical safeguards that regulated entities must implement to protect the confidentiality, integrity, and availability of ePHI. Compliance with the Security Rule became mandatory as of April 20, 2005, for most covered entities, and April 20, 2006, for small health plans.

In 2009, the Health Information Technology for Economic and Clinical Health (HITECH) Act was enacted as part of the American Recovery and Reinvestment Act. The HITECH Act amended HIPAA by strengthening enforcement provisions, expanding the application of HIPAA requirements to business associates, and requiring the notification of breaches involving unsecured PHI. These statutory changes were implemented and clarified by the HIPAA Omnibus Rule, which was finalized on March 26, 2013, with a compliance deadline of September 23, 2013. The Omnibus Rule confirmed that business associates must comply directly with the Security Rule and certain provisions of the Privacy Rule. It also requires business associates to ensure that subcontractors who handle ePHI agree to comply with applicable HIPAA requirements through written agreements. Covered entities must enter into business associate agreements that contain terms ensuring Security Rule compliance, including terms that require subcontractors to do the same.[5] Business associates must also report security incidents, including breaches, to the covered entity.

In 2021, the HITECH Act was further amended to require HHS to consider whether a covered entity or business associate has implemented recognized security practices (RSPs) when determining the amount of a CMP, the scope and duration of an audit, and any associated remedies under the HIPAA Security Rule. RSPs may include those developed under the NIST CSF, Section 405(d) of the Cybersecurity Act of 2015, or other practices established under applicable law. This amendment does not create a safe harbor or prevent the imposition of penalties for violations. However, if an entity can demonstrate that it has implemented RSPs consistently and across its operations for the 12 months prior to a security incident, that information may be considered as a mitigating factor during enforcement. The absence of RSPs will not be treated as an aggravating factor. This provision applies only to HIPAA Security Rule investigations and does not apply to Privacy Rule violations or other areas of enforcement. Implementation of RSPs remains voluntary.

In April 2024, HHS finalized a rule amending the HIPAA Privacy Rule to prohibit the disclosure of PHI related to lawful reproductive health care in certain circumstances.[6] Additional information is set forth in 45 C.F.R. §§ 164.502(a)(5)(iii) and 164.509.[7]

The HIPAA Privacy Rule,[8] Security Rule,[9] and Breach Notification Rule[10] form the basis for how covered entities and business associates must protect and manage PHI. These rules focus on regulatory objectives and allow flexibility in how those objectives are met. Privacy, security, and other frameworks may support compliance, but they do not replace these regulatory requirements. HHS, through its Office for Civil Rights (HHS OCR), is responsible for the interpretation and enforcement of these rules. HHS OCR conducts investigations, audits, and compliance reviews, and it may impose civil money penalties for violations. In certain cases, HHS OCR may also refer matters for criminal enforcement to the U.S. Department of Justice.[11]

Individuals who believe that a covered entity or business associate has violated the HIPAA Privacy, Security, or Breach Notification Rules may file a complaint with HHS OCR. Complaints must be submitted in writing electronically via the *OCR Complaint Portal*. HHS. *File a Health Information Privacy Complaint*. https://www.hhs.gov/hipaa/filing-a-complaint. HHS OCR is authorized to investigate such complaints and may resolve them through technical assistance, corrective action, or by imposing civil money penalties, as appropriate, under Section 1176 of the Social Security Act (42 U.S.C. § 1320d-5), as amended by the HITECH Act.

Together, the HIPAA Privacy Rule, Security Rule, and Breach Notification Rule establish the core federal regulatory requirements for protecting health information in the United States. These rules apply to covered entities and business associates and define how PHI must be used, disclosed, safeguarded, and—when regulatory requirements so dictate—how breaches of such information must be reported.

6.2.1 Civil Money Penalties and the HIPAA Omnibus Rule

The HIPAA Omnibus Rule, issued in 2013, significantly expanded the enforcement provisions of HIPAA, particularly in connection with civil money penalties (also referred to as civil monetary penalties) (CMPs). It implemented key provisions of the HITECH Act and marked a major shift in how HHS, through the OCR, applies CMPs to violations of the HIPAA Privacy, Security, and Breach Notification Rules.[12]

Prior to the HITECH Act and the Omnibus Rule, HHS OCR had broad discretion to resolve HIPAA violations through informal measures such as technical assistance or voluntary compliance, often without issuing financial penalties. The Omnibus Rule changed that approach by implementing a tiered penalty structure, established by the HITECH Act, based on the level of an organization's culpability. This structure sets minimum and maximum penalties for violations and limits HHS OCR's discretion in many cases.

The CMP structure includes four tiers:

- Tier 1—lack of knowledge: The organization did not know, and by exercising reasonable diligence would not have known, that a violation occurred.
- Tier 2—reasonable cause: The violation occurred due to reasonable cause and not willful neglect.
- Tier 3—willful neglect (corrected): The violation was the result of willful neglect but was corrected within the required time period.
- Tier 4—willful neglect (not corrected): The violation resulted from willful neglect and was not corrected within the permitted timeframe.

Each tier includes a corresponding range of per-violation penalties. Additionally, there are annual maximum caps for each category of violation. While these caps were originally uniform across tiers, HHS later clarified through a Notice of Enforcement Discretion that annual caps would vary by tier. These caps are updated periodically to reflect inflation and current enforcement priorities.

These penalties apply to all covered entities and to business associates as well. The Omnibus Rule also expanded the scope of liability, allowing HHS OCR to hold organizations accountable for the actions of their agents, regardless of whether a formal business associate agreement is in place, based on the level of authority and control involved.

CMPs are not limited to data breaches. They can be imposed for any violation of the HIPAA Rules, including but not limited to impermissible disclosures of PHI, failure to provide timely access to individuals, or insufficient safeguards. Penalties may be assessed, including in the absence of individual harm, such as when noncompliance is systemic or sustained.

This highlights the importance of covered entities and business associates establishing and maintaining robust compliance programs. This includes but is not limited to documented policies, regular workforce training, risk assessments, and timely remediation of identified vulnerabilities.

6.3 HIPAA—Spotlight on Covered Entities, Organized Health Care Arrangements, and Business Associates

The HIPAA Rules apply to covered entities, business associates, and subcontractors of business associates. A covered entity is a health care provider, health plan, or health care clearinghouse that transmits health information electronically in connection with certain standard transactions, such as billing or eligibility checks.[13]

A health care provider includes professionals or organizations such as doctors, dentists, psychologists, pharmacies, nursing homes, clinics, and chiropractors—but only if they transmit any health information electronically in connection with a transaction for which HHS has adopted a standard.[14]

A health plan includes health insurance companies, HMOs, employer-sponsored health coverage, and government health programs like Medicare, Medicaid, and military and veterans' health programs.[15]

A health care clearinghouse is an entity that processes health information received from another entity into a standard format, or vice versa—for example, converting nonstandard billing data from a provider into a standard format used for claims submission.[16]

A business associate is a person or organization that performs certain functions or services on behalf of, or provides services to, a covered entity that involve the creation, receipt, maintenance, or transmission of PHI. Business associates include a wide range of vendors and service providers such as billing companies, IT contractors, consultants, cloud storage providers, and legal or accounting firms that create, receive, transmit, or maintain PHI.[17]

Covered entities must have a written business associate agreement in place that specifies the work to be performed and requires the business associate to comply with the HIPAA Rules. Business associates are also directly liable under HIPAA for violations of the applicable provisions of the Rules. They are required to comply with the HIPAA Rules when performing functions or services that involve the creation, receipt, maintenance, or transmission of PHI.[18]

Subcontractors of business associates are also covered under HIPAA if they create, receive, maintain, or transmit PHI on behalf of the business associate. Each such subcontractor is required to comply with the HIPAA Rules and must have a written agreement in place with the business associate or upstream contractor that engages them.[19]

HIPAA also applies to covered entities that participate in an organized health care arrangement (OHCA). An OHCA is a legally distinct group of covered entities that participate in joint activities such as shared electronic health records or joint billing operations. OHCAs are permitted to share PHI among participants for operational purposes without needing separate authorizations from individuals. However, each participant in an OHCA is still responsible for complying with HIPAA independently, including if they issue a joint Notice of Privacy Practices or coordinate compliance activities.[20]

6.4 HHS OCR Enforcement and HIPAA

HHS OCR's enforcement actions—especially those involving resolution agreements (RAs) and corrective action plans (CAPs)—have provided invaluable guidance to the healthcare and public health sector on HIPAA compliance. The involvement of RAs and CAPs addresses specific HIPAA violations. However, many healthcare stakeholders take note of the lessons learned. Thus, RAs and CAPs provide guidance that healthcare organizations can use to help improve their privacy and security postures.

HHS OCR's enforcement activities have led many healthcare organizations to strengthen their security and compliance programs across a range of operational areas. Common actions taken in response to RAs and CAPs include:

- Conducting accurate, thorough, and enterprise-wide risk analyses
- Developing and maintaining risk management plans based on identified threats and vulnerabilities
- Developing and maintaining a robust vulnerability management program, including timely application of patches
- Enhancing HIPAA privacy and security training, including workforce security awareness
- Implementing and testing contingency plans, including data backup, disaster recovery, and business continuity procedures
- Strengthening technical safeguards such as encryption, access controls, and authentication mechanisms
- Improving identity and access management, including the principle of least privilege and user provisioning practices

- Reviewing and updating business associate agreements to ensure proper safeguards and responsibilities are in place
- Enhancing third-party risk management and cybersecurity supply chain risk management
- Monitoring for and responding to potential insider threats through auditing, logging, and workforce sanctions where appropriate
- Updating and enforcing physical safeguards to protect systems and data at all locations, including off-site and administrative offices
- Establishing procedures for timely breach detection, reporting, and response in accordance with HIPAA requirements
- Implementing proactive access controls and user activity monitoring to detect and prevent electronic health record (EHR) snooping or other unauthorized access to patient records
- Addressing risks associated with shadow IT, including unapproved web tools that handle ePHI without proper oversight[21]

As stated by HHS:

> A resolution agreement is a settlement agreement signed by HHS and a covered entity or business associate in which the covered entity or business associate agrees to perform certain obligations and make reports to HHS, generally for a period of three years. During the period, HHS monitors the covered entity's compliance with its obligations. A resolution agreement may include the payment of a resolution amount. If HHS cannot reach a satisfactory resolution through the covered entity's demonstrated compliance or corrective action through other informal means, including a resolution agreement, civil monetary penalties (CMPs) may be imposed for noncompliance against a covered entity.
>
> HHS. *Resolution Agreements*. https://www.hhs.gov/hipaa/for-professionals/compliance-enforcement/agreements/index.html.

6.5 Common HIPAA Violations

Certain types of HIPAA violations are especially common—and have frequently resulted in enforcement actions and CMPs. These include the unauthorized access (snooping) of patient records; failing to conduct a risk analysis or manage known security risks; not entering into HIPAA business associate agreements; denying or delaying patients' access to their health records; inadequate access controls; failure to encrypt portable devices containing ePHI; improper disposal of PHI; exceeding the 60-day deadline for breach notification under HIPAA; and impermissible disclosures of patient data.[22] These issues highlight recurring compliance failures and highlight the importance of administrative, physical, and technical safeguards and, generally, HIPAA compliance.

6.6 Stark Law Exception and Anti-Kickback Statute Safe Harbor for Cybersecurity Technology and Services Donations (2020)

An organization's policies and procedures help to establish the approach to managing cybersecurity risk. However, many affiliated or independent providers may not necessarily have the resources to implement adequate safeguards for a robust cybersecurity program. Healthcare organizations may need to support others to reduce shared risk. Recent changes to federal law and regulations allow certain cybersecurity donations without violating the Stark Law or Anti-Kickback Statute.

HHS issued revisions to the regulations implementing the Stark Law and the Anti-Kickback Statute to address cybersecurity.

On December 2, 2020, the Centers for Medicare & Medicaid Services published a final rule updating the Stark Law regulations, and the Office of Inspector General published a separate final rule revising the safe harbors under the Anti-Kickback Statute. These regulatory changes include new provisions that permit the donation of cybersecurity technology and services under specific conditions. Both rules became effective on January 19, 2021.[23]

The Centers for Medicare & Medicaid Services issued a final rule on December 2, 2020, titled *Medicare Program; Modernizing and Clarifying the Physician Self-Referral Regulations*. This rule updates the Stark Law to reduce administrative burden and better support value-based care. It includes a new exception that allows healthcare organizations to donate cybersecurity technology and related services to physicians without violating self-referral prohibitions. It also revises the existing exception for EHR donations. These changes clarify how providers can support secure health IT infrastructure while remaining compliant with the Stark Law.

On December 2, 2020, the Office of Inspector General issued a separate final rule titled *Medicare and State Health Care Programs: Fraud and Abuse; Revisions to Safe Harbors Under the Anti-Kickback Statute, and Civil Monetary Penalty Rules Regarding Beneficiary Inducements*.[24] This rule includes two safe harbors related to cybersecurity under the Anti-Kickback Statute. The first is a new safe harbor that protects certain donations of cybersecurity technology and services. The second updates the existing safe harbor for EHRs to allow cybersecurity items and services to be included as part of an EHR donation arrangement.

The revisions are designed to allow healthcare entities to lawfully donate cybersecurity technology and services, recognizing the growing risk posed by cyber threats.

The Stark Law, also known as the Physician Self-Referral Law and codified at 42 U.S.C. § 1395nn, prohibits physicians from referring Medicare patients to an entity with which the physician or an immediate family member has a financial relationship, unless an exception applies. It is a civil statute enforced by the Centers for Medicare & Medicaid Services. The law's purpose is to protect against conflicts of interest and unnecessary care that can drive up costs.

The Anti-Kickback Statute, codified at 42 U.S.C. § 1320a–7b(b), is a criminal statute that prohibits offering, paying, soliciting, or receiving remuneration in exchange for referrals of items or services reimbursable under a federal healthcare program. The Office of Inspector General is responsible for enforcement and issues safe harbors that describe conduct not subject to prosecution.

6.7 2021 HITECH Act Amendment

Under the 2021 amendment to the HITECH Act (Public Law 116–321),[25] HHS is required to consider whether a covered entity or business associate has adequately demonstrated the implementation of RSPs during the prior 12-month period when making certain HIPAA enforcement decisions. Specifically, the Secretary of Health and Human Services must take such practices into account when determining the amount of a CMP, the extent and duration of an audit, or the terms of any RA related to a potential violation of the HIPAA Security Rule.[26]

As specifically set forth in the 2021 amendment to the HITECH Act—

> The term "recognized security practices" means the standards, guidelines, best practices, methodologies, procedures, and processes developed under section 2(c)(15) of the National Institute of Standards and Technology Act, the approaches promulgated under section 405(d) of the Cybersecurity Act of 2015, and other programs and processes that address cybersecurity and that are developed, recognized, or promulgated through regulations under other statutory authorities. Such practices shall be determined by the covered entity or business associate, in accordance with 42 U.S.C. § 17941.[27]

Implementation of *recognized security practices* is entirely voluntary. A covered entity or business associate that chooses not to implement such practices is not subject to increased penalties or additional audit scrutiny. However, HHS OCR may treat the implementation of these practices as a mitigating factor during investigations or audits involving the HIPAA Security Rule. HHS OCR may request documentation from entities demonstrating that recognized practices have been in continuous use for at least 12 months. Where entities rely on "other" security practices, they must provide appropriate legal or regulatory citations showing that such practices were developed, recognized, or promulgated under applicable statutory authority.[28]

As stated by HHS OCR in an educational video on RSPs under the HITECH Act[29]:

> The 2021 amendment to the Health Information Technology for Economic and Clinical Health (HITECH) Act (Public Law 116–321) requires the Secretary of Health and Human Services to consider the implementation of "recognized security practices" by covered entities and business associates when determining enforcement actions under the HIPAA Security Rule. Specifically, the Secretary must consider these practices when assessing the amount of a civil monetary penalty, the length and scope of an audit, or the terms of a resolution agreement.
>
> Covered entities and business associates may submit evidence demonstrating that they have implemented recognized security practices continuously for at least twelve months prior to the start of an OCR audit or investigation. OCR may then consider this implementation as a mitigating factor when deciding the severity of any enforcement action. In addition to HICP and NIST frameworks, organizations may also rely on other cybersecurity practices—provided they can supply statutory or regulatory authority to show that the practices were developed, recognized, or promulgated as required by the law.[30]
>
> The 2021 amendment to the HITECH Act does not relieve covered entities or business associates of their obligations under the HIPAA Security Rule, nor does it prevent OCR from enforcing applicable requirements. Rather, it gives regulated entities the opportunity to reduce exposure to enforcement risks by documenting and sustaining the use of recognized security practices over time.[31]
>
> *The implementation of recognized security practices is not mandatory according to OCR.* The purpose of the amendment is to incentivize the voluntary adoption of robust cybersecurity practices, particularly those that are demonstrable and align with sector-specific threats and risk mitigation strategies.[32]

- Recognized security practice #1: Practices developed by the National Institute of Standards and Technology (NIST) under section 2(c)(15) of the NIST Act.
  - *This includes cybersecurity practices and controls that are implemented in alignment with the NIST Cybersecurity Framework.*

- Recognized Security Practice #2: Approaches promulgated under section 405(d) of the Cybersecurity Act of 2015.
  - The Health Industry Cybersecurity Practices (HICP), developed under section 405(d), specifically are within this definition. HICP is a voluntary set of guidelines intended to strengthen cybersecurity across the healthcare and public health (HPH) sector. The HICP suite includes:
    - A main document that sets forth key cybersecurity threats facing healthcare organizations and ten corresponding mitigation practices.
    - Technical volume 1, which offers tailored guidance for small healthcare organizations.
    - Technical volume 2, which provides more advanced and scalable implementation guidance for medium and large healthcare organizations.
- Recognized Security Practice #3: Other cybersecurity programs and processes that are developed, recognized, or promulgated by statute or regulation.
  - Organizations may also rely on other cybersecurity practices—provided they can supply statutory or regulatory authority to show that the practices were developed, recognized, or promulgated as required by the law.

6.8 Spotlight on Recognized Security Practices (RSPs) under the HITECH Act

Adoption of RSPs is voluntary at the present time. However, for those organizations that choose to adopt them, organizations must also demonstrate that these practices are being implemented consistently over time. The *following* information is based on guidance provided by HHS OCR in a YouTube video published on October 31, 2022.[33]

Documentation plays a central role in establishing compliance. Entities may provide policies and procedures that show how RSPs are adopted and applied, implementation records such as project plans and meeting minutes, and operational evidence, including screenshots, application reports, or vendor contracts. Additional forms of documentation may include training materials and records verifying that RSPs have been continuously in place for the previous 12 months.

Examples of recognized cybersecurity practices include the NIST CSF and the Health Industry Cybersecurity Practices (HICP) developed under the HHS 405(d) program. Other cybersecurity practices may also qualify if they are recognized by statute or regulation. These recognized security practices provide structured, risk-based models designed for healthcare environments. Aligning with them strengthens an organization's security posture and supports its readiness for regulatory review.

Providing evidence of RSP implementation allows an organization to show that it has taken reasonable and appropriate steps to manage cybersecurity risk. In some cases, this may result in reduced penalties or a more favorable enforcement outcome. By contrast, organizations that do not adopt RSPs are not penalized for that decision alone—but they lose the opportunity to cite these practices as a mitigating factor during enforcement proceedings.

Organizations should evaluate current practices against recognized security practices like NIST CSF or HICP, develop a roadmap for implementation, document progress thoroughly, involve key stakeholders from across the organization, and update practices regularly to reflect new threats or regulatory changes.

While adoption of RSPs remains optional at the present time, it offers a meaningful advantage to organizations that take cybersecurity and compliance seriously. It positions them to better defend against threats, protect PHI, and demonstrate accountability under the HIPAA Security Rule.

6.9 HIPAA Privacy Rule

The HIPAA Privacy Rule is set forth in 45 C.F.R. Part 160 and Subparts A and E of Part 164. It sets national standards for how PHI may be used and disclosed, and it applies to covered entities and business associates. Covered entities include health care providers that conduct certain standard transactions electronically, health plans, and health care clearinghouses. Business associates are also subject to the Privacy Rule when handling PHI on behalf of a covered entity or another business associate.

6.9.1 Protected Health Information

Protected health information, or PHI, is defined at 45 C.F.R. § 160.103 (definitions). PHI is individually identifiable health information that relates to an individual's past, present, or future physical or mental health or condition, the provision of health care, or payment for health care, and that either directly identifies the individual or could reasonably be used to identify the individual. The Privacy Rule applies to all forms of PHI—whether electronic, paper, or oral.

PHI can be generally understood as identifying or identifiable information about an individual in the context of their health care. PHI is a subset of individually identifiable health information (IIHI). IIHI is defined at 45 C.F.R. § 160.103 as information, including demographic data, that is created or received by a health care provider, health plan, employer, or health care clearinghouse, and that (1) relates to the past, present, or future physical or mental health or condition of an individual, the provision of health care to an individual, or the past, present, or future payment for the provision of health care to an individual, and (2) identifies the individual or for which there is a reasonable basis to believe the information can be used to identify the individual.

PHI is defined at 45 C.F.R. § 160.103 to mean IIHI that is transmitted by electronic media, maintained in electronic media, or transmitted or maintained in any other form or medium. PHI excludes IIHI in education records covered by the Family Educational Rights and Privacy Act (FERPA) (20 U.S.C. § 1232g); in records described at 20 U.S.C. § 1232g(a)(4)(B)(iv) (treatment records of students at postsecondary institutions that are not considered "education records" under FERPA, but are still governed by FERPA and excluded from HIPAA); in employment records held by a covered entity in its role as employer; and regarding a person who has been deceased for more than 50 years.

PHI may include information that is either identifying of an individual or identifiable about an individual. Thus, the identifiers may be direct or indirect. PHI includes direct identifiers such as names, medical record numbers, and diagnosis codes. It also includes other identifiers that may not directly identify an individual but may render the information identifying or identifiable with respect to an individual, either on their own or in combination with other information.

Examples of such identifiers that may constitute PHI include the following:

- Names
- All geographic subdivisions smaller than a state, including

  - Street address
  - City
  - County
  - Precinct
  - ZIP code and equivalent geocodes
    - Note: The initial three digits of a ZIP code may be retained if, according to current publicly available U.S. Census Bureau data:
      - The geographic unit formed by combining all ZIP codes with the same three initial digits contains more than 20,000 people; and
      - For any geographic unit with 20,000 or fewer people, the ZIP code must be changed to 000
- All elements of dates (except year) directly related to an individual, including
  - Birth date
  - Admission date
  - Discharge date
  - Date of death
  - All ages over 89 and all elements of dates (including year) indicative of such age
    - Note: These may be aggregated into a single category of "age 90 or older"
  - Telephone numbers
  - Fax numbers
  - Email addresses
  - Social Security numbers
  - Medical record numbers
  - Health plan beneficiary numbers
  - Account numbers
  - Certificate or license numbers
  - Vehicle identifiers and serial numbers, including license plate numbers
  - Device identifiers and serial numbers
  - Web Universal Resource Locators (URLs)
  - Internet Protocol (IP) address numbers
  - Biometric identifiers, including
  - Fingerprints
  - Voice prints
  - Full-face photographic images and any comparable images
- Any other unique identifying number, characteristic, or code (unless permitted solely for re-identification purposes under 45 C.F.R. § 164.514(c), and only if specific safeguards are followed, including that the code is not derived from or related to information about the individual and is not used or disclosed for re-identification)

6.9.2 De-Identified Health Information

The HIPAA Privacy Rule permits the use or disclosure of de-identified health information that does not identify an individual and for which there is no reasonable basis to believe that the information can be used to identify the individual (45 C.F.R. § 164.514(a)). One permitted method for de-identification is the Safe Harbor method (45 C.F.R. § 164.514(b)(2)). Under this method, 18 specific identifiers of the individual or of relatives, employers, or household members must be removed. These identifiers include names; geographic subdivisions smaller than a state (with certain exceptions for ZIP codes); all elements of dates (except year) related to birth, admission, discharge, or death; all ages over 89 and all elements of dates (including year) indicative of such age, except that such ages and elements may be aggregated into a single category of age 90 or older; telephone numbers; email addresses; Social Security numbers; medical record numbers; health plan beneficiary numbers; account numbers; certificate or license numbers; vehicle identifiers and serial numbers; device identifiers and serial numbers; URLs; IP addresses; biometric identifiers (such as fingerprints or retinal scans); full-face photographs and comparable images; and any other unique identifying number, characteristic, or code. In addition to removing these elements, the covered entity or business associate must not have actual knowledge that the remaining information could be used alone or in combination with other data to identify the individual.[34]

The second method permitted for de-identification is the Expert Determination method under 45 C.F.R. § 164.514(b)(1), which requires a qualified expert to determine that the risk of re-identification is very small and to document the methods and results of the analysis.[35]

If either the first method (Safe Harbor) or the second method (Expert Determination) of de-identification of health information is satisfied, the information is not considered PHI and is no longer subject to the HIPAA Privacy Rule.[36]

6.9.3 Treatment, Payment, and Health Care Operations

The HIPAA Privacy Rule permits certain uses and disclosures of PHI without the individual's written authorization—such as for treatment, payment, and health care operations (TPO). Other uses and disclosures generally require prior written authorization, unless a specific exception applies under HIPAA or other applicable law or regulation.

Under the HIPAA Privacy Rule, covered entities may use or disclose PHI without the individual's written authorization for purposes of TPO. The following definitions of treatment, payment, and health care operations reflect the essential elements, but these definitions are more fully set forth in the actual regulatory text at 45 C.F.R. § 164.501.

Treatment refers to the provision, coordination, or management of health care and related services by one or more health care providers. This includes coordination or management of care with third parties, consultations between providers about a patient, and referrals of a patient from one provider to another.[37]

Payment refers to activities to obtain reimbursement for services, determine eligibility or coverage, billing, collection, claims adjudication, and related tasks by health care providers or health plans.[38]

Health care operations refer to specific administrative, quality improvement, legal, financial, and business activities undertaken by a covered entity that are necessary to manage and support its core functions. As set forth in 45 C.F.R. § 164.501, these activities include the following:

- Quality assessment and improvement initiatives (excluding research), patient safety activities, population-based efforts to improve health or reduce costs, protocol development, case management, and care coordination;
- Evaluation of provider qualifications and performance, practitioner training, and credentialing functions such as accreditation, certification, and licensing;
- Underwriting and related insurance functions (subject to applicable restrictions);
- Legal, auditing, and compliance-related services, including fraud and abuse detection;

- Business planning and development, such as formulary design and coverage policy development; and
- General administrative tasks, including Privacy Rule compliance, customer service, internal grievance resolution, business transactions (e.g., sale or merger), creation of de-identified data or limited data sets, and fundraising for the benefit of the covered entity.

These activities must relate to the covered entity's health care operations functions and are distinct from treatment and payment, though they support the operation of the healthcare system overall.[39]

6.9.4 Minimum Necessary Standard and TPO

The minimum necessary standard (also referred to as the Minimum Necessary Rule) applies to the use and disclosure of PHI for payment and health care operations, as set forth in 45 C.F.R. § 164.502(b). Covered entities must implement policies and procedures to reasonably limit such disclosures to the least amount of information needed to accomplish the intended purpose. This includes applying role-based access controls so that only workforce members with a legitimate need may access relevant information.

While the minimum necessary standard applies to most uses and disclosures of PHI, there are specific exceptions. For example, it does not apply to: disclosures for treatment; to the individual; when made pursuant to a valid authorization; when required by law; or when made to the Secretary of Health and Human Services. These and other exceptions are more fully set forth in 45 C.F.R. § 164.502(b)(2).

6.9.5 Written HIPAA Authorizations

The HIPAA authorization must meet the requirements set forth in 45 C.F.R. § 164.508(c), including being written in plain language and containing the following core elements:[40]

- A specific and meaningful description of the information to be used or disclosed.
- The name or specific identification of the person(s) or class of persons authorized to make the requested use or disclosure.
- The name or specific identification of the person(s) or class of persons to whom the covered entity may make the requested use or disclosure.
- A description of each purpose of the requested use or disclosure. If the individual initiates the authorization and elects not to specify a purpose, the statement "at the request of the individual" is sufficient.
- An expiration date or expiration event that relates to the individual or the purpose of the disclosure. For research purposes, the authorization may state "end of the research study," "none," or similar language.
- Signature of the individual and date. If signed by a personal representative, the authorization must also include a description of the representative's authority to act on the individual's behalf.

Additional information about HIPAA authorizations is more fully set forth in 45 C.F.R. § 164.508. HHS. *Authorizations.* https://www.hhs.gov/hipaa/for-professionals/faq/authorizations/index.html.

6.9.6 Patient Rights

The HIPAA Privacy Rule grants individuals specific rights, including the right to access and obtain a copy of their health records (45 C.F.R. § 164.524)[41]; request amendments or corrections (45 C.F.R. § 164.526); request an accounting of certain disclosures (45 C.F.R. § 164.528)[42]; and request confidential communications (45 C.F.R. § 164.522(b))—that is, to receive communications of PHI by alternative means or at alternative locations.[43]

Individuals may also request restrictions on certain uses and disclosures of their PHI, as provided under 45 C.F.R. § 164.522(a).[44] A covered entity must agree to a requested restriction on disclosures to a health plan if the disclosure is for payment or health care operations (and not otherwise required by law), and the individual has paid the healthcare provider in full out of pocket for the item or service (45 C.F.R. § 164.522(a)(1)(vi)).[45]

Individuals also have the right to direct a covered entity to transmit a copy of their protected health information directly to another person designated by the individual. The request must be in writing, signed by the individual, and clearly identify the designated person and the location where the protected health information should be sent (45 C.F.R. § 164.524(c)(3)(ii)).[46]

6.9.7 De-Identified Health Information

The Privacy Rule also addresses de-identified health information. Health information is considered de-identified, and therefore not subject to the HIPAA Rules, if it meets the requirements of 45 C.F.R. § 164.514. There are two acceptable methods: (1) the removal of specific identifiers under the Safe Harbor method and the absence of actual knowledge that the remaining information could be used to identify the individual, or (2) a documented determination by a qualified expert that the risk of re-identification is very small. However, if information can be reasonably re-identified, it is not considered de-identified under HIPAA. The process of de-identification must be carried out carefully, and any re-identification must be deliberate, documented, and consistent with applicable standards.

6.9.8 HIPAA Privacy Rule Violations

Failure to comply with the requirements of the HIPAA Privacy Rule may result in enforcement actions by HHS OCR. Under Section 1176 of the Social Security Act, as amended by the HITECH Act, HHS OCR has the authority to impose CMPs for such violations. In some cases, HHS OCR may instead resolve violations through RAs that include a monetary settlement and a CAP, rather than through formal penalties.

6.10 The Impact of the HITECH Act and HIPAA Omnibus Rule on the HIPAA Privacy Rule

6.10.1 Business Associate Accountability

The HITECH Act requires that business associates of covered entities comply with the HIPAA Security Rule and certain Privacy Rule provisions and makes them directly liable for violations. This requirement is found in HITECH Act § 13401. The HIPAA Omnibus Rule implemented this requirement by revising 45 C.F.R. § 164.502(e) to apply specific Privacy Rule obligations—such as impermissible uses and disclosures and compliance with minimum necessary standards—directly to business associates. The rule also amended 45 C.F.R. § 160.103 to expand the definition of "business associate" to include subcontractors, meaning downstream vendors who create, receive, maintain, or transmit PHI on behalf of a business associate are now subject to the same legal obligations.

6.10.2 Individual Right to Electronic Access

The HITECH Act required covered entities to provide individuals with access to PHI in electronic format when the PHI is maintained in an EHR. This requirement is set forth in HITECH Act § 13405(e). The HIPAA Omnibus Rule implemented this requirement and extended it to any protected health information maintained in an electronic designated record set as set forth in 45 C.F.R. §§ 164.524(c)(2)(ii) and 164.524(c)(3)(ii). The rule expanded the right to include any PHI maintained in an electronic designated record set. It also required that electronic copies be provided in the form and format requested by the individual if readily producible or in another agreed-upon readable format if not. Individuals may also request that the covered entity transmit the electronic copy directly to a third party designated by the individual.

6.10.3 Right to Restrict Disclosures to Health Plans

The HITECH Act required that covered entities comply with an individual's request to restrict the disclosure of PHI to a health plan when the PHI relates to a service that the individual paid for entirely out-of-pocket. This requirement is found in HITECH Act § 13405(a). The HIPAA Omnibus Rule implemented this provision in 45 C.F.R. § 164.522(a)(1)(vi). The rule clarified that covered entities must honor the restriction only if the disclosure is for payment or health care operations and only for the specific item or service that was paid for in full. It also clarified that the restriction does not apply if disclosure is required by law.

6.10.4 Prohibition on Sale of PHI

The HITECH Act prohibited the sale of PHI without individual authorization except in limited circumstances. This requirement is found in HITECH Act § 13405(d). The HIPAA Omnibus Rule implemented this prohibition in 45 C.F.R. § 164.508(a)(4). The rule defined "sale" broadly to include disclosures of PHI in exchange for direct or indirect remuneration and clarified the limited exceptions. It also required that an authorization explicitly state that the disclosure involves remuneration.

6.10.5 Limits on Use of PHI for Marketing

The HITECH Act required that covered entities obtain individual authorization before using PHI for marketing communications if the communication involves financial remuneration from a third party. This requirement is found in HITECH Act § 13406(a). The HIPAA Omnibus Rule implemented this requirement in 45 C.F.R. § 164.508(a)(3). The rule defined "marketing" to include communications that promote a product or service and clarified that an authorization is required if a third party provides financial remuneration to the covered entity for making the communication.

6.10.6 Use of PHI for Fundraising

The HITECH Act permitted the use of certain PHI for fundraising purposes and required that individuals be given an opportunity to opt out of future communications. This requirement is found in HITECH Act § 13406(b). The HIPAA Omnibus Rule implemented this requirement in 45 C.F.R. § 164.514(f). The rule required that fundraising communications include a clear and easy method for opting out. It also limited the categories of PHI that may be used for fundraising to specific data elements such as demographic information and dates of health care provided to the individual.

6.10.7 Prohibition on Use of Genetic Information for Underwriting

The Genetic Information Nondiscrimination Act (GINA) prohibited the use of genetic information for underwriting by health plans. The HIPAA Omnibus Rule implemented this prohibition in 45 C.F.R. § 164.502(a)(5)(i). The rule defined genetic information as a type of PHI and prohibited health plans from using or disclosing genetic information for underwriting purposes.

6.10.8 Civil Money Penalties

6.10.8.1 Civil Money Penalties and the HIPAA Omnibus Rule

The HIPAA Omnibus Rule, issued in 2013, significantly expanded the enforcement provisions of HIPAA, particularly in connection with CMPs. It implemented key provisions of the HITECH Act and marked a major shift in how HHS, through HHS OCR, applies penalties to violations of the HIPAA Privacy, Security, and Breach Notification Rules.

Prior to the HITECH Act and the Omnibus Rule, HHS OCR had broad discretion to resolve HIPAA violations through informal measures such as technical assistance or voluntary compliance, often without issuing financial penalties. The Omnibus Rule changed that landscape by establishing a tiered penalty structure based on the level of an organization's culpability. This structure mandates minimum penalties for certain violations and sets maximum caps, thereby removing OCR's discretion in many cases.

The CMP structure includes four tiers:

- Tier 1—lack of knowledge: The covered entity or business associate did not know and, by exercising reasonable diligence, would not have known that a violation occurred.
- Tier 2—reasonable cause: The violation was due to reasonable cause and not willful neglect.
- Tier 3—willful neglect (corrected): The violation was the result of willful neglect, but it was corrected within the required time period.
- Tier 4—willful neglect (not corrected): The violation resulted from willful neglect and was not corrected.

These penalties apply to all types of covered entities and, following the Omnibus Rule, to business associates as well.

The Omnibus Rule also broadened the scope of liability. Business associates are now directly subject to the HIPAA Rules, including potential CMPs for violations. In addition, covered entities and business associates may be held liable for the acts of their agents, regardless of whether a formal business associate agreement is in place, depending on the degree of control the entity exercises over the agent's activities.

CMPs are not limited to breaches involving large-scale breaches. They may be imposed for any violation of the Privacy Rule, such as impermissible uses or disclosures of PHI, failure to provide access to PHI, or noncompliance with authorization or notice requirements. Penalties may be applied, including in the absence of harm to individuals, particularly when the violation reflects systemic issues or a pattern of noncompliance.

The HIPAA Omnibus Rule reinforces the expectation that covered entities and business associates must implement comprehensive, ongoing compliance programs. Documentation, workforce training, security assessments, and prompt response to identified vulnerabilities are critical elements in reducing the risk of enforcement and potential penalties.

6.11 HIPAA Security Rule

The HIPAA Security Rule establishes national standards for safeguarding ePHI. It applies to all HIPAA-covered entities—healthcare providers, health plans, and healthcare clearinghouses—that transmit health information in electronic form, as well as their business associates. The rule took effect on April 20, 2005, for most covered entities.[47]

The purpose of the Security Rule is to ensure the confidentiality, integrity, and availability of ePHI. Confidentiality means that information is not disclosed to unauthorized individuals or processes. Integrity means that information is not altered or destroyed in an unauthorized manner. Availability means that information is accessible and usable when needed by authorized individuals.[48]

The Security Rule complements the HIPAA Privacy Rule and the Breach Notification Rule. While the Privacy Rule governs how PHI may be used and disclosed, and the Breach Notification Rule requires reporting of certain incidents involving unauthorized access or disclosures, the Security Rule focuses on the safeguards that must be in place to protect electronic data from such events.[49]

The Security Rule does not prescribe specific technologies or tools, or means to accomplish the objectives within the regulation. Regulated entities (i.e., covered entities and business associate) must assess their own size, complexity, capabilities, infrastructure, and the risks to ePHI. Based on those factors, they are expected to implement safeguards that are reasonable and appropriate. The Security Rule is designed to be scalable and technology-neutral to accommodate different types and sizes of organizations.[50]

6.11.1 Security Standards: General Rules (45 C.F.R. § 164.306)

Covered entities and business associates are required to implement security measures that protect ePHI. Specifically, they must:

- Ensure the confidentiality, integrity, and availability of all ePHI they create, receive, maintain, or transmit.
- Protect against any reasonably anticipated threats or hazards to the security or integrity of that information.
- Protect against any reasonably anticipated uses or disclosures of that information not permitted or required under the HIPAA Privacy Rule (subpart E).
- Ensure that the workforce complies with these requirements.

6.11.1.1 Flexibility of Approach *(45 C.F.R. § 164.306)*

Covered entities and business associates are not limited to a specific set of technologies or methods. They may implement any security measures that allow them to reasonably and appropriately meet the requirements of the Security Rule.

In determining which security measures to implement, the following factors must be considered:

- The size, complexity, and capabilities of the organization
- The technical infrastructure, hardware, and software security capabilities
- The cost of the proposed security measures
- The probability and potential impact of risks to ePHI

6.11.2 Standards and Implementation Specifications

Covered entities and business associates must comply with the applicable standards outlined in 45 C.F.R. § 164.306 (security standards: general rules) and in 45 C.F.R. § 164.308 (administrative safeguards), 45 C.F.R. § 164.310 (physical safeguards), 45 C.F.R. § 164.312 (technical safeguards), 45 C.F.R. § 164.314 (organizational requirements), and 45 C.F.R. § 164.316 (policies and procedures and documentation requirements).

Implementation specifications are classified as either required or addressable. If the specification is required, it must be implemented.

If the implementation specification is addressable, the organization must:

- Assess whether the specification is reasonable and appropriate for its environment, based on its contribution to protecting ePHI.
  - If the answer is yes, the implementation specification must be implemented.
  - If not, the organization must:
    - Document why implementation is not reasonable and appropriate; and
    - Implement an equivalent alternative measure if it is reasonable and appropriate to do so.

6.11.2.1 Maintenance *(45 C.F.R. § 164.306(e))*

Security measures must be reviewed and modified as necessary to ensure continued reasonable and appropriate protection of ePHI, as required by 45 C.F.R. § 164.306(e). Documentation must be updated to reflect those changes, as required by 45 C.F.R. § 164.316(b)(2)(iii).

Note: This refers to the security measures that were implemented to comply with the required or addressable implementation specifications under the HIPAA Security Rule.

The HIPAA Security Rule at 45 C.F.R. § 164.304 states: "Security or Security measures encompass all of the administrative, physical, and technical safeguards in an information system."

6.11.3 Safeguards under the HIPAA Security Rule—How They Are Structured

Safeguards are divided into three categories: administrative, physical, and technical. Within each category, there are required standards and implementation specifications. The standards define the security objectives that must be met to protect ePHI. All standards are required and must be implemented by covered entities and business associates. Each standard may include one or more implementation specifications, which provide detailed instructions for how to meet the standard.[51]

6.11.4 Implementation Specifications

Implementation specifications are classified as either "required" or "addressable." Required specifications must be implemented as stated. Addressable specifications must also be considered, but regulated entities have discretion in how to comply. Addressable does not mean optional. If an addressable specification is not implemented, the organization must document the decision, justify it based on risk, and implement an alternative that meets the intent of the standard, provided that such an alternative is reasonable and appropriate in the context of the organization's circumstances.[52]

This structure allows the HIPAA Security Rule to establish baseline requirements through its required standards and implementation specifications, while providing reasonable flexibility through its addressable implementation specifications. This enables regulated entities to meet security objectives in a manner that is appropriate for their size, environment, resources, and workflow.

6.11.5 Administrative Safeguards

As set forth in the HIPAA Security Rule at 45 C.F.R. § 164.308,[53] administrative safeguards mean administrative actions, policies, and procedures to manage the selection, development, implementation, and maintenance of security measures to protect ePHI and to manage the conduct of the covered entity's or business associate's workforce in relation to the protection of that information.

Administrative safeguards include the designation of a security official, workforce security measures, information access controls, security awareness training, and incident response procedures. A risk analysis is a foundational requirement. Organizations must assess the risks and vulnerabilities to ePHI and implement risk management strategies to reduce those risks. Risk analysis is not a one-time task; it must be reviewed and updated regularly to reflect operational changes and new threats.[54] An example of an administrative safeguard is the security management process standard at 45 C.F.R. § 164.308(a)(1). The implementation specifications are risk analysis, risk management, sanction policy, and information system activity review—all of which are required as set forth in 45 C.F.R. § 164.308.[55]

Another example of an administrative safeguard is the contingency plan as set forth in 45 C.F.R. § 164.308(a)(7). This includes the required implementation specifications of data backup plan, disaster recovery plan, emergency-mode operation plan, testing and revision procedures, and applications and data criticality analysis. Testing and revision procedures (45 C.F.R. § 164.308(a)(7)(ii)(D)) and applications and data criticality analysis (45 C.F.R. § 164.308(a)(7)(ii)(E)) are addressable implementation specifications of the contingency plan standard. However, the data backup plan, disaster recovery plan, and emergency mode operation plan are all required implementation specifications as set forth in the HIPAA Security Rule under 45 C.F.R. § 164.308(a)(7).[56] Additional administrative safeguards as currently set forth in the regulation are summarized (Table 6.1) (45 C.F.R. § 164.308).

6.11.6 Technical Safeguards

As set forth in the HIPAA Security Rule at 45 C.F.R. § 164.312, technical safeguards mean the technology and the policy and procedures for its use that protect ePHI and control access to it. Technical safeguards apply to all forms of electronic media that create, receive, maintain, or transmit ePHI, including systems, devices, applications, and networks.

Technical safeguards include access controls, audit controls, integrity controls, authentication mechanisms, and transmission security. An example of a technical safeguard is the access

Table 6.1 Administrative Safeguards (HIPAA Security Rule)—45 C.F.R. § 164.308

Standard	*Implementation Specification*	*Required or Addressable*
Security Management Process (§ 164.308(a)(1))	Risk Analysis	Required
	Risk Management	Required
	Sanction Policy	Required
	Information System Activity Review	Required
Assigned Security Responsibility (§ 164.308(a)(2))	Security Official Designation	Required
Workforce Security (§ 164.308(a)(3))	Authorization and/or Supervision	Addressable
	Workforce Clearance Procedure	Addressable
	Termination Procedures	Addressable
Information Access Management (§ 164.308(a)(4))	Isolating Health Care Clearinghouse Functions	Required
	Access Authorization	Addressable
	Access Establishment and Modification	Addressable
Security Awareness and Training (§ 164.308(a)(5))	Security Reminders	Addressable
	Protection from Malicious Software	Addressable
	Log-In Monitoring	Addressable
	Password Management	Addressable
Security Incident Procedures (§ 164.308(a)(6))	Response and Reporting	Required
Contingency Plan (§ 164.308(a)(7))	Data Backup Plan	Required
	Disaster Recovery Plan	Required
	Emergency Mode Operation Plan	Required
	Testing and Revision Procedures	Addressable
	Applications and Data Criticality Analysis	Addressable
Evaluation (§ 164.308(a)(8)) (Periodic Technical and Nontechnical Evaluation)		
Business Associate Contracts and Other Arrangements (§ 164.308(b))	Written Contract or Other Arrangement	Required

control standard at 45 C.F.R. § 164.312(a)(1). The implementation specifications are unique user identification, emergency access procedure, automatic logoff, and encryption and decryption. Of these, unique user identification and emergency access procedures are required. Automatic logoff, encryption, and decryption are addressable implementation specifications.

Another example of a technical safeguard is the audit controls standard at 45 C.F.R. § 164.312(b). This requires the implementation of hardware, software, and procedural mechanisms that record and examine activity in systems that contain or use ePHI.

The integrity standard is found at 45 C.F.R. § 164.312(c)(1). Covered entities and business associates must implement policies and procedures to protect ePHI from improper alteration or destruction. An example implementation is the use of digital signatures or hashing mechanisms to verify that information has not been modified in an unauthorized manner, both of which are addressable. The Security Rule includes an addressable implementation specification requiring a mechanism to authenticate electronic protected health information, as set forth in 45 C.F.R. § 164.312(c)(2), to corroborate that ePHI has not been altered or destroyed in an unauthorized manner.

Transmission security is another technical safeguard as set forth in 45 C.F.R. § 164.312(e)(1). The implementation specifications are integrity controls and encryption.

Encryption is yet another technical safeguard as set forth in 45 C.F.R. § 164.312(e)(2). Although it is an addressable safeguard, addressable does not mean optional. If encryption is reasonable and appropriate, the entity must implement it. If it is not, the entity must document why it is not reasonable and appropriate and, when suitable, implement an equivalent alternative measure that achieves the same purpose.

Authentication is addressed under 45 C.F.R. § 164.312(d). This standard requires procedures to verify that a person or entity seeking access to ePHI is the one claimed. Multi-factor authentication and secure logon procedures are examples. Additional technical safeguards as currently set forth in the regulation are summarized (Table 6.2) (45 C.F.R. § 164.312).

Table 6.2 Technical Safeguards (HIPAA Security Rule)—45 C.F.R. § 164.312

Standard	*Implementation Specification*	*Required or Addressable*
Access Control (§ 164.312(a)(1))	Unique User Identification	Required
	Emergency Access Procedure	Required
	Automatic Logoff	Addressable
	Encryption and Decryption	Addressable
Audit Controls (§ 164.312(b))	Mechanisms to Record and Examine Activity	Required
Integrity (§ 164.312(c)(1))	Mechanism to Authenticate ePHI	Addressable
Person or Entity Authentication (§ 164.312(d))	Verification of Identity	Required
Transmission Security (§ 164.312(e)(1))	Integrity Controls	Addressable
	Encryption	Addressable

6.11.7 Physical Safeguards

As set forth in the HIPAA Security Rule at 45 C.F.R. § 164.310, physical safeguards mean physical measures, policies, and procedures to protect electronic information systems and related buildings and equipment from natural and environmental hazards, and unauthorized intrusion.

Physical safeguards include facility access controls, workstation use, workstation security, and device and media controls. An example of a physical safeguard is the facility access controls standard at 45 C.F.R. § 164.310(a)(1). The implementation specifications are contingency operations, facility security plan, access control and validation procedures, and maintenance records. All of these are addressable implementation specifications.

The contingency operations implementation specification requires procedures that allow facility access in support of data restoration under a disaster recovery plan or emergency-mode operations plan. The facility security plan requires policies to protect the facility and its equipment from unauthorized access, tampering, or theft. Access control and validation procedures focus on controlling and validating physical access to facilities based on role or function, including visitor control. Maintenance records require documentation of facility-related security repairs and modifications.

Another physical safeguard is workstation use (45 C.F.R. § 164.310(b)). Covered entities and business associates must implement policies and procedures specifying the functions to be performed, how those functions are to be performed, and the physical environment in which workstations that access ePHI are used.

Workstation security is yet another physical safeguard (45 C.F.R. § 164.310(c)). It mandates the use of physical safeguards to restrict workstation access to authorized users only. Examples include physical locks, screen barriers, or locating workstations in secure areas.

Device and media controls are also physical safeguards (45 C.F.R. § 164.310(d)(1)). The implementation specifications are disposal and media re-use (both required), and accountability and data backup and storage (both addressable). Disposal procedures must ensure that hardware or media containing ePHI is rendered unusable or inaccessible. Media re-use procedures must ensure that no ePHI remains before reuse. Accountability measures include maintaining records of device movement and responsible personnel. Data backup and storage procedures ensure that a retrievable, exact copy of ePHI is created prior to equipment relocation. Additional physical safeguards are summarized (Table 6.3) (45 C.F.R. § 164.310).

Table 6.3 Physical Safeguards (HIPAA Security Rule)—45 C.F.R. § 164.310

Standard	*Implementation Specification*	*Required or Addressable*
Facility Access Controls (§ 164.310(a)(1))	Contingency Operations	Addressable
	Facility Security Plan	Addressable
	Access Control and Validation Procedures	Addressable
	Maintenance Records	Addressable
Workstation Use (§ 164.310(b))		Required

Table 6.3 (Continued) Physical Safeguards (HIPAA Security Rule)—45 C.F.R. § 164.310

Standard	*Implementation Specification*	*Required or Addressable*
Workstation Security (§ 164.310(c))		Required
Device and Media Controls (§ 164.310(d)(1))	Disposal	Required
	Media Re-Use	Required
	Accountability	Addressable
	Data Backup and Storage	Addressable

6.11.8 Summary—Administrative, Physical, and Technical Safeguards

Administrative, technical, and physical safeguards should be aligned to support the organization's people, processes, and technology to help reduce cybersecurity risk.

When an implementation specification is labeled addressable, it does not mean optional. Instead, the covered entity or business associate must assess whether the safeguard is reasonable and appropriate in its particular environment, based on the risk to ePHI.

Standards and implementation specifications include—

§ 164.308 (administrative safeguards)
§ 164.310 (physical safeguards)
§ 164.312 (technical safeguards)
§ 164.314 (organizational requirements); and
§ 164.316 (policies and procedures and documentation requirements).

6.11.9 Organizational Requirements (45 C.F.R. § 164.314)

Covered entities and business associates must enter into business associate contracts (also referred to as business associate agreements)[57] or other arrangements that ensure the protection of ePHI. These agreements must require business associates to comply with applicable security requirements, ensure their subcontractors are also bound by these obligations, and report any known security incidents, including breaches, to the covered entity.

In the case of group health plans, the plan documents of the group health plan must be amended to incorporate provisions to require the plan sponsor to:

- Implement administrative, physical, and technical safeguards that reasonably and appropriately protect the confidentiality, integrity, and availability of the ePHI that it creates, receives, maintains, or transmits on behalf of the group health plan.
- Ensure that the adequate separation required by 45 C.F.R. § 164.504(f)(2)(iii) is supported by reasonable and appropriate security measures.[58]
- Ensure that any agent to whom it provides this information agrees to implement reasonable and appropriate security measures to protect the information; and
- Report to the group health plan any security incident of which it becomes aware.

6.11.10 Policies and Procedures and Documentation Requirements (45 C.F.R. § 164.316)

Covered entities and business associates must implement reasonable and appropriate policies and procedures to comply with the Security Rule. These policies and procedures must be maintained in written form (electronic or paper), and any required actions, activities, or assessments must be documented. All documentation must be retained for at least six years from the date it was created or last was in effect, whichever is later. It must be made available to those responsible for implementing the relevant procedures and updated as needed in response to changes in the environment or operations that affect the security of ePHI.[59]

6.11.11 Business Associates Directly Liable for HIPAA—HITECH Act

Business associates must comply with the Security Rule directly, as required by HITECH Act amendments implemented through the HIPAA Omnibus Rule. Business associates are also required to ensure that any subcontractors that create, receive, maintain, or transmit ePHI on their behalf agree to comply with the Security Rule by entering into a written agreement. Covered entities are required to enter into written business associate agreements that include terms ensuring compliance with the Security Rule. These agreements must also require that any subcontractors who handle ePHI do the same. Business associates must report security incidents, including breaches, to the covered entity.[60]

6.12 HIPAA Omnibus Rule and Its Impact on the HIPAA Security Rule

The HIPAA Omnibus Rule, which became effective on March 26, 2013, implemented and clarified several provisions of the HITECH Act. It included a compliance deadline of September 23, 2013. The rule imposed direct compliance obligations on business associates and their subcontractors, including requirements to implement administrative, physical, and technical safeguards.

6.12.1 Spotlight on Recognized Security Practices: NIST CSF and the HIPAA Security Rule

In 2021, the HITECH Act was amended to include a new provision concerning RSPs.[61] Under this amendment, HHS is required to consider whether a regulated entity has adopted and been using RSPs continuously for the 12 months prior to a security incident. This applies during investigations or enforcement actions related to the HIPAA Security Rule.

RSPs may include those developed under the NIST CSF, those created through the HHS 405(d) program[62] under the Cybersecurity Act of 2015,[63] or other practices that are established under applicable law or regulation.[64]

To benefit from this provision, an organization must demonstrate that RSPs have been fully implemented and actively used throughout the enterprise. Providing documentation that merely describes plans for future implementation is not sufficient. Evidence must show that the practices have been in place and used consistently for at least the preceding 12 months.[65]

The implementation of RSPs under the 2021 amendment to the HITECH Act is voluntary at the present time. The amendment does not create a safe harbor and does not prevent the government from imposing CMPs if violations of the HIPAA Security Rule are found. However, if a covered entity or business associate can demonstrate that RSPs have been in place for at least the past 12 months, the government may take that into account when determining the amount of any penalty, the scope and duration of an audit, and any associated remedies.

The HIPAA Security Rule establishes the baseline safeguards for protecting ePHI. It requires covered entities and business associates to implement administrative, physical, and technical safeguards that are reasonable and appropriate based on their size, complexity, and risk environment. These requirements are legally binding and focus on protecting the confidentiality, integrity, and availability of ePHI.

The NIST CSF, including its core functions—Govern, Identify, Protect, Detect, Respond, and Recover—offers a useful structure for organizing and implementing the requirements of the Security Rule.

The functions of the NIST CSF can be used as a practical lens for understanding how the HIPAA Security Rule supports and strengthens an organization's cybersecurity program. However, the HIPAA Security Rule's provisions align with, and can be mapped to, the key operational outcomes described in the NIST CSF.

6.13 HIPAA Breach Notification Rule

The HIPAA Breach Notification Rule, at 45 C.F.R. §§ 164.400–414, requires covered entities and business associates to provide notification when a breach of unsecured PHI occurs.[66] Other breach notification requirements apply to vendors of personal health records and their third-party service providers under Section 13407 of the HITECH Act—the Health Breach Notification Rule—which is enforced by the Federal Trade Commission.[67]

A breach is generally defined as an impermissible use or disclosure of PHI under the Privacy Rule that compromises the privacy or security of the information. An impermissible use or disclosure is presumed to be a breach unless the covered entity or business associate demonstrates, through a documented risk assessment, that there is a low probability the PHI has been compromised as set forth in 45 C.F.R. § 164.402.

The risk assessment must consider at least four of the following factors:

- The nature and extent of the PHI involved (including the likelihood of re-identification)
- Who received or accessed the information
- Whether the PHI was actually acquired or viewed, and
- The extent to which the risk has been mitigated.

Covered entities and business associates may also choose to notify affected individuals without conducting a risk assessment.[68]

There are three exceptions to what qualifies as a breach. The first is when a workforce member or individual acting under the authority of a covered entity or business associate unintentionally accesses, acquires, or uses PHI in good faith and within the scope of their role. The second is when PHI is inadvertently disclosed by someone authorized to access it to another person who is also authorized to access it within the same organization or arrangement. In both of these cases, the PHI must not be further used or disclosed in a way that violates the Privacy Rule. The third exception applies when the covered entity or business associate has a good faith belief that the unauthorized recipient of the information would not be able to retain it.[69]

The HIPAA Breach Notification Rule applies only to breaches involving unsecured PHI. PHI is considered "unsecured" if it has not been rendered unusable, unreadable, or indecipherable to unauthorized individuals using the technologies and methodologies specified in HHS guidance pursuant to HITECH Act § 13402(h). If PHI is properly secured according to that guidance, the breach notification requirements do not apply.[70] HHS. *Guidance to Render Unsecured Protected Health Information Unusable, Unreadable, or Indecipherable to Unauthorized Individuals.* https://www.hhs.gov/hipaa/for-professionals/breach-notification/guidance/index.html.

See also 74 Fed. Reg. 19006 (Apr. 27, 2009). Guidance Specifying the Technologies and Methodologies That Render Protected Health Information Unusable, Unreadable, or Indecipherable to Unauthorized Individuals. https://www.hhs.gov/hipaa/for-professionals/breach-notification/guidance/index.html.

When a breach of unsecured PHI occurs, covered entities must notify affected individuals, the Secretary of HHS, and in some cases, the media. Business associates must notify the covered entity if the breach occurs at or by the business associate.

Notice to individuals must be provided without unreasonable delay and no later than 60 days after discovery of the breach. Notice must be in writing by first-class mail or by email if the individual has agreed to electronic communications. If contact information is unavailable for 10 or more individuals, substitute notice must be provided through a website posting or media announcement. If fewer than 10 individuals are affected and cannot be contacted, alternative methods such as telephone or other forms of notice may be used. The notification must include a brief description of the breach, what types of information were involved, steps individuals should take, what the entity is doing to investigate and mitigate the breach, and contact information.[71]

If a breach affects more than 500 residents of a state or jurisdiction, the covered entity must also notify prominent media outlets serving the affected area. This media notice must be provided without unreasonable delay and in no case later than 60 calendar days after the discovery of the breach. The media notice must include the same information required in the individual notifications.[72]

Covered entities are also required to notify the Secretary of Health and Human Services of all breaches involving unsecured PHI. For breaches involving 500 or more individuals, the covered entity must notify the Secretary without unreasonable delay and in no case later than 60 calendar days after discovery of the breach. For breaches involving fewer than 500 individuals, the covered entity may report them to the Secretary on an annual basis. These reports must be submitted no later than 60 days after the end of the calendar year in which the breaches were discovered. Notification to the Secretary must be made using the electronic breach reporting form available on the HHS OCR website. Business associates must notify the covered entity of any breach of unsecured PHI that occurs at or by the business associate, without unreasonable delay and no later than 60 days after discovery. To the extent possible, the business associate should provide the covered entity with the identity of each affected individual and any other information needed for the individual notifications.[73]

Covered entities and business associates are responsible for demonstrating that all required notifications were made or that a breach did not occur. This includes maintaining documentation of notifications or conducting a risk assessment showing a low probability of compromise. It also includes applying any exceptions to the definition of breach.[74]

Covered entities are also required to have written policies and procedures in place for breach notification, to train workforce members on those procedures, and to impose appropriate sanctions when policies are not followed.[75]

6.14 Spotlight on Encryption and the HIPAA Breach Notification Rule

Under the HIPAA Breach Notification Rule (45 C.F.R. §§ 164.400–414), a breach is presumed to have occurred unless the covered entity or business associate "demonstrates that there is a low probability that the PHI has been compromised based on a risk assessment." This requirement is set forth in 45 C.F.R. § 164.402.

The required *risk assessment* must consider at least the following four factors:

- The nature and extent of the PHI involved, including the types of identifiers and the likelihood of re-identification
- The unauthorized person who used the PHI or to whom the disclosure was made
- Whether the PHI was actually acquired or viewed
- The extent to which the risk to the PHI has been mitigated

Encryption may be a key mitigating factor in such assessments. However, it must be implemented using strong, modern algorithms and sound cryptographic practices. Weak encryption—such as outdated or easily broken ciphers—may not meaningfully reduce risk. For example, the Caesar cipher applies a fixed letter shift and is trivially reversible. A ROT+3 *Caesar cipher*[76] converts "John Doe" into "Mrkq Grh."[77] Such encryption offers no meaningful protection and would not generally support a determination that the probability of compromise is low.

The effectiveness of encryption depends on multiple factors, including the robustness of the cryptographic algorithm, the entropy—or unpredictability—of the encryption key, and how the decryption key is managed.[78] If the decryption key is stored on the same device as the encrypted data, or is otherwise accessible due to poor key management practices, the data remain exposed. In such cases, the probability of compromise may remain high, and breach notification *may* still be required.

Practical tip: The determination of whether a breach notification is required under HIPAA—or under any other federal, state, or international law or regulation such as the EU General Data Protection Regulation (GDPR),[79] or in accordance with contractual requirements—should involve consultation with in-house legal counsel and, where appropriate, retained outside counsel with relevant qualifications and expertise.

6.15 Summary—HIPAA, HIPAA Privacy Rule, HIPAA Security Rule, and HIPAA Breach Notification Rule

The HIPAA Privacy Rule, Security Rule, and Breach Notification Rules set forth the regulatory requirements for protecting PHI. The Privacy Rule governs how PHI is permitted to be or is required to be used or disclosed. It applies to all forms of PHI, whether paper, electronic, or oral. The Security Rule applies specifically to ePHI and requires administrative, physical, and technical safeguards. The Breach Notification Rule requires notification to individuals, the Secretary, and in some cases, the media when unsecured PHI is compromised. These rules work together to establish what covered entities and business associates must do to safeguard health information and respond to incidents.

The rules set the objectives but do not prescribe the specific manner or means by which those objectives must be met. However, security frameworks help address how the objectives of the Security Rule can be met; they also provide additional objectives and guidance to support a more robust and risk-based approach to safeguarding information.

Other breach reporting obligations may also apply, including those under foreign laws such as the EU General Data Protection Regulation (GDPR), sector-specific data protection mandates, or contractual requirements that impose stricter or earlier notification timelines than those required by law. Accordingly, when a breach occurs, it is possible that multiple state, federal, international, and contractual breach notification requirements may apply. Certain state laws may also impose additional privacy and security obligations.[80]

6.16 NIST Privacy Framework

The NIST Privacy Framework is a voluntary framework designed to help organizations manage privacy risk through structured governance, operational controls, and risk-based decision-making. It is intended to complement legal and regulatory requirements. Like the NIST CSF, it provides a flexible structure that organizations can adapt based on their size, complexity, risk tolerance, and data environment.[81]

The NIST Privacy Framework explains that privacy risk arises from how data is processed. Processing refers to how the data is collected, used, shared, stored, and retained over time. Privacy risks also can arise from a loss of confidentiality, integrity, or availability during processing, such as data theft by external attackers or the unauthorized access or use of data by employees, which reflects insider-threat concerns. To manage these risks, organizations should implement administrative, technical, and physical controls that address privacy requirements and reduce the likelihood and impact of adverse outcomes.

The NIST Privacy Framework also helps organizations examine whether their data practices could lead to problems for individuals, such as loss of autonomy, discrimination, or lack of transparency. These concerns are especially relevant in contexts such as AI, where data-driven decisions may be opaque or affect individual rights.[82]

The NIST Privacy Framework is organized into three components: the Core, Profiles, and Implementation Tiers.[83]

The Core of the NIST Privacy Framework defines a set of privacy-related outcomes and activities that support risk management. It is organized around five functions[84]:

- Identify-P involves understanding how data is processed and mapping the privacy risks that result.
- Govern-P focuses on establishing policies, roles, training, and oversight to manage those risks.
- Control-P includes technical and procedural controls such as access restrictions, data minimization, consent mechanisms, and purpose specification.

- Communicate-P emphasizes transparency with individuals and external stakeholders, including notices, disclosures, and responses to inquiries.
- Protect-P addresses privacy safeguards that overlap with traditional cybersecurity controls, such as encryption and user authentication.[85]

Each Core function is divided into categories and subcategories that provide more specific outcomes an organization may implement or assess against.[86]

Profiles allow organizations to describe their current privacy posture and to define a target state. A current profile reflects outcomes that are being achieved today, while a target profile reflects desired outcomes. Comparing the two helps organizations identify gaps and establish priorities.[87]

The Implementation Tiers describe how integrated and repeatable an organization's privacy risk management practices are. Tiers range from Tier 1 (Partial) to Tier 4 (Adaptive) and reflect how well privacy risk management is embedded in enterprise processes, culture, and decision-making—not just whether specific controls are in place.[88]

The NIST Privacy Framework is designed to work in conjunction with the NIST CSF. Organizations often address privacy and cybersecurity together. Cybersecurity focuses on protecting data from unauthorized access or loss, while privacy focuses on how data is handled, including when systems function correctly. The two frameworks share a common structure and language, which allows organizations to align governance activities, internal controls, and risk assessments across both domains.[89]

Although voluntary, the Privacy Framework provides valuable guidance for healthcare organizations seeking to strengthen privacy governance, particularly in areas not fully addressed by HIPAA. It is increasingly relevant in environments where AI and large-scale data analytics are used, helping organizations assess how automated systems may affect individuals and whether additional privacy safeguards or accountability mechanisms are needed.[90] Crosswalks that map the provisions of laws, regulations, standards, and frameworks to the NIST Privacy Framework are available on the NIST Privacy Framework *Crosswalks* web page. NIST. *Crosswalks.* https://www.nist.gov/privacy-framework/resource-repository/browse/crosswalks.

6.17 NIST Cybersecurity Framework

The NIST CSF 2.0 provides guidance to all organizations—regardless of sector, size, or type—on how to manage and communicate cybersecurity risk. The Framework is flexible and scalable, making it suitable for a wide range of operational environments. It is also widely used to communicate cybersecurity risk across organizational levels, including executive leadership and boards of directors, to support informed decision-making and shared accountability.

For U.S. federal agencies, certain NIST guidelines and standards as required by the Office of Management and Budget (OMB) are mandatory under the *Federal Information Security Modernization Act (FISMA).*[91] They also may be contractually required for certain government contractors and subcontractors. In the private sector, NIST guidance is voluntary, but it is widely adopted as a recognized source of best practice—especially in regulated industries such as healthcare, financial services, and other critical infrastructure sectors. (The healthcare and public health sector is 1 of the 16 recognized critical infrastructure sectors according to the U.S. Department of Homeland Security.)

While NIST CSF Versions 1.0 and 1.1 were directed to critical infrastructure stakeholders, NIST CSF 2.0 is intended for use by any organization, regardless of size, industry, or whether it is part of a *critical infrastructure sector.*[92]

By way of history, the NIST CSF 1.0 was officially released on February 12, 2014,[93] following a public stakeholder input process involving multiple workshops. NIST engaged industry, academia, and government representatives in shaping the Framework's content and priorities.[94] Version 1.1 was released on April 16, 2018, incorporating updates based on stakeholder feedback and evolving security practices.[95]

Most recently, on February 26, 2024, NIST released CSF 2.0. This version introduced the addition of a sixth core function: Govern. The Framework's six core functions—Govern, Identify, Protect, Detect, Respond, and Recover—represent the key areas of cybersecurity risk management. The Govern Function provides the structural foundation. It defines the organization's cybersecurity risk management strategy, establishes oversight mechanisms, clarifies roles and responsibilities, and informs policy development. The Govern Function serves as the structural hub that supports and enables the other five functions (Figure 6.1).

The Framework has *Tiers* to characterize the rigor of an organization's cybersecurity risk governance and management practices. The four Tiers—*Tier 1 (Partial), Tier 2 (Risk Informed), Tier 3 (Repeatable), and Tier 4 (Adaptive)*—describe a progression from informal, ad hoc practices to approaches that are agile, risk-informed, and continuously improving. The Tiers provide context for how an organization views cybersecurity risk and the processes it uses to manage that risk. Organizations may use Tiers to inform their Current and Target Profiles and to set the tone for how cybersecurity risk is addressed across the enterprise. Progression to higher Tiers may be appropriate when risks are greater, when external mandates require stronger risk management practices, or when a cost–benefit analysis supports more rigorous approaches. The Tiers are intended to complement, not replace, an organization's existing cybersecurity risk management methodology.

In addition to Tiers, organizations may use Organizational Profiles to describe their cybersecurity posture in terms of the CSF Core outcomes. A Current Profile specifies which outcomes the organization is presently achieving or working to achieve. A Target Profile identifies the prioritized outcomes the organization aims to achieve in the future based on its mission, risk environment, requirements, and stakeholder expectations.

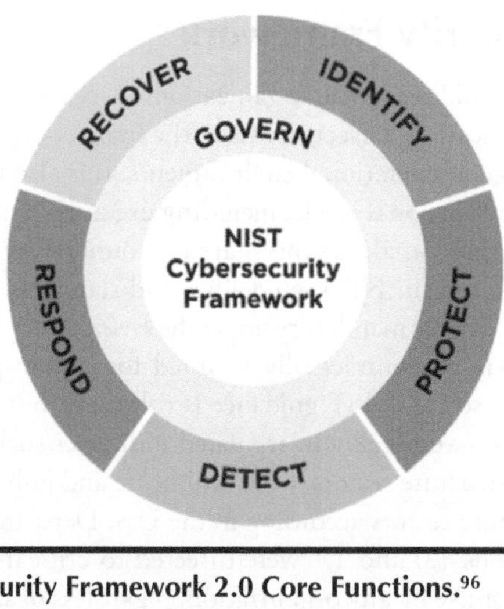

Figure 6.1 NIST Cybersecurity Framework 2.0 Core Functions.[96]

Organizational Profiles help organizations assess their current state, define future goals, and create an action plan to close gaps. Profiles can be scoped broadly (e.g., enterprise-wide) or narrowly (e.g., systems handling sensitive data or responding to a specific threat type). The process includes defining scope, gathering relevant inputs, documenting the Profile, analyzing differences between Current and Target states, and implementing an action plan to address those gaps.

Profiles can also support communication with external stakeholders. A Current Profile can describe existing capabilities, while a Target Profile can be used to express cybersecurity expectations to partners or third parties. Community Profiles—developed for sectors, technologies, or use cases—can also serve as starting points for an organization's own Target Profile.

Many healthcare organizations use the NIST CSF as a framework for managing cybersecurity risk. Its flexibility supports alignment with the HIPAA Security Rule. Under the HITECH Act, as amended in 2021, the NIST CSF is recognized as one of the "recognized security practices" that may be considered during enforcement or investigations.

Security decisions must be grounded in a comprehensive risk assessment. Administrative, physical, and technical safeguards must be selected and implemented based on the organization's specific risk profile and in accordance with applicable legal, regulatory, and contractual requirements. Governance provides the structure needed to ensure that these safeguards are implemented consistently, evaluated regularly, and adjusted as conditions change. NIST CSF 2.0 offers a structured, widely adopted foundation for establishing, implementing, and improving cybersecurity governance.

The NIST CSF 2.0 is designed to integrate with and complement other NIST guidance, providing a flexible foundation for managing cybersecurity risk. It supports alignment with NIST's broad range of resources, including guidance on engineering trustworthy systems[97] and developing cyber-resilient systems.[98] Organizations can also refer to NIST Special Publication 800–53 Revision 5, which offers a comprehensive catalog of security and privacy controls to support risk assessment and safeguard selection. In addition, the NIST Privacy Framework may be relevant, as cybersecurity incidents frequently involve privacy-related considerations. Together, these resources enable a coordinated, risk-based approach to security and resilience. Please also see the NIST CSF 2.0 Informative References resource and implementation examples. NIST. *CSF 2.0 Informative References.* https://www.nist.gov/cyberframework/informative-references.

6.18 Spotlight on Core Functions of the NIST Cybersecurity Framework

6.18.1 Core Function: Govern

The Govern Function defines the structure, strategy, policies, and responsibilities required to manage cybersecurity risk across the organization. Governance sets the direction for how cybersecurity decisions are made, who is responsible for implementing them, how accountability is maintained, and how progress is monitored. The cybersecurity program must operate as an integrated, enterprise-wide effort that aligns with the organization's mission, obligations, and risk environment.[99]

C-SCRM is one of the core governance activities within the Govern Function, highlighting the need to identify, assess, and manage risks associated with third-party suppliers, vendors, and service providers that could impact the organization's cybersecurity posture.[100]

Governance provides the structure to coordinate security actions, assign responsibility, and support consistent implementation. It enables accountability and sets the foundation for continuous improvement across all areas of cybersecurity risk management.[101]

6.18.1.1 Govern—Organizational Context

Governance begins with a clear understanding of the organization's context. This includes its mission, size, purpose, leadership structure, and vision. It also includes internal factors such as staffing levels, technical capabilities, and available budget. The organization must also understand its obligations under relevant laws, regulations, industry standards, and contracts. Dependencies—such as vendors, cloud providers, and third-party services—must also be identified.

Understanding this context allows the organization to identify which assets, systems, and functions are critical to its mission and operations, what risks are relevant, and how to prioritize security activities accordingly. This understanding provides the basis for setting realistic expectations, developing appropriate policies, and selecting safeguards that align with the organization's size, staffing, budget, and operational constraints.

6.18.1.2 Govern—Risk Management Strategy[102]

Governance includes establishing a cybersecurity risk management strategy that aligns with the organization's broader ERM program.[103] This strategy defines how cybersecurity risk is addressed and integrated into the overall management of organizational risk, including financial, operational, legal, reputational, and supply chain risks.

Key considerations include:

- *Defined objectives.* Risk management objectives must reflect mission priorities and stakeholder expectations. These objectives guide decision-making and tradeoffs and should be developed collaboratively and reviewed periodically.
- *Risk appetite and tolerance.* The organization must define what levels and types of risk are acceptable and translate these into specific, measurable risk tolerance statements.
- *Risk treatment.* The organization must determine how different types of risk will be accepted, mitigated, avoided, or transferred.
- *Third-party risk management and supply chain risks.* Supply chain risks must be identified, assessed, prioritized, and incorporated into ERM. Contracts should contain cybersecurity requirements, and third-party risk must be evaluated and monitored through structured processes. This should be done in coordination with the legal department, vendor management office, and others, as appropriate.
- *Change management.* Risk management practices must remain current and aligned with the organization's environment. They should be updated through a defined change management process based on risk assessments, incident reviews, audits, regulatory updates, and organizational changes such as mergers or restructuring.
- *Overall cross-functional coordination.* Effective risk management requires coordination across legal, compliance, finance, operations, IT, security teams, and the vendor management office.

When governance is effective, cybersecurity serves as a business enabler. It supports informed decision-making, aligns with enterprise priorities, and allows the organization to manage risk in a structured and coordinated way. Governance is not static. It is a continuous function that must adapt as the organization, fiscal priorities, and operating environment evolve.

Governance adapts as lessons learned from privacy and security incidents emerge and as the organization undergoes structural changes such as restructuring, mergers, acquisitions, or divestitures. Effective governance also requires attention to resource allocation; workforce capabilities; legal, regulatory, and contractual obligations; and emerging risks that may influence strategic and tactical decisions.

6.18.1.3 Govern—Roles, Responsibilities, and Reporting Structure

In the cybersecurity context, governance defines how cybersecurity responsibilities are structured, assigned, and coordinated across the organization.
Key considerations include:

- *Accountability.* Organizations should define who is accountable for cybersecurity risk, who makes decisions about risk posture, and how risk management responsibilities are documented, communicated, and enforced.
- *Responsibilities.* Responsibilities must be matched with the authority to carry them out and supported by adequate resources, skills, and organizational structures.
- *Accountability mechanisms.* Performance expectations, escalation paths, and review procedures should be clearly defined and consistently applied.

The roles, responsibilities, and reporting structure enables the organization to assign risk ownership, track risk response actions, and evaluate workforce readiness in a manner aligned with defined responsibilities and the organization's risk management strategy.

6.18.1.4 Govern—Policy and Enforcement

Governance defines how the organization creates, communicates, and enforces cybersecurity policies.

Key considerations include:

- *Establishing policies.* Policies are established on the basis of organizational context, cybersecurity strategy, and priorities, and they must be clearly communicated and consistently enforced through processes that verify compliance and address instances of noncompliance.
- *Policy scope.* Policies must reflect the organization's mission, risk appetite, legal and regulatory obligations, and resource constraints.
- *Documentation of policies.* Policies must be formally documented, approved by senior leadership, communicated clearly to personnel (e.g., announcements, training, and the like), and implemented through supporting standards, procedures, and guidelines.
- *Acknowledgment of policies.* The workforce should read and acknowledge policies, follow procedures, and receive training on how to comply with them.
- *Review of policies. Policies must be regularly reviewed to ensure that they address business needs and requirements as well as meet federal, legal, regulatory, and contractual requirements.*
- *Change management.* Changes in mission, technology, business structure, personnel, or infrastructure may require timely policy updates through a defined change management process.
- *Policy enforcement.* Noncompliance must be addressed using corrective or disciplinary mechanisms that are applied consistently across the organization.

6.18.1.5 Govern—Oversight and Performance Evaluation

Governance includes formal oversight of cybersecurity strategy and operations. Oversight mechanisms are used to monitor whether objectives are being met, whether controls are working as intended, and whether policies and procedures are being followed. These mechanisms must be clearly defined and supported by documented roles, processes, and reporting requirements.

Performance of the cybersecurity program must be evaluated using key indicators, including both outcome-oriented metrics (such as security events prevented or mitigated) and process-oriented metrics (such as training completion rates, incident response times, and control effectiveness). Metrics are quantitative measures used to evaluate whether objectives are being met. Without such measurement, it is not possible to determine whether the program is performing effectively or improving over time. Metrics also support transparency and accountability. They are essential for communicating the status and effectiveness of the cybersecurity program to senior leadership, boards of directors, and other stakeholders who require clear, data-driven reporting to inform oversight and decision-making. Evaluation of the program's performance is based on multiple inputs, including audit findings, incident reports, operational data, and stakeholder feedback. This enables leadership to assess the overall effectiveness of the cybersecurity program and to make targeted adjustments when deficiencies or performance issues are identified.

Oversight includes both internal review and communication with executive leadership. Governance ensures that cybersecurity performance is monitored through structured processes and reported to senior management at defined intervals. Cybersecurity risk information must be aligned with enterprise risk reporting and integrated into ongoing performance and risk discussions.

Cybersecurity risk management must be incorporated into enterprise risk governance at the board level. The board must be positioned to understand how cybersecurity risk affects mission, strategy, and operations, and to evaluate whether governance processes support effective risk oversight and accountability.

6.18.1.6 Summary—Core Function: Govern

Governance defines how cybersecurity risk is directed and managed across the organization. It establishes the strategy, roles, policies, oversight mechanisms, and third-party management practices needed to maintain a consistent, integrated, and accountable cybersecurity program. Governance applies across the organization. It covers employees, executives, contractors, service providers, and others who interact with organizational systems, data, or processes. It ensures that roles are clearly defined and that expectations are aligned with the organization's mission, business objectives, and risk posture.

Governance is also about people. It defines how individuals and teams share information, coordinate actions, and carry out responsibilities. It ensures clarity around who does what, how decisions are made, and how information flows across functional and organizational lines.

Applicable legal, regulatory, and contractual obligations must be met, while aligning cybersecurity risk management with the organization's strategic objectives and operational priorities. It provides the structure necessary to assign accountability, make risk-informed decisions, monitor performance, and drive continuous improvement.

Internal oversight and communication with executive leadership and the board are necessary for effective governance. Governance must also evolve based on changing risk conditions, environmental context, lessons learned, and stakeholder expectations.

The Govern Function sets organizational expectations, defines roles and responsibilities, and aligns cybersecurity activities with enterprise risk objectives. It provides the foundation upon which the Identify Function determines what is most critical, the Protect and Detect Functions build their safeguards and monitoring, and the Respond and Recover Functions execute coordinated actions during and after an incident. Together, these relationships enable a consistent, measurable, and sustainable cybersecurity program.

6.18.2 Core Function: Identify

The Identify Function establishes the foundation for managing cybersecurity risk. Its purpose is to develop a comprehensive understanding of the environment, including what the organization must protect and what risks it faces.

Key considerations include:

- *Inventory.* An inventory of what systems, applications, networks, devices, configurations, data, personnel, and assets exist in the environment; how these support business functions and critical services; and what exposures or dependencies may introduce risk.
- *Cross-disciplinary work.* Establish a cross-disciplinary team of cybersecurity, privacy, governance, compliance, IT, operations, legal, human resources, finance, and other stakeholders. Each group helps to identify the assets, including knowing which assets are most important, which handle sensitive data, and which could cause serious problems if they stopped working, were lost, failed, or compromised. Understand the impact regarding consequences of what could happen to the assets.
- *Life cycle management.* Cybersecurity, privacy, and governance teams must coordinate to track assets from acquisition through deployment, use, maintenance, and decommissioning.[104]
- *Federal requirements.* For U.S. federal agencies, certain NIST guidelines and standards as required by the Office of Management and Budget (OMB) are mandatory under the Federal Information Security Modernization Act (FISMA). They also may be mandatory for federal contractors and other entities when required by their contracts, grant requirements, or federal acquisition regulations.[105]
- *Integration with other core functions.* Governance and cybersecurity supply chain risk management (C-SCRM) considerations must also be included to understand organizational risk.[106]

6.18.2.1 Identify—Risk Assessment

The organization must *identify, assess, and document* cybersecurity risks that affect its assets, operations, and people. Risk assessments must include the identification of vulnerabilities, the evaluation of potential threat events, validation of known weaknesses, and review of the technical, physical, and administrative safeguards in place.

Insider threats and external threats must be accounted for. Insider threats may include employee misuse, process failures, or unauthorized workarounds that bypass established controls.

External threats may include ransomware actors, phishing campaigns, denial-of-service attacks, or third-party compromise. Threat intelligence sources and information sharing partnerships must be used to monitor emerging attack techniques and indicators of compromise.

Each risk scenario must include an evaluation of likelihood and potential impact. These assessments must be documented, typically in a formal risk register or equivalent system. Business leaders and security professionals must work together to ensure risks are characterized in terms relevant to mission, operations, compliance, and strategic objectives. Cascading risks—such as those affecting multiple interconnected systems or business processes—must also be identified.

Risk assessments help organizations understand how threats and vulnerabilities may affect mission, operations, assets, and people. Traditionally, organizations have used qualitative ratings (such as high, medium, or low) to describe likelihood and impact. Increasingly, however, organizations are adopting quantitative methods that estimate factors such as financial loss, downtime, or probability to support clearer comparisons and more informed decision-making. Hybrid approaches that combine qualitative judgment with quantitative modeling are also becoming more common.[107]

Some organizations use the FAIR (Factor Analysis of Information Risk) model to perform quantitative risk assessments. FAIR provides a structured way to estimate how often a cybersecurity event might happen and what the financial impact could be. The approach relies on measurable data and estimates to calculate risk in quantitative terms. This helps organizations compare risks, support cybersecurity decisions, and communicate risk in a way that aligns with business needs.[108]

6.18.2.2 Identify—Business Context and Criticality

Understanding business context is essential to identifying what must be protected and why. This includes determining which business functions are critical to mission success, which systems and data flows support those functions, and how disruption could affect operations. These insights come from working closely with operational and functional leaders to identify time-sensitive services, systems with low tolerance for downtime, and the potential impacts of compromise—including safety concerns, legal exposure, or loss of trust.

Asset classification and data sensitivity levels must reflect this business context. In this context, an "asset" includes information, systems, applications, devices, networks, and other resources that create, store, transmit, or process data. It is essential to maintain an accurate understanding of what assets exist, where they reside, and how they are accessed and used. This includes understanding how information flows across systems and who has access to it.

Asset classification schemes should be clearly defined, documented, and applied consistently across the organization to support effective cybersecurity risk management.[109] After assets are classified, those with higher sensitivity or operational criticality may require stronger or more specialized safeguards, such as enhanced monitoring, tighter access controls, segmentation, or additional resilience measures.

Criticality assessments help determine which assets are most essential to the continuity of operations and patient safety, guiding prioritization in protection, detection, response, and recovery planning.

6.18.2.3 Identify—Change Management and Risk-Based Planning

The Identify Function includes the ability to monitor, adjust, and improve cybersecurity efforts over time. As the organization changes, cybersecurity risk must be re-evaluated. Risk assessments, audit results, threat intelligence, and security reviews help identify outdated assumptions, gaps, or other areas where adjustments are needed.

Changes to systems, applications, networks, devices, configurations, data, or other resources must be reviewed for cybersecurity implications. Maintaining accurate asset inventories, asset and data classifications, and data flows ensures that the organization can evaluate how a change affects existing risks, whether new risks are introduced, and whether updates to the risk register are required.

Change management processes must include steps to evaluate how proposed changes could introduce risk, identify when exceptions may be necessary, and define how those exceptions will be documented and monitored.[110] Deferred actions or temporary workarounds must be documented, justified, and reviewed regularly. Exceptions should be granted sparingly and approved through a defined governance process.

The Identify Function also enables prioritization of cybersecurity efforts. By combining information about assets, threats, vulnerabilities, and business impact, organizations can make informed, risk-based decisions.[111]

6.18.3 Core Function: Protect

The Protect Function focuses on implementing safeguards in place so the organization can operate securely. Its purpose is to reduce cybersecurity risk by managing access; securing systems, applications, networks, devices, configurations, data, and other resources; protecting confidential, protected, proprietary, or sensitive information; and ensuring people understand their responsibilities.

Defense-in-depth relies on multiple layers of safeguards that work together to prevent, detect, and mitigate threats.

Key safeguards include:

- Access control. Access must be limited to authorized individuals or systems and based on clearly defined conditions. Identity should be verified using multi-factor authentication (MFA) or passwordless FIDO2 phishing-resistant authentication methods, which may rely on biometrics, PINs, or physical security keys.
- Network protection. Both on-premises and cloud environments require strong defenses. Network segmentation helps control communication pathways and restricts the spread of risk. Protections must also extend to remote users and hybrid work environments.
- Application and device security. Websites, web applications, mobile applications, medical devices, and Internet of Things (IoT) systems must be protected with secure design practices, vulnerability testing, and appropriate technical controls such as web application firewalls (WAFs).
- Legacy system management. Legacy systems may require compensating controls—including isolation, restricted access, or enhanced monitoring—to reduce risk. Organizations should plan to modernize outdated systems and reduce technical debt.[113]
- Secure configuration and maintenance. Systems, applications, networks, and devices must be securely configured, maintained, and updated. Physical access to sensitive systems and areas must be monitored and controlled.
- Data protection. Data must be protected throughout its life cycle—at rest, in transit, and when archived.
- Cybersecurity supply chain risk management (C-SCRM) must be integrated into both cybersecurity and enterprise risk management programs to address third party risks.[114]

The Protect Function relies on insights from the Identify Function to determine what must be secured. It aligns with the strategy and policies from the Govern Function and supports the visibility and awareness needed for the Detect Function. Together, these functions create a cohesive approach to safeguarding the organization's assets and operations.

6.18.4 Core Function: Detect

The Detect Function helps the organization recognize when a cybersecurity event is happening or may have already occurred. It ensures that the organization can observe its environment, notice signs of unusual or risky activity. Early detection helps reduce harm; supports timely response; and protects systems, applications, networks, devices, configurations, data, and other resources.

Effective detection begins with establishing awareness of normal activity and behaviors. This requires observing systems, applications, networks, devices, and users to identify activity or behavior that does not match expected patterns and knowing what the normal baseline looks like. This includes login patterns, typical system or device activity, expected network activity, user activity, and data and network flows.

Baselines help define what is typical in terms of system, device, network, application, and data usage, login patterns, the movement of data, network connections, and processes. These baselines can be defined only when the organization has sufficient visibility into how its systems, applications, networks, devices, configurations, data, and other resources operate. Activity or behavior that deviates from these baselines may indicate unusual or risky activity and must be detected and analyzed.

Threat intelligence is another key component of detection. Threat intelligence includes vetted information used to support decision-making and defensive actions. It may come from internal monitoring, industry reports, trusted vendors, government agencies, or vetted information sharing groups that focus on cybersecurity.

Detection must also account for activity in the physical environment. Repeated failed badge attempts, unusual after-hours access, or attempts to enter restricted locations—such as server rooms or data centers—may produce physical anomalies that warrant investigation. Physical indicators should be integrated into the organization's overall monitoring program.

Continuous monitoring is necessary to observe both physical and cyber environments for changes and patterns in real time or near real time. Monitoring helps detect activity that may signal threats such as malware, insider misuse, compromised accounts, or attempted exploitation. It includes both external and internal activity.

Once baselines and deviations from what is normal are understood, alerts can be generated when activity falls outside these expectations.

Alerts are notifications that something unusual or suspicious may be occurring. These alerts are generated by monitoring and detection tools such as the following:

- Security Information and Event Management (SIEM) systems that collect and analyze logs from many sources;
- Security Orchestration, Automation, and Response (SOAR) platforms that automate security operations workflows, integrate data and alerts from multiple security technologies, and coordinate response actions to improve the speed and consistency of incident handling
- Endpoint Detection and Response (EDR) platforms that monitor individual systems for suspicious changes, behavioral indicators, or activities
- Network Detection and Response (NDR) platforms that analyze network traffic for anomalies or indicators of compromise

- Intrusion Detection and Prevention Systems (IDPS) that inspect network traffic for known threats or unusual patterns
- Extended Detection and Response (XDR) platforms that integrate data from endpoints, networks, identities, cloud platforms, and email to improve correlation and detection accuracy
- Cloud monitoring tools that provide visibility into activity across cloud-based systems
- User and Entity Behavior Analytics (UEBA) tools that can detect insider threats, compromised accounts, and abnormal user or system behavior or activity
- Deception technologies such as honeypots or decoy assets that alert when accessed improperly

These monitoring and detection tools help detect threats such as phishing-related account compromise, ransomware activity, unauthorized access, unusual privilege escalation, or insider misuse.

Once an alert is triggered, it must be reviewed to determine whether it qualifies as a cybersecurity incident. Each organization is responsible for defining what constitutes a cybersecurity incident based on its environment, risk posture, legal, regulatory, and contractual requirements, and mission.

It is important for organizations to define which cybersecurity incidents are significant versus non-significant incidents. These definitions may be documented in incident response plans, security policies, or operational playbooks. Clear definitions support consistency in how events are evaluated, triaged, and escalated.

Significant security incidents may include events that disrupt critical services or impact critical assets; involve confidential, protected, proprietary, or sensitive information; require notification under legal, regulatory, or contractual reporting obligations; or have the potential for widespread operational, reputational, financial, or safety impact or otherwise carry significant legal implications.

Considerations for determining whether a cybersecurity incident is significant include:

- The type and importance of the systems or data affected
- The scope and scale of the event (e.g., how many users, systems, devices, departments, or business units are impacted)
- The duration and nature of the disruption
- Potential legal, regulatory, contractual, financial, safety, or other consequences
- Any external reporting or notification requirements

Some incidents—particularly significant ones—are difficult to detect. Nation-state actors may use long-term, stealthy techniques designed to blend in with routine operations. Adversaries often rely on "living off the land" (LOTL) methods, using built-in administrative tools and legitimate processes to evade detection.[112] These threats may generate little to no alerting and are difficult to identify without a strong understanding of normal behavior across systems, networks, applications, devices, and data—as well as how employees, contractors, vendors, business associates, and others typically interact with them.

The Detect Function provides visibility needed to recognize threats early, determine what may be at risk, and take appropriate action to protect assets, operations, finances, and people.

6.18.5 Core Function: Respond

The Respond Function focuses on taking action when a potential, suspected, or confirmed cybersecurity incident is detected. It includes confirming what is occurring, coordinating the response, containing the threat, and restoring affected systems and services. The goal is to manage the incident in a way that minimizes harm and supports recovery.

Effectively responding to an incident requires preparation, coordination, and timely decisions based on both technical and operational considerations. Coordination with legal, compliance, communications, executive leadership, operational teams, and the board of directors may be necessary depending on the scope and impact of the incident. Maintaining situational awareness of external threat activity improves an organization's ability to prepare for and respond to cyber risks. Trusted information sharing groups across the HPH sector and other critical infrastructure sectors provide updates on current threats, relevant indicators, and effective response techniques. These exchanges contribute to awareness, preparedness, and continuous improvement across the cybersecurity community.[115]

Potential, suspected, or confirmed incidents should be reported promptly to the appropriate points of contact, supported by a culture that encourages reporting and minimizes delays in initiating incident response activities. Incidents may be identified through workforce reporting, technical detection mechanisms, or both. Organizations must be prepared to respond, regardless of how an incident is discovered.

During the incident response process, several actions are taken to manage and address the incident. *Triage* refers to the initial evaluation and classification of the event to determine its severity, scope, and priority for response. *Containment* focuses on limiting the spread or impact of the incident—for example, by isolating a system, disabling an account, or removing unauthorized access. *Eradication* refers to removing the root cause of the incident, such as deleting malware, closing open ports, or correcting misconfigurations. Remediation involves restoring affected systems and services to normal operation, addressing underlying weaknesses, and putting safeguards in place to reduce the chance of recurrence.

Many incident response activities and decisions depend on human analysis, professional judgment, and context. However, AI and automation are increasingly used to assist with detection and response. In the future, some aspects of incident response may be handled by AI-enabled systems with less direct human involvement. This may improve speed and consistency, particularly for well-defined or recurring issues.

Some systems include automated vulnerability detection and remediation—often described as *self-healing capabilities*. These systems can identify certain types of flaws, apply patches, or restore configurations automatically. These responses still require oversight and must operate within defined parameters, but they can strengthen response by reducing time to containment and minimizing disruption. Organizations must determine where automation is appropriate and ensure that human judgment is applied where necessary.

The Respond Function builds on the visibility provided by the Detect Function, enabling organizations to take swift and coordinated action when an event occurs. It relies on the strategy, roles, and decision-making structures established through the Govern Function. It also relies on the asset understanding and risk prioritization developed in the Identify Function. Effective incident response also depends on the protections implemented under the Protect Function, which help contain incidents and limit their impact. Together, these functions enable organizations to manage incidents efficiently, reduce harm, and maintain the continuity of critical operations.

6.18.6 Core Function: Recover

The Recover Function focuses on restoring services and operations following a cybersecurity incident. It supports both immediate recovery actions and long-term improvements that enhance the organization's ability to recover in the future. Recovery involves technical processes, business coordination, and clear communication to restore confidence and sustain operations.

There are two distinct phases of recovery. The short-term recovery phase aims to resume essential business operations as soon as possible. This may involve switching to alternate systems, restoring data from backups, or re-establishing network access. The long-term recovery phase focuses on improving overall resilience by addressing the root causes of the incident, identifying process gaps, and strengthening safeguards to reduce the likelihood and impact of future incidents.

To guide recovery activities, organizations use defined measures such as:

- Recovery time objective (RTO): The targeted maximum time allowed to restore a specific system or service before the impact becomes unacceptable.
- Recovery point objective (RPO): The maximum tolerable amount of data loss, measured from the most recent valid backup.
- Mean time to recover (MTTR): The average time it takes to fully restore systems or services after an incident.
- Key considerations include:
  - *Recovery targets.* Recovery targets—such as RTO, RPO, and MTTR—help determine how systems are prioritized and which backup, failover, or redundancy methods are used. (A failover method allows a backup system to begin operating when a primary system becomes unavailable. It helps ensure that critical services continue with minimal interruption.)
  - *Recovery planning and testing.* Recovery planning includes developing, maintaining, and updating business continuity and disaster recovery plans, policies, and procedures. Business continuity focuses on maintaining or rapidly restoring essential functions and requires regular testing and validation to ensure that recovery processes operate effectively during an incident.
  - *Lessons learned.* Recovery also involves learning from the incident. This includes conducting after-action reviews, identifying what went well and what did not, updating documentation, and incorporating lessons learned into future planning.
  - *Effective communications.* Communication must be timely, accurate, and aligned with legal, regulatory, contractual, reputational, and other obligations.

The Recover Function builds on the strengths of the other CSF functions. It depends on the governance structures and risk decisions established in Govern, the asset and risk visibility gained through Identify, the safeguards implemented through Protect, and the timely detection and coordinated actions carried out under Detect and Respond. Together, these functions enable the organization to restore operations, maintain continuity of care, and strengthen resilience for future events.

6.19 Applying NIST Cybersecurity Framework to Common Scenarios

6.19.1 Scenario 1: Day-to-Day Operations

Cybersecurity efforts are ongoing and do not start only after an incident has been confirmed. In healthcare and other critical infrastructure sectors, attempts to gain unauthorized access are very frequent. Attackers probe systems, scan for weaknesses, and look for opportunities to exploit configuration errors, outdated systems, or human behavior. These activities often occur without being immediately detected. The absence of a known incident does not mean the environment is secure. NIST CSF 2.0 provides structure for how the organization manages risk, makes decisions, and maintains security across all areas.

6.19.1.1 Govern Function

The Govern Function defines the foundation. It establishes how the cybersecurity program is directed, resourced, and monitored. This includes assigning responsibilities, clarifying roles, and ensuring that policies and procedures are in place and followed. Governance ensures that decisions about access, change management, third-party oversight, and risk escalation are made consistently and with accountability. It defines how the organization sets its cybersecurity strategy, how performance is measured, and how issues are reported to leadership. Without this structure, other security functions are less likely to be applied effectively or consistently.

6.19.1.2 Identify Function

The Identify Function supports day-to-day security by maintaining visibility. The organization must know what systems, assets, data, and services exist—and which of those are essential to operations. This includes inventories of hardware, software, cloud platforms, and vendor services. It also includes classification of assets, data, systems, applications, networks, devices, and other resources based on their sensitivity, criticality, and value to the organization. Dependencies must be identified and monitored, including reliance on third-party providers. This understanding supports risk-based decision-making and ensures that safeguards are applied where they are most needed.

6.19.1.3 Protect Function

The Protect Function addresses administrative, physical, and technical safeguards put in place to reduce the likelihood and impact of cybersecurity events. These include access controls, authentication, encryption, network segmentation, endpoint protection, and secure configuration management. Security awareness programs, acceptable use policies, and badge access are other examples.

6.19.1.4 Detect Function

The Detect Function enables the organization to recognize events that could indicate unauthorized or harmful activity. This includes monitoring for anomalies in network traffic, system logs, and user activity. Detection tools such as SIEMs, SOAR (Security Orchestration, Automation, and Response), EDR, intrusion detection systems, and intrusion detection and prevention systems (IDPS) are used to identify deviations from established normal authorized activity. It is important to have a baseline of normal activity because it allows the organization to identify behaviors or events that may indicate compromise, misuse of assets, or other malicious or undesirable activity.

6.19.1.5 Respond Function

The Respond Function enables the organization to have incident response procedures in place. This includes clearly defining who is responsible for what, how issues are reported and passed along to the right people, and how communication occurs during an incident. More serious or complex incidents must be escalated to the appropriate personnel or leadership. (This is also known as an escalation path.)[116]

6.19.1.6 Recover Function

The Recover Function ensures that the organization can restore affected systems and services. This may include restoring files from backup, reimaging systems,[117] or applying configuration changes. Recovery also involves reviewing what occurred and updating policies or controls as needed. This process supports continuous improvement and helps reduce the risk of recurrence.

In daily operations, applying the NIST CSF ensures that cybersecurity is not treated as a separate activity but is integrated into how the organization functions. Governance ensures coordination and accountability across all of the Framework's core functions (Govern, Identify, Protect, Detect, Respond, and Recover). This structured approach supports operational continuity, awareness, communications, and alignment, including when there is no visible incident.

Even if monitoring tools do not show signs of compromise, this does not necessarily mean the environment is safe. *Assume the breach.* Threats can exist below the threshold of detection (e.g., quiet, low-level activity that is not flagged by detection systems). It may take time, context, or more advanced techniques and tools to uncover what is actually happening. The inability to detect something does not confirm it is not there. It may simply be operating below the detection threshold.

6.19.2 Scenario 2: Ransomware Attack Originating from a Compromised Vendor

A ransomware incident involving a third-party vendor demonstrates how external compromise may lead to compromise of internal systems and networks. Consider the following scenario:

An employee in the billing department received an email that appeared to come from a medical billing company the organization routinely works with. The message stated that updated reimbursement guidance was attached and required immediate review. The employee opened the attachment and enabled the macro when prompted, believing it was part of a standard document update. Enabling the macro installed malware on the device. This initial infection gave the attacker a foothold inside the organization's environment. The attacker then deployed a self-propagating ransomware worm that spread laterally across clinical and administrative systems, encrypting shared drives and disrupting access to electronic health records and other critical services.

This scenario demonstrates how an attack originating outside the organization can lead to significant internal harm.

6.19.2.1 Govern Function

The Govern Function establishes how an organization manages both vendor risk and insider threat. In this case, governance determines how responsibilities are divided when a vendor-related incident occurs—such as a phishing attack sent from a compromised vendor account. Vendor contracts must clearly state cybersecurity requirements, including reporting expectations and safeguards for email and other communication channels, including authentication, filtering, and monitoring. Internally, the organization must define who is responsible for reviewing vendor activity, approving access, and responding when external incidents affect internal operations. These expectations should be written down and actively monitored and enforced.

In this scenario, the organization relied on its governance structures to manage the vendor-related incident. Governance determined who was responsible for contacting the compromised billing vendor, reviewing the vendor's contractual cybersecurity obligations, and escalating the matter to privacy, security, and executive leadership. Established policies and reporting lines ensured that the event was treated as a vendor-originated security incident and that internal teams responded in a coordinated and accountable manner.

6.19.2.2 Identify Function

The Identify Function enables the organization to understand how it relies on the affected vendor. It is essential to map which systems, business units, and personnel interact with the vendor. This includes knowing whether the vendor handles sensitive information, supports critical workflows, or maintains email-based relationships with key staff. In this example, identifying the employees who regularly receive documents from the vendor helps determine where risk may be concentrated and where monitoring should be focused.

In this scenario, the organization determined which internal departments interacted with the compromised billing vendor, which systems exchanged data with the vendor, and which employees routinely received attachments from the vendor. This information helped the organization pinpoint the path of exposure, identify which systems and services the ransomware worm affected, and understand the areas placed at risk by the vendor compromise.

6.19.2.3 Protect Function

The Protect Function is about limiting the organization's exposure before the incident occurs. This includes having email security controls in place—such as link scanning, attachment filtering, and malware detection. Endpoint protection must be deployed and maintained across user devices. Vendor access must be defined, limited, and monitored. MFA, secure email protocols, and encryption must be applied consistently across communication channels.

In this scenario, the organization had implemented protective safeguards—such as email filtering, attachment scanning, endpoint protection, and MFA—but the phishing email from the vendor's compromised account bypassed these controls. The event revealed gaps in the organization's protective measures, including limitations in email filtering against trusted external partners and the need for stronger validation of vendor-supplied documents. Protection activities also included assessing whether vendor access to organizational systems was properly limited and whether additional safeguards were needed to reduce the likelihood of similar incidents in the future.

6.19.2.4 Detect Function

The Detect Function helps the organization recognize that something is wrong. In this scenario, alerts may come from unusual login activity, suspicious file access, or lateral movement from the initial infected device. Detection tools must be configured to highlight deviations from normal activity, particularly among staff who interact with vendors. Systems should be monitored for indicators of compromise (IOC), and threat intelligence should be used to help validate alerts and understand whether a known malware strain or attack technique is involved.

Threat intelligence enhances situational awareness by providing vetted information about current threats, threat actors, IOC, attack techniques, and other relevant details. It helps the organization understand what to look for and how known threats may present themselves in the environment.

In this scenario, the organization's detection tools flagged several indicators of compromise. Endpoint and SIEM alerts showed that the employee's workstation executed a malicious macro shortly after the email from the billing vendor was opened. Network monitoring tools detected abnormal lateral movement as the ransomware worm attempted to spread to shared drives and clinical systems. File-integrity monitoring (FIM) alerts and user and entity behavior analytics (UEBA) detections indicated rapid encryption activity and system behaviors that were inconsistent with normal operations. At the same time, logs confirmed that the phishing email originated from the vendor's compromised account, which explained why it passed initial trust checks. These correlated detections enabled the organization to recognize that a vendor-originated compromise had triggered a ransomware infection inside its environment and to act quickly to contain the threat.

6.19.2.5 Respond Function

The Respond Function is activated once the phishing email is reported or malicious activity has been observed. This includes isolating the affected device, terminating unauthorized sessions, revoking credentials, and communicating with the vendor to confirm the compromise. Legal and compliance teams must determine whether the incident triggers regulatory or contractual reporting obligations. Actions must be documented, and decision-making roles should be clear. The goal is to contain the threat, understand the scope, and coordinate with all internal and external stakeholders.

In this scenario, the response team isolated the organization's infected billing department workstation, disabled the affected internal user account, and halted network connectivity to prevent the ransomware worm from spreading further. The team contacted the billing vendor to report the suspicious email activity, confirm that the vendor's email account had been compromised, and request that the vendor secure its environment and notify other clients as needed. The organization documented each step taken to contain the attack and coordinated with the vendor's technical and security staff as part of the response. Legal, compliance, and leadership teams reviewed the incident to determine regulatory and contractual reporting obligations and coordinated internal and external communications throughout the response.

6.19.2.6 Recover Function

The Recover Function includes both short-term and long-term recovery. Short-term recovery focuses on restoring systems and services so the organization can resume normal operations. This may involve restoring data from backups, reimaging affected devices, and verifying that systems are no longer compromised.

Long-term recovery involves analyzing the incident to understand what allowed it to occur and identifying how similar events can be prevented in the future. For example, this may include reviewing why a phishing message was not filtered, or whether a vendor had access to systems, services, or data that were not necessary for their role. Recovery efforts may result in one or more of the following, for example, depending on the situation: updated policies and procedures, updated configurations, enhanced technical, administrative, and physical safeguards, enhanced training, more efficient communications, and upgraded software, systems, and infrastructure. This supports greater resilience and helps reduce the likelihood and impact of future incidents.

In this scenario, recovery activities included restoring encrypted systems from backup, reimaging compromised devices, and validating that clinical and administrative services could resume safely. Longer-term recovery required reviewing how the malicious vendor email bypassed filtering, assessing whether vendor access needed to be restricted, and updating policies, safeguards, and training to address gaps exposed by the incident. Lessons learned were documented and used to strengthen the organization's vendor-risk management and cybersecurity practices.

6.19.3 Scenario 3: Negligent Insider Using Public Large Language Model

An employee at a healthcare organization uses a publicly available large language model to help draft letters to patients about their diagnoses and treatment plans. In doing so, the employee copies and pastes sensitive patient information—such as name, address, diagnosis, and other personal details—into the AI tool's input field. The employee intends to use the AI to improve the clarity and tone of the communication, but does not realize that the tool is hosted by a third party and is not approved by the organization. The data is processed by an external system that is not covered by a HIPAA business associate agreement and may retain the input for training or other purposes.

The employee has disclosed PHI to an unauthorized external party, even if the action was unintentional. The use of a public tool without proper controls or agreements in place constitutes an impermissible disclosure and introduces significant privacy risk.

6.19.3.1 Govern Function

The *Govern Function* must address the use of unapproved AI tools when handling PHI and other sensitive information. The governance approach must explicitly define expectations for the appropriate use of AI tools, including restrictions on processing PHI and other categories of sensitive, confidential, proprietary, or protected information. An acceptable use policy—one that addresses the safe and responsible use of trustworthy AI tools—must be clearly communicated and consistently enforced through training, monitoring, and oversight. Policies must also explicitly prohibit the use of public AI tools or other forms of shadow AI for processing PHI. Policies should require workforce members to use only approved and sanctioned systems, tools, and platforms that are managed by the organization.

In this scenario, the organization had policies that prohibited entering PHI into public AI tools and required workforce members to use only approved, sanctioned systems. These governance structures made clear that copying patient information into a public large language model violated acceptable-use standards and patient-privacy requirements. Governance also established the oversight responsibilities of privacy, compliance, and HR teams, enabling the organization to investigate the disclosure, take corrective action, and reinforce policy compliance across the workforce.

6.19.3.2 Identify Function

The *Identify Function* supports organizational awareness of where sensitive data resides, how data is accessed, and which AI tools or services are in use across the environment. This includes identifying whether AI tools are being accessed from organizational devices, cloud services, or browser extensions. These tools must be evaluated for security risks and compliance with legal, regulatory, and contractual requirements. A comprehensive data map should identify where PHI, other sensitive personal data, and proprietary organizational information are created, received, transmitted, or maintained. This data map helps the organization maintain visibility and apply appropriate safeguards when assessing how tools, such as AI, interact with sensitive and other types of confidential and proprietary information.

In this scenario, the organization used its access records, audit logs, and data-mapping information to determine which employee used the public AI tool and what PHI was copied into it. Because the organization had identified where sensitive data reside and which users are permitted to access them, it was able to confirm that the workforce member retrieved patient records and then entered that information into an unsanctioned AI platform, allowing the organization to understand the scope of the data involved.

6.19.3.3 Protect Function

The *Protect Function* involves putting safeguards in place to prevent the unauthorized use or exposure of data. These safeguards include technical, administrative, and physical controls that work together to reduce cybersecurity risk.

One important safeguard is intrusion detection. According to NIST SP 800-94, *Guide to Intrusion Detection and Prevention Systems (IDPS)*, "[i]ntrusion detection is the process of monitoring the events occurring in a computer system or network and analyzing them for signs of possible incidents, which are violations or imminent threats of violation of computer security policies, acceptable use policies, or standard security practices." NIST. *Guide to Intrusion Detection and Prevention Systems (IDPS) (SP 800-94).* https://nvlpubs.nist.gov/nistpubs/legacy/sp/nistspecialpublication800-94.pdf.

In practice, intrusion detection requires continuous analysis of activity across systems and networks to identify events that may indicate a threat.

Intrusion prevention builds on detection by attempting to block the threat before it can succeed. NIST defines intrusion prevention as "the process of performing intrusion detection and attempting to stop detected possible incidents." In other words, when a potential threat is detected, the system takes action—such as rejecting malicious traffic or terminating a suspicious session—to stop it from proceeding further.

These capabilities are often integrated into a single system, known as an Intrusion Detection and Prevention System (IDPS). NIST Special Publication 800–94[118] describes IDPS as tools that identify potential incidents, log and report those incidents, and, in many cases, attempt to stop the threat. IDPS can be used to document threats. By documenting information about threats, IDPS may provide data that can be used to understand how attackers operate, identify patterns over time, and improve the organization's defenses. Security teams may use this information to help them to investigate incidents, determine root causes, and take corrective actions. Some organizations may deploy standalone detection (Intrusion Detection Systems) or standalone prevention tools (Intrusion Prevention Systems), while others use integrated *IDPS* solutions. The choice depends on organizational needs, infrastructure, and available resources (including, without limitation, budget and workflow considerations).

By using IDPS—or standalone intrusion detection systems (IDS) and intrusion prevention systems (IPS)—organizations can monitor activity across their environment and take action when necessary to identify, contain, and mitigate threats. These threats may include the use of shadow IT or shadow AI by employees or contractors when they use tools, services, or platforms that are not approved, managed, or governed by the organization's IT department, the unauthorized exfiltration of sensitive or personal information (including, but not limited to, PHI and personally identifiable information (PII)), and other events that violate organizational policies or are otherwise prohibited. Other safeguards, such as Data Loss Prevention (DLP) tools, can monitor outbound data movement and help prevent PHI—as well as other confidential, proprietary or sensitive information—from being copied or transmitted to unapproved AI platforms.

Alongside technical safeguards, the workforce—including employees, contractors, and others—must be trained to understand how to handle PHI as well as confidential, proprietary, and sensitive information. This includes knowing how internal systems are intended to be used, recognizing risks associated with unsanctioned tools, and complying with organizational policies.

Robust prevention, threat detection, and enforcement of safeguards—in addition to appropriate and efficient incident response—all work in coordination to protect the organization and reduce cybersecurity risk.

In this scenario, the organization implemented safeguards that should have prevented PHI from being entered into a public large language model. Technical safeguards such as DLP tools could have flagged or blocked the attempted copy-and-paste of PHI into an unsanctioned website, and web-filtering controls could have restricted access to public AI platforms from organizational devices. Administrative safeguards, including policies prohibiting shadow AI, and workforce training on appropriate use, were already in place but were not followed. These protections, when enforced collectively, help reduce the likelihood that PHI will be disclosed to unauthorized external systems.

6.19.3.4 Detect Function

The *Detect Function* is necessary to identify potential indicators of compromise, such as unauthorized access, use, disclosure, or exfiltration of data, including when those activities involve unsanctioned AI platforms (shadow AI). Detection activities must focus on correlating access to sensitive data with the use of unapproved or unsanctioned tools, platforms, or services. Monitoring user activity, system logs, outbound data transfers, and the use of unsanctioned or unapproved applications can help uncover misuse.

In this scenario, detection tools flagged that the workforce member accessed certain patient records within a short amount of time. Web filtering logs showed that the same individual then navigated to a public large language model website. These correlated events indicated that PHI was entered into the unapproved and unsanctioned AI tool.

6.19.3.5 Respond Function

The *Respond Function* ensures that the organization investigates unauthorized access, use, or disclosure of data, determines what data may have been exposed, and takes the appropriate actions. Legal and compliance teams must assess whether this constitutes a reportable breach under HIPAA. Depending on the findings, the employee may need additional training or, in some cases, disciplinary action.

In this scenario, the response team reviewed the system logs showing which patient records the workforce member accessed, analyzed the web-filtering logs confirming that the individual used a public large language model, and verified exactly what PHI had been entered into the unsanctioned AI tool. The organization documented the sequence of events, evaluated whether any affected patients needed to be notified, and took corrective actions to prevent recurrence. This included retraining the workforce member on the organization's acceptable use policy and related requirements.

6.19.3.6 Recover Function

The *Recover* Function supports the organization's ability to recover and strengthen its security posture after an incident involving the unauthorized use of an AI tool or other unsanctioned technology. This includes evaluating how the incident occurred, identifying gaps in training or safeguards, and updating policies to address emerging technologies like AI. Lessons learned must be documented and used to inform future risk assessments and controls.

This scenario illustrates how well-intentioned use of technology can still result in harm if controls and awareness are lacking. It highlights the need for governance, safeguards, monitoring, and response mechanisms to work together—especially as AI tools become more prevalent in healthcare environments.

6.19.4 Scenario 4: Malicious Insider—Theft of Patient Information

A nurse at a hospital used his legitimate access to the hospital's EHR system to steal patient demographic and insurance information. Over the course of several months, the nurse accessed dozens of records that were not related to his assigned patients or job duties. This information was then sold to a third party and used to commit medical identity theft. The organization did not discover the activity until six months later, when unusual billing complaints were raised by affected patients and flagged by the privacy office.

This is an example of a malicious insider—in this case, an employee with authorized access who intentionally misused that access. The nurse accessed patient records that were not related to his clinical responsibilities and had no legitimate connection to his assigned patients or job duties. While he had access to the system as part of his role, he used that access inappropriately and without authorization. This type of misuse represents a clear violation of both policy and patient privacy, and it highlights the challenges of detecting insider threats when users operate within systems they are allowed to access.

Malicious insider activity like this is unlikely to be flagged unless the organization understands what normal authorized activity looks like and can detect when someone deviates from it. However, if there is no clear, defined understanding, then viewing records without a legitimate reason may not be recognized as suspicious. Monitoring must be designed to detect these types of abnormal activities, including when the user is using valid credentials.

6.19.4.1 Govern Function

Governance sets the foundation for managing insider risk. The organization must have clear policies that define appropriate access and use of EHR systems, including role-based access controls and patient data confidentiality requirements. Staff must be trained on these expectations, and policies must be consistently enforced. The hospital's leadership and compliance teams must ensure that there is proper oversight and that insider threats are addressed as part of the organization's risk management strategy. This includes having procedures for reporting suspicious activity, conducting internal investigations, and taking disciplinary action. A culture of accountability and shared responsibility is also essential—where staff are encouraged to speak up if they observe access that is unusual, inappropriate, or unauthorized.

In this scenario, the organization had policies the nurse violated, including role-based access expectations, patient-privacy requirements, and procedures for reporting suspicious activity. Governance also established the oversight responsibilities of the privacy, compliance, and HR teams, which enabled the organization to investigate the misconduct, enforce disciplinary actions, and address the insider threat as part of its broader risk management strategy.

6.19.4.2 Identify Function

The organization must understand which systems and data are sensitive, who is authorized to access them, and under what circumstances. This includes mapping which job functions are allowed to view specific types of patient information and ensuring that access is provisioned accordingly. In this case, the nurse's access should have been limited to patients under his care. Asset and access inventories must be kept current so that deviations from established normal (authorized) activity can be evaluated. The Identify Function also includes recognizing dependencies—such as user directories, access management platforms, and audit logging systems—that support accountability and monitoring.

In this scenario, the organization had identified which systems contained sensitive patient information, which job roles were authorized to access those systems, and the legitimate circumstances under which such access could occur. This made it possible to determine that the nurse's repeated access to unrelated patient records fell outside his authorized role and represented a misuse of access.

6.19.4.3 Protect Function

Controls must be in place to prevent unauthorized access or misuse of sensitive data. This includes enforcing least privilege and role-based access controls so that users can only access what they legitimately need. Technical safeguards—such as session timeouts, data masking, and access logging—can help reduce the risk of misuse. Administrative safeguards like workforce training, confidentiality agreements, and regular access reviews also contribute to protection. While technical controls alone cannot prevent all insider threats, they reduce the opportunity for abuse and support enforcement of policy.

In this scenario, the organization had established safeguards—such as role-based access controls, confidentiality agreements, and periodic access reviews—but these protections were not sufficient to prevent the nurse from intentionally misusing his legitimate access. Although technical controls enforced least privilege, the nurse still used permitted access pathways to view records he was not authorized to access, demonstrating that protective measures alone cannot stop all forms of insider abuse.

6.19.4.4 Detect Function

Malicious insiders can be difficult to detect because they have legitimate access—whether physical or virtual—and their actions may appear normal on the surface. In some cases, behavioral warning signs may be missed or dismissed, and staff may hesitate to report concerns about colleagues. Additionally, the organization must know what normal authorized activity looks like so that deviations can be identified. For example, if a nurse accesses a large number of records without any corresponding patient interactions or assignments, this should raise a red flag. Monitoring must be capable of identifying access to unrelated patient records or bulk viewing of charts. Alerts must be configured to flag unusual activity, and logs must be regularly reviewed.

In this scenario, the organization eventually detected the misconduct only after unusual billing complaints were reported, prompting a review of EHR audit logs. If real-time monitoring rules had been in place to identify abnormal unauthorized activity—such as repeated access to patient records unrelated to the nurse's clinical duties—the suspicious activity could have been detected much earlier.

6.19.4.5 Respond Function

When the privacy office received complaints about suspicious billing, the organization initiated an investigation. Responding to this type of incident requires coordination among privacy, compliance, HR, IT, and legal teams. The hospital must confirm whether any data was exfiltrated and to what extent. Immediate steps to contain the incident are necessary, such as suspending the user's access (if the organization deems that this is appropriate), preserving logs and audit trails, and securing evidence that may be needed for investigation, disciplinary action, or other purposes. The response plan must clearly set forth roles and responsibilities, escalation procedures, communication protocols, and legal obligations.

Depending on the confirmed scope of the incident and applicable legal or regulatory requirements and implications, law enforcement may be contacted. The organization must decide whether it wants to report the incident to law enforcement and whether it is required to report the breach under applicable breach notification requirements, such as the HIPAA Breach Notification Rule, state breach laws, contractual obligations, or other relevant mandates. All investigative steps, decisions made, and actions taken must be thoroughly documented to ensure accountability and traceability. Coordination between teams is essential to ensure a well-managed and consistent response process.

In this scenario, the organization suspended the nurse's access, preserved the relevant audit logs, and coordinated an internal investigation to confirm the scope of the unauthorized access and determine whether PHI had been exfiltrated. Privacy, compliance, HR, IT, and legal teams collaborated to assess regulatory obligations, evaluate whether breach notification was required, and determine appropriate disciplinary actions.

6.19.4.6 Recover Function

Recovery involves both short-term and long-term efforts. In the short term, the organization must take steps to stabilize the situation and return to normal operations. This may include disabling the user's access, completing the investigation, and coordinating with legal, privacy, and compliance teams. Affected individuals must be notified if PHI was compromised, and the organization may offer identity protection services or other support depending on the nature of the exposure. Internal documentation must be completed, and any immediate corrective actions must be implemented.

Long-term recovery focuses on ensuring that the incident does not happen again. This includes identifying gaps that contributed to the incident—such as insufficient access controls, lack of activity-based monitoring, or gaps in training. Lessons learned should inform updates to technical safeguards, policies, user monitoring practices, and governance structures. Recovery also involves reinforcing awareness of insider threat risks and supporting a culture of accountability. In this way, recovery is about restoring services as well as building greater resilience for the future.

In this scenario, the organization notified affected individuals, completed internal documentation, and implemented immediate corrective actions such as disabling the nurse's access. Longer term recovery included strengthening access-review procedures, improving monitoring for abnormal user activity, updating policies and workforce training, and reinforcing organizational awareness of insider threat risks. Lessons learned were formally documented and used to update safeguards and governance practices, supporting greater organizational resilience and helping to reduce the likelihood of similar incidents in the future.

6.19.5 Scenario 5: Business Email Compromise (BEC)

A healthcare organization received a fraudulent email that appeared to come from its main billing company, a trusted third-party vendor responsible for handling patient invoicing and insurance billing. The attacker used an email address that closely resembled the vendor's real domain and sent a message instructing the organization to update the vendor's bank account details for future payments. The email appeared legitimate because the attacker used a look-alike domain that appeared nearly identical to the vendor's actual domain. This is known as a homoglyph attack.

An employee in the finance department processed the request and initiated a large wire transfer without verifying the change directly with the vendor using its official and previously known contact information. Because of the amount involved, the transaction required CFO approval. The CFO, under pressure to meet a major deadline for an upcoming board presentation, briefly reviewed the request and approved it without further inquiry. Notably, the CFO had recently declined to complete the organization's phishing awareness training, despite repeated reminders.

6.19.5.1 Govern Function

Governance helps to set the security expectations that apply across the organization—including to executives and external vendors. In this case, the organization lacked clearly defined requirements around verifying vendor payment changes and did not ensure those expectations were consistently enforced. A more mature governance approach would include role-specific training for all personnel, including executives, tailored to their responsibilities and constraints. For example, executive training could be shorter and more focused on decision-making risks, but participation should not be optional. In addition, vendor management policies should require business partners to implement basic email authentication controls (such as Sender Policy Framework (SPF), DomainKeys Identified Mail (DKIM), and Domain-based Message Authentication, Reporting, and Conformance (DMARC) to reduce the risk of spoofed or impersonated messages reaching the organization.

As explained by CISA:

> Sender Policy Framework (SPF) is an authentication protocol that lists IP addresses in a DNS TXT record that are authorized to send email on behalf of domains. A sent email message will be checked for an SPF record and checked against an authorized sender list. If the valid SPF record exists, a policy of "PASS" or "FAIL" will be applied. Failed policy application should result in the message being routed to a spam folder. DomainKeys Identified Mail (DKIM) adds a digital signature to email headers to ensure email content has not changed. A sent email message will include a private key to encrypt the email signature. The public key is included in a DNS TXT record. The message recipient validates the signature by comparing the public/private keys. Domain-based Message Authentication, Reporting, and Conformance (DMARC) is an email authentication protocol that uses SPF and DKIM to validate the sender and block fraudulent messaging. It enables a domain owner to specify a policy for handling unauthenticated messages. These tools ensure that an email message is genuine and is coming from a validated source. These protocols are not intended to work in isolation and should be implemented together.

Cybersecurity Infrastructure and Security Agency (CISA). *Implement SPF, DKIM, and DMARC Email Authentication Methods (CM0055).* https://www.cisa.gov/eviction-strategies-tool/info-countermeasures/CM0055.

Governance also requires that processes like payment change approvals be governed by defined roles and responsibilities—such as enforcing *separation of duties*. No single employee, regardless of role, should be able to complete a high-risk financial transaction from start to finish. Formal policies must codify these expectations and establish clear escalation paths if anomalies are detected or approvals are rushed.

In this scenario, the organization lacked governance controls that required verification of vendor payment changes, did not enforce mandatory executive training, and did not require vendors to implement email-authentication protections. These governance gaps allowed the fraudulent payment request to be processed without proper validation, escalated review, or adherence to established oversight expectations.

6.19.5.2 Identify Function

The healthcare organization failed to recognize that vendor payment processing, particularly when involving high-dollar wire transfers, is a high-value target. A more effective approach would include identifying critical processes (such as vendor payment changes), understanding who can edit or authorize those changes, and determining what external systems (e.g., email from vendors) those processes rely on. This also includes identifying vendors that support essential functions or financial services and evaluating their email security posture as part of third-party risk assessments.

In this scenario, the organization had not identified vendor payment changes as a high-risk process or mapped which roles and systems could initiate or approve banking updates. Because these risks were not identified, the fraudulent request was treated as routine rather than a transaction requiring additional verification.

6.19.5.3 Protect Function

A better security posture from a protection perspective would involve multiple layers of technical and administrative controls. This includes *separation of duties*—ensuring that no single person can complete a high-risk transaction without oversight. For example, one individual may initiate a change to vendor banking information, but a second, independent person must verify and approve it. Additional safeguards would include dual verification of payment changes, role-based restrictions on who can access or edit vendor records, and mandatory hold periods for large wire transfers. Email authentication protocols such as SPF, DKIM, and DMARC should be implemented by the organization and required of vendors.[119] Email security systems may also be configured to detect domain spoofing, impersonation attempts, or policy violations.

Executives and staff should also be trained to recognize BEC tactics, understand verification procedures, and follow them—regardless of urgency. In this scenario, the Chief Financial Officer (CFO) approved a large payment without adequate review while under deadline pressure and had recently bypassed the organization's phishing awareness training.

In this scenario, protective safeguards—such as mandatory dual verification, role-based restrictions, and separation of duties—were not in place or not enforced. These gaps allowed both the finance employee and the CFO to process the fraudulent request without independent validation or adherence to policy.

6.19.5.4 Detect Function

This incident went undetected because there were no alerts or checkpoints to identify the suspicious activity. The vendor payment change was processed without a second layer of review, and the attacker's email was not flagged by phishing detection systems. A more effective detection strategy would include automated rules or analytics to identify anomalous transactions—such as changes to vendor bank details followed by high-dollar transfers. These events should be treated as red flags and routed to compliance or internal audit personnel for secondary review.

Email systems should also be configured to detect failures in authentication checks (SPF, DKIM, DMARC), or characteristics that suggest impersonation—such as email originating from a newly registered domain. However, these defenses depend on vendors implementing authentication protocols on their own domains. Because of this, organizations may wish to include such requirements in vendor contracts to reduce the risk of impersonation.

These layers of protection and detection illustrate *defense in depth*—a strategy that applies multiple, redundant security controls at various levels to protect against failure. Even if one safeguard (such as training) is bypassed (or otherwise fails), other controls (such as detection rules or dual verification) may still catch the issue. Defense in depth improves the likelihood of catching harmful activity early and preventing it from spreading or causing harm.

In this scenario, the organization had no automated detection rules to flag unusual financial activity, and the spoofed domain was not identified by email security controls. Because no alerts were generated, the fraudulent transaction proceeded without being detected until after the wire transfer had been completed.

6.19.5.5 Respond Function

Responding to the incident required coordinated action across internal teams. The healthcare organization convened an emergency board meeting and, with authorization from the board and senior leadership, contacted law enforcement in less than 4 hours from the time of the unauthorized wire transfer. Although law enforcement cannot guarantee recovery of funds in every case, the prompt action in this instance enabled law enforcement to intervene and work with the financial institution to successfully recover the transferred funds.[120]

This rapid response depended on prompt escalation, clear internal communication, and documentation of events. A strong response plan includes pre-defined roles and legal considerations—including which parties are responsible for initiating contact with law enforcement or outside counsel. The organization also must assess whether the incident is reportable under applicable breach notification laws, including HIPAA (if PHI was compromised), state data breach laws, or contractual provisions.

In this scenario, the organization escalated the issue quickly, coordinated with law enforcement and its financial institution, and recovered the misdirected funds. These actions relied on internal communication protocols and clearly defined response responsibilities.

6.19.5.6 Recover Function

Short-term recovery included confirming that no further unauthorized changes had been made and securing payment workflows to prevent recurrence. The organization conducted a full review of vendor access rights, email filtering rules, and internal finance procedures. Longer-term recovery efforts included updating policies to clarify separation of duties, enhancing training programs for all staff including executives, and revising contractual language with vendors to ensure they implement adequate email authentication protections.

This incident also prompted an internal audit of high-risk processes involving vendor communication and the development of a targeted fraud detection system for payment-related changes. Recovery is not just about restoring normal operations—it is also about improving the organization's long-term resilience so that similar threats can be identified, reported, and prevented in the future.

In this scenario, recovery efforts included updating finance procedures, enhancing executive training, strengthening vendor-management requirements, and implementing fraud-detection analytics. Lessons learned were incorporated into policies and controls to improve long-term resilience and reduce the likelihood of similar incidents.

6.19.6 Scenario 6: Mobile Device (BYOD) + International Travel

A clinical manager at a healthcare organization traveled internationally to visit the organization's new affiliate. He brought his personal smartphone, which he also used for work-related communications and to access the healthcare organization's apps and data. The organization permitted the use of personal devices for work—commonly referred to as "bring your own device" or BYOD—but did not have a formal BYOD policy in place. (BYOD refers to an arrangement where employees are allowed to use their own smartphones, tablets, or laptops to access organizational systems, apps, or data.) The organization also lacked a formal policy or guidelines regarding international travel.

Although the organization had a mobile device management (MDM) system in place, the employee's personal phone was too old to be supported by the MDM platform and was therefore not enrolled or covered under that system. During the trip, the employee lost the device. Sensitive internal data was stored locally on the phone and was also accessible remotely through cloud services. The healthcare organization was not able to locate or remotely wipe the device. A remote wipe refers to the ability of an IT administrator or organization to delete data from a lost or stolen device to prevent unauthorized access to sensitive information. Because the device was unmanaged and outside of the organization's mobile control infrastructure, these actions could not be performed.

Please note: Whether an organization can remotely wipe a personal device may depend on applicable laws and regulations, policy, contractual agreements, company policy, and the employee's (or other individual's) informed consent.

6.19.6.1 Govern Function

Governance was insufficient in this scenario. The organization lacked a formal BYOD policy and had no international travel guidelines—despite allowing personal devices to access sensitive internal data. Governance structures must establish clear and enforceable policies for BYOD use, including device eligibility, user responsibilities, data protection expectations, and monitoring capabilities. Policies should address international travel.

In this scenario, the organization had not established governance controls to define which personal devices were eligible for work use, did not require enrollment in MDM, and had no international travel-security policy. These governance gaps allowed an outdated, unmanaged device to access internal systems during international travel, creating conditions under which the device could be lost without any organizational ability to locate or wipe it.

6.19.6.2 Identify Function

The lack of visibility into BYOD devices not enrolled in MDM left the organization unaware of what data was stored or accessible from the device. Identification processes should include an asset inventory that accounts for all devices used to access organizational data—whether BYOD devices or company-owned devices.

In this scenario, the organization did not identify or inventory the employee's personal device as an asset accessing internal systems, did not track what data was stored locally on it, and did not identify the risks associated with the device's outdated operating system and lack of MDM enrollment. This lack of visibility made it impossible for the organization to determine the full extent of exposure once the device was lost.

6.19.6.3 Protect Function

The organization had limited protective measures in place. The absence of mandatory enrollment in MDM for BYOD devices and the lack of a secure workspace or sandbox meant that sensitive data could be stored on an unmanaged personal device. A stronger protective approach would include clear BYOD eligibility criteria (e.g., minimum operating system versions), mandatory MDM enrollment of mobile devices, remote wipe capabilities, and guidance for using secure communications channels while abroad. Travel-specific controls could include providing loaner or burner devices, discouraging the use of public Wi-Fi and charging stations, and limiting or containerizing access to sensitive data. Strong encryption and MFA (or robust passwordless authentication) should be required for remote access.

In this scenario, the organization had no protective mechanisms requiring the employee's device to meet minimum security standards, did not enforce MDM enrollment, and had not implemented containerization or secure workspaces to prevent sensitive data from being stored locally. These missing protections allowed sensitive information to reside on an unsupported, unmanaged device that could not be remotely wiped once lost during international travel.

6.19.6.4 Detect Function

Detecting security issues on mobile devices requires visibility into device status, activity, and compliance. Effective detection includes monitoring for unusual access attempts, unauthorized device types connecting to systems, and failed MDM enrollment. It should also include monitoring for abnormal geographic access patterns, such as logins from foreign countries not normally associated with business operations. Without MDM enrollment or device health reporting, the organization cannot reliably detect when a personal device is out of compliance, operating on outdated software, or storing sensitive data in an insecure manner. Detection capabilities should also include alerting when devices fall outside policy requirements (e.g., unsupported operating systems), when sensitive data is accessed through unmanaged devices, or when cloud logins originate from risky locations.

In this scenario, the organization had no ability to detect that the employee's personal device lacked MDM enrollment, did not meet security requirements, or was accessing sensitive data from abroad. Because there were no alerts tied to foreign access, unsupported operating systems, or unmanaged devices accessing internal apps, the organization received no indication that the device posed a risk until it was reported lost.

6.19.6.5 Respond Function

The Respond Function ensures that the organization initiates investigative and containment actions when a device containing sensitive data is lost. A proper response includes disabling access from the lost device, reviewing logs to determine what information was accessible, and assessing whether any unauthorized login attempts occurred after the loss. Legal, privacy, and compliance teams must determine whether the loss constitutes a reportable breach under HIPAA or other applicable laws.

In this scenario, the organization took all available steps within its technical limitations: it disabled the employee's access from the lost device, reviewed cloud-service logs to determine which internal data had been accessed from the phone, and attempted—but was unable—to initiate a remote wipe because the device had never been enrolled in MDM and was unsupported by the organization's management tools. The organization documented the loss, evaluated whether any PHI or sensitive internal information had been stored locally on the phone, and began assessing regulatory and contractual reporting obligations.

6.19.6.6 Recover Function

Recovery involves restoring secure operations and reducing future risk. Short-term recovery includes completing the investigation, finalizing breach-notification steps if required, and updating internal documentation. Longer-term recovery efforts focus on strengthening policies and controls to prevent similar incidents.

In this scenario, the organization completed its investigation, updated internal records, and—if required—provided notifications to affected individuals. Longer-term recovery included creating a formal BYOD policy, defining minimum device-security standards, enforcing mandatory MDM enrollment for all devices accessing internal systems, establishing international-travel requirements, and offering additional training for staff who use personal devices for work. Lessons learned were incorporated into policies, safeguards, and governance structures to strengthen resilience and reduce the likelihood of similar incidents in the future.

6.19.7 Scenario 7: Deepfake Impersonation + Telehealth

A senior government official appeared to join a scheduled telehealth video consultation through the healthcare organization's platform. The call looked legitimate: the person used the official's name and title, and the face and voice on screen closely matched public footage of the official. During the call, the individual asked for clarification about his own recent test results. Believing the request was authentic, the clinician—thinking he was speaking directly with the official—shared information about the individual's medical condition and prognosis.

This turned out to be a case of deepfake impersonation. A threat actor used AI to simulate the likeness and voice of the official, likely drawing from widely available video and audio clips online. The actor exploited weaknesses in the authentication process to access sensitive health information under false pretenses. The organization did not discover the deception until the real official's office contacted the health system days later, asking about an unusual notification it had received regarding a follow-up appointment.

This scenario highlights the evolving risks posed by AI-enabled deepfakes, especially when communicating virtually, such as with telehealth. It also shows the importance of verifying identity through more than appearance or voice alone.

Since at least 2019,[121] attackers have begun using AI to enhance phishing and impersonation campaigns—including deepfake audio and AI-generated content—targeting organizations of all types and sizes, including healthcare and beyond. AI-powered tools make it easier to mimic trusted individuals, craft convincing messages, and deceive users. As these techniques become more advanced, the use of AI in cyber defense is no longer optional. We now need AI to help identify and counter threats that are increasingly AI-driven. In other words, organizations increasingly require AI-driven defense capabilities to counter AI-enabled threats.

6.19.7.1 Govern Function

Governance structures must establish clear, enforceable policies for verifying patient identity in telehealth encounters—particularly when sensitive information is being discussed. In this case, the organization failed to implement or enforce sufficient verification procedures, relying primarily on superficial indicators like the individual's name and visual appearance. Governance should require robust patient identity verification prior to any disclosure of medical information, such as confirmation through a secure portal, MFA, or other pre-established channels. Governance must also ensure that staff understand when and how to escalate suspicious or unusual interactions, and must continuously evaluate emerging risks—such as AI-driven impersonation—as part of the organization's broader cyber and privacy risk management.

In this scenario, the organization lacked governance controls requiring strong identity verification before releasing sensitive medical information for telehealth sessions. The organization also had no policies directing clinicians to escalate unusual or high-risk interactions. Governance gaps allowed the clinician to rely on appearance and name alone, enabling the deepfake impersonator to obtain sensitive medical information.

6.19.7.2 Identify Function

This incident revealed weaknesses in the organization's identity verification process during virtual sessions. The impersonator (i.e., deepfake threat actor) was able to schedule and join a telehealth appointment using publicly available information and visual likeness alone. The organization did not use contextual or risk-based indicators—such as confirmation through official contact methods, device reputation, location awareness, or MFA—to validate the individual's identity. A stronger approach would include layered verification mechanisms that do not rely solely on appearance or name, and that can detect anomalies or deviations from established normal, authorized activity.

In this scenario, the organization failed to verify the individual's identity, beyond name and likeness, and the telehealth system treated the deepfake impersonator as legitimate because no identity-verification controls—such as secure-portal authentication, MFA, or validated contact methods—were enforced. Without these checks, the deepfake impersonator was able to join the session and obtain sensitive medical information.

6.19.7.3 Protect Function

The system did not have strong enough safeguards to prevent impersonation or to protect sensitive health information from being shared inappropriately. The organization did not require confirmed patient identity verification before discussing diagnostic or prognostic information. Staff should be trained to recognize potential deepfakes and other signs of impersonation.

In this scenario, the organization had no protective safeguards requiring strong identity verification before releasing sensitive medical information during a telehealth session. Because no protective controls were in place to validate the individual's identity, the clinician disclosed PHI directly to a deepfake impersonator.

6.19.7.4 Detect Function

The threat actor's deepfake video and audio passed undetected by the telehealth system and personnel. Detect capabilities should include tools or procedures to flag anomalies, such as mismatched metadata (e.g., device and IP location). Emerging solutions such as deepfake detection software may be considered. Clinicians must know how to escalate concerns and document irregularities.

In this scenario, the organization had no detection mechanisms that could reliably identify signs of deepfake audio or video. Because no alerts or anomaly indicators were triggered during the telehealth session, the impersonation was not detected until the real government official's office contacted the organization days later.

6.19.7.5 Respond Function

The organization had no clear process for escalating unexpected or suspicious telehealth interactions. When concerns arose, an internal review was launched to assess what information had been shared and whether a reportable breach had occurred. A stronger response would have included clearly defined escalation pathways and designated roles for clinical, privacy, legal, compliance, and IT teams. Incident response plans should be updated to reflect emerging tactics like AI-generated deepfakes and impersonation attempts.

In this scenario, once the deception was discovered, the organization initiated an investigation to determine what PHI had been disclosed, whether the breach was reportable, and what steps were needed to contain further exposure. Privacy, legal, compliance, and IT teams collaborated to assess obligations, notify internal leaders, and document the incident.

6.19.7.6 Recover Function

In the aftermath, the organization notified relevant internal stakeholders and began evaluating whether breach notification obligations applied. Recovery efforts focused on identifying what went wrong and implementing corrective measures. The organization reviewed and tightened access controls for telehealth sessions, updated clinician guidance on confirming identity, and established additional safeguards for handling high-profile or unusual encounters. This incident highlighted that remote services require security practices that are tailored to the virtual environment. It also demonstrated the need for continuous evaluation of emerging risks such as deepfakes. As part of long-term recovery, the organization committed to tracking emerging risks, upgrading technology solutions to invest in appropriate deepfake detection technologies, and educating staff about deepfakes and how to handle these situations.[122]

In this scenario, the organization revised its telehealth identity verification procedures, updated policies for high-risk virtual encounters, invested in stronger authentication and enhanced deepfake detection capabilities, and incorporated lessons to reduce the likelihood of similar impersonation incidents.

6.19.8 Scenario 8: Leaky Bucket—Exposed to Public

The issue involved a misconfigured cloud storage bucket that was created by a staff member outside of IT without going through the organization's standard provisioning process. The bucket was used to store internal documents, including sensitive healthcare operational data, but it was left open to the public internet. The individual who created it did not realize that the default settings allowed anyone to access the data without authentication. Because IT was unaware of the bucket's existence, there were no monitoring or protective controls in place.

This type of incident is referred to as a "leaky bucket." It occurs when cloud storage is misconfigured in a manner that unintentionally exposes data to unauthorized users. If the organization does not have a centralized way to detect or inventory all externally facing cloud assets, these types of exposures can go unnoticed. A security researcher may discover the publicly accessible cloud storage bucket and notify the organization of the issue.

6.19.8.1 Govern Function

This incident exposed a lack of governance over cloud storage provisioning. The organization did not have clear policies restricting who could create cloud storage buckets or how those resources should be configured and monitored. Governance structures should include requirements for centralized control, review, and approval of any cloud-based storage, regardless of the user's department or role. Policies must define what types of data may be stored in the cloud, what security settings must be applied, and how visibility into these resources will be maintained. Governance also includes education—staff must understand the consequences of setting up cloud environments outside official channels.

In this scenario, the organization had general governance processes for cloud use, but they did not extend to or effectively control staff-initiated cloud storage creation outside the formal provisioning workflow. Existing policies did not clearly restrict who could create cloud storage buckets, did not require centralized review or approval, and did not prohibit employees from setting up cloud storage independently. These governance gaps allowed a misconfigured public bucket to be created without IT awareness, despite the presence of broader governance structures elsewhere in the organization. As a result, the cloud storage bucket was provisioned outside established oversight processes, directly contributing to the exposure.

6.19.8.2 Identify Function

The organization lacked visibility into its cloud storage footprint. Because the cloud storage bucket was not provisioned through IT, it was not included in the organization's asset inventory or monitored through standard tooling. Identification activities should include routine scanning for unauthorized or unmanaged cloud resources, including buckets that are publicly accessible. Inventories should reflect not just what the organization has deployed internally, but also any external or shadow assets that may pose risk. Without knowing what exists, it is impossible to assess exposure or risk.

In this scenario, the organization failed to identify the cloud storage bucket because it was never added to the cloud asset inventory. The bucket had no associated owner in IT. Accordingly, the bucket was not monitored for configuration or access changes. The organization lacked visibility into the bucket and did not recognize that it was exposed. An external security researcher identified the issue using an online service that catalogs publicly exposed cloud storage buckets. The researcher then notified the organization of the exposure.

6.19.8.3 Protect Function

There were no protective controls applied to the cloud storage bucket because it was created without going through the organization's approved cloud-deployment process. Stronger protection requires restricting who is allowed to create cloud storage and ensuring that any new resource is automatically checked against required configuration standards. Misconfiguration prevention tools can alert users or block deployments that do not meet baseline security criteria (e.g., unauthenticated public access). Encryption should be enforced for all data stored in the cloud, and strong authentication should be required for anyone accessing it. Guardrails like default-deny settings and policy-as-code approaches can also help prevent accidental exposures.

In this scenario, the organization had no protective mechanisms—such as controlled cloud storage provisioning, policy-as-code guardrails (automated rules that enforce required security configurations before deployment), or automated misconfiguration checks—because the cloud storage bucket was created outside the organization's approved cloud deployment process. As a result, the cloud storage bucket was created in a configuration that exposed internal files and data to the public internet, with no encryption or authentication to restrict access.

6.19.8.4 Detect Function

The organization did not detect the exposure until long after the cloud storage bucket had been created. There were no alerts triggered because the resource was not known to IT and not included in the organization's monitoring systems. A better detection posture would involve continuous scanning of cloud infrastructure for policy violations or signs of public exposure. External threat intelligence or attack surface management tools may also help flag unexpected cloud resources or changes in access posture. Cloud activity should be logged so systems can flag unusual download patterns or access from unfamiliar locations.

In this scenario, no detection alerts were generated because the cloud storage bucket was unknown to the organization's monitoring tools, was not included in cloud security scanning, and had no logging enabled. As a result, IT had no visibility into public access, geographic anomalies, or download activity, and the exposure remained undetected until it was reported by an external party.

6.19.8.5 Respond Function

Once the exposure was discovered, the organization had to quickly assess what information had been exposed and for how long. The response required coordination among IT, compliance, privacy, and legal teams. Incident response plans should account for misconfigurations of cloud-based assets and take note of steps for containment (e.g., access restriction or deletion), internal and external communication, forensic review, and—if required—breach notification. In this case, the lack of visibility and audit trails delayed response and made it difficult to determine exactly what had been accessed.

In this scenario, the organization scrambled to restrict public access to the cloud storage bucket, determine what data had been exposed, and coordinate with privacy, compliance, and legal teams to evaluate breach-notification obligations. Because audit trails were missing, the incident response team had limited ability to reconstruct access history, extending the time required to assess the scope of the incident.

6.19.8.6 Recover Function

After the incident, the organization needed to restore trust and correct the conditions that led to the exposure. Recovery steps included decommissioning the unauthorized cloud storage bucket, updating cloud governance policies, restricting self-service provisioning, and launching an internal awareness campaign about secure cloud use. The IT team also implemented regular scanning for external cloud assets to detect similar issues in the future.

In this scenario, the organization removed the unauthorized cloud storage bucket, updated its cloud governance framework, implemented guardrails to prevent unmanaged provisioning, and adopted continuous scanning to detect future misconfigured cloud storage. Lessons learned were incorporated into training and policy updates to reduce the likelihood of recurrence.

6.19.9 Cultural Alignment of Privacy and Cybersecurity—Working Together

Protecting sensitive health information requires cultural alignment between privacy and cybersecurity functions. When privacy and security are integrated, organizations can address data protection in a holistic sense. Privacy is a fundamental component of security, and meaningful security cannot exist without privacy. Although these functions share the common goal of protecting patient data, they often approach it from different perspectives. Security teams may seek broad visibility into operations, relying on detailed logs, audit trails, real-time alerts, and comprehensive monitoring.

Privacy teams often emphasize limiting the collection, use, and retention of sensitive or personal data. Privacy teams may want to know whether collecting data is justified, whether storing it creates risk, whether sharing it aligns with the individual's rights and expectations. Privacy focuses on authorization, necessity, and proportionality.

However, each team must understand that the other is not operating in opposition. The friction comes from different roles, different incentives, and different operational environments. That means each team needs to understand the other in very specific terms: the terminology they use, the risks they track, the controls they rely on, and the environment they operate in. Terms such as "control," "access," "retention," and "incident" can have different meanings in privacy and security contexts. But it is important for each team to understand the other's terminology and operational context.

Understanding also requires awareness of each team's priorities. Security may prioritize incident detection, mitigation, remediation, threat intelligence, system hardening, access control, network visibility, log integrity, vulnerability management, encryption, identity assurance, and system availability.

Security may respond immediately to stop a threat without fully considering how the containment approach affects individuals. For example, containment steps may expose, redirect, or copy personal data. Privacy may object to or block a technical control without recognizing how the decision affects the organization's ability to contain, isolate, or recover from a threat.

Privacy and security teams need to build a common roadmap. That means aligning on what the organization is protecting, which risks matter most, and how responsibilities are assigned across both functions. Teams also need to see how decisions are made, what tradeoffs are considered, and where each team's constraints come from.

Security teams may focus on identifying the threat vector, containing the threat, and restoring systems. Privacy teams may assess whether personal data was exposed, what obligations apply, who must be notified, and within what timeframe. A common playbook ensures both teams know how to act, when to engage each other, and how to coordinate.

6.19.10 Developing Privacy and Security Policies and Procedures

Privacy and security policies serve as foundational governance instruments for any organization that handles sensitive data, operates digital infrastructure, or engages with regulatory obligations. These policies are not optional. They define the expectations, roles, and controls required to manage risk, meet compliance requirements, and preserve the confidentiality, integrity, and availability of information systems. In the modern environment, these policies must also account for the rapid integration of AI technologies, which introduce both unprecedented opportunities and complex new risks.

Robust governance ensures that personnel are aware of the organization's policies, are trained on their content, and understand how the requirements apply to their specific responsibilities. Policies must be written with specificity and clarity. They must be structured to be enforceable and maintained through a continuous review cycle. The policy must use clear and accessible language. It must avoid technical jargon unless necessary, and when technical terms are used, they must be clearly defined and used consistently throughout. A well-governed policy must be easy to read and logically organized. It should also be focused on practical application. The layout must support usability by using structured sections that address specific functions or user groups directly. Content must be tailored to the needs, responsibilities, and risks of the intended audience. What matters to a system administrator may differ from what matters to someone in human resources, legal, or finance. The policy must acknowledge these differences in emphasis and tone.

Each policy should include a designated point of contact who can provide authoritative guidance, respond to questions, and help resolve ambiguity. Individuals must know whom to approach when they are uncertain about a policy requirement, and they must be encouraged to do so before acting on assumptions. Understanding of policies must be reinforced through training that is mandatory, timely, and role-specific. This includes onboarding for new personnel, annual refreshers, post-incident re-education, and targeted sessions following material updates to the policy itself. Where policy violations have occurred, training must be used to correct activity and address knowledge gaps. This training must be documented, tracked, and evaluated for effectiveness. A centralized system must be used to record delivery, completion, and attestation so the organization can verify compliance.

Policies should align with how work is performed in practice. If a policy diverges from actual practice, the policy must be reevaluated. A well-governed policy reflects current workflows, risk tolerance, and the practical capabilities of the workforce. Where policy deviations occur consistently, the organization must examine whether the policy is outdated, misaligned, or insufficiently communicated.

Policy development should incorporate regular feedback from personnel who use or rely on the policy. When developing or revising a policy, the organization must consult with all relevant stakeholders, including human resources, legal, compliance, operations, and any business unit that will be affected. AI governance, in particular, demands early and ongoing involvement from those deploying or managing AI tools to ensure that the policy reflects actual risk exposure, data practices, and acceptable activities.

When significant changes are expected, policies should be piloted with a representative group. A test user group or representative user base should be asked to review and apply the policy in a controlled setting. Their input should inform policy revisions prior to broad rollout of the policy.

Each policy should explain its purpose. It should describe the risks it addresses. It should also state how the policy supports the organization's operations and functions. When personnel understand the rationale behind the policy, compliance improves and enforcement becomes more straightforward.

A high number of policy exceptions may indicate that the policy needs review or adjustment. These issues may include outdated requirements, unclear expectations, or inadequate training. They must be investigated and corrected. If the documented expectations in the policy do not match actual practice, the gap must be addressed directly. The organization must determine whether the policy itself is outdated or whether the staff require additional training or clarification. Policies and procedures may need revision to align more closely with workflows, systems, or staffing models. At the same time, personnel must be re-trained to reinforce expectations, close knowledge gaps, and correct habits that have deviated from defined protocols.

Policy enforcement, version control, training, exception management, and update cycles are interconnected. Weakness in one area affects the others. For this reason, organizations should manage privacy and security policies through a single, coordinated governance program that is precise, enforceable, and regularly updated. This need increases as AI becomes more integrated into business operations, clinical systems, and administrative workflows.

6.19.10.1 When and Why to Update Policies and Procedures

Policies and procedures should be reviewed regularly to ensure they are accurate, effective, and aligned with changes in the organization's risk landscape. A fixed review schedule should be established for each policy and followed consistently. Policies should be reviewed at least annually. Some circumstances may require more frequent review. Higher risk areas, such as those involving patient data, critical infrastructure, or AI, may require semi-annual or quarterly review. Each policy and procedure should identify a responsible owner and a defined review cadence.

Organizations should also be prepared to conduct unscheduled reviews. This may be due to changes in the business, such as mergers, acquisitions, or divestitures, which can introduce new risks and data governance obligations. Significant staffing changes, including the departure of key personnel, onboarding of executives, reductions in force, or outsourcing, may also require immediate updates to policies and procedures.

Technology changes can also require updates to policies and procedures. The implementation of new systems, cloud migrations, the deployment of AI, or the adoption of zero trust architectures[123] should all be reflected in the policy framework to ensure that controls remain relevant and enforceable.

Legal and regulatory updates should be reflected in the policies on a timely basis, especially when they affect data handling, breach notification, or privacy rights. New contractual obligations with vendors, partners, or customers may also require updates to the policies and procedures.

Security incidents, especially those involving policy violations, generally warrant a review of the playbooks, plans, policies, and procedures. The lessons learned from incident investigations and post-mortem analyses provide critical insight, such as procedural gaps, enforcement weaknesses, or communication failures.

Internal or external audit findings may reveal deficiencies that require remediation, such as clarified language, improved controls, or updated policies and procedures.

Emerging threats, such as newly discovered vulnerabilities, attacker techniques, or sector-specific risks, may also require review and adjustments to policies and procedures.

Written policies should reflect the current environment and threat landscape, not what was true 12 months ago or 3 years ago. Strong governance involves both a fixed review schedule and a readiness to act when situations occur such as a breach or policy violation.

6.19.11 Anatomy and Life Cycle of Security Policies

A security policy is a formal document that defines the organization's position on a specific information security issue, such as access control, encryption, acceptable use, or remote access. Each policy must follow a consistent structure and format to support clarity, enforceability, and review. It must define specific requirements and be organized so those requirements can be applied consistently across the organization.

A policy typically begins with a title and standard metadata, including the policy ID or number, version, date of publication, last review date, and the name of the responsible author or reviewer. These metadata support version control and audit tracking.

The first section is the purpose statement. It explains the intent of the policy. It also lists key objectives, including minimizing security risk, protecting sensitive systems, and preserving business continuity. The purpose must clearly state how the policy supports confidentiality, integrity, and availability. It should also note any legal, regulatory, or contractual obligations the policy addresses.

The second section is the scope. This defines what systems, business units, data types, or environments are covered by the policy. Examples may include physical facilities, network infrastructure, mobile devices, cloud services, or specific applications. Scope must be precise. A policy does not apply to all systems by default. If certain systems are excluded, that should be stated.

The third section is applicability. Applicability defines who is subject to the policy. This may include internal staff, contractors, third-party service providers, and remote workers. Applicability must be clearly stated to avoid confusion during enforcement. For example, a policy may apply to all employees accessing production systems but exclude vendors with no system access.

Roles and responsibilities must then be set forth. It should be clear who is responsible for maintaining the policy, applying its controls, and enforcing compliance. Common roles include information security staff, department heads, system owners, human resources, and legal counsel. Each role must be linked to specific duties to support accountability.

The core section of the policy contains the policy requirements. These may include mandatory actions, required controls, or reporting expectations. Requirements must be written in clear, direct language.

Following the requirements, a policy may include references to applicable laws, regulations, and contractual obligations. It may also contain enforcement language that defines how violations will be addressed, which teams will be involved, and what disciplinary actions may apply. A contact section should also be included, designating a person or role to handle questions or provide clarification. Regarding enforcement, human resources can be consulted to help determine what the enforcement should be—especially if this is relevant to their domain, such as employee discipline, performance reviews, and the like.

Policies should be formatted for readability. Use headings, spacing, and short paragraphs to ensure that information can be found and understood quickly.

Before formal approval, the policy must be reviewed by all relevant stakeholders. This typically includes personnel from information security, privacy, information technology, finance, legal, compliance, human resources, and the affected business units. These stakeholders must be given the opportunity to review the draft and provide input to ensure the policy is accurate, practical, and aligned with operational, legal, and regulatory expectations. After feedback is collected, the policy should be revised accordingly, and the updated version must then proceed through the organization's established approval process. The approving entity may vary depending on the context, but commonly includes executive leadership, a designated governance committee, or the Chief Information Security Officer.

Before final approval, the organization should consider piloting the draft policy with a small group of representative users. This group may include operational staff, system administrators, or team leads who will be directly responsible for complying with or enforcing the policy. The purpose of the pilot is to assess whether the policy is clearly written, practical to implement, and aligned with actual workflows. Feedback from the pilot may reveal ambiguous language, unrealistic requirements, or operational conflicts that must be resolved. Any necessary revisions should be completed before the policy is submitted for final approval.

Once approved, the policy should be distributed using secure and accessible platforms. All personnel to whom the policy applies should receive it and formally acknowledge receipt and understanding. Training should occur at all applicable stages of the policy life cycle. Individuals should be trained on the content and intent of the policy before any enforcement action is taken. This includes initial training for newly affected personnel, refresher training when material changes are made, and targeted re-education following policy violations or implementation failures.

Policies should be reviewed at least annually. In some cases, a six-month or quarterly review may be appropriate, depending on the associated risk. In addition to the scheduled cycle, policies must be reviewed and updated when specific events occur. These may include the implementation of new technology, changes to staffing, a legal or regulatory update, the signing of a new contract, the outcome of a security audit, or the occurrence of a security incident. If a policy is no longer aligned with how work is performed, it must be revised.

Each policy defines how the organization protects its assets. A well-written policy supports consistent decision-making, reduces risk, and promotes accountability. A poorly written policy creates confusion, enables inconsistency, and increases exposure. For that reason, the content, structure, and maintenance of each policy must be treated with the same rigor as the systems and data it is meant to protect.

While a policy articulates what is required or prohibited, it does not describe how to carry out those requirements in operational terms. That level of detail is defined in a corresponding procedure. A procedure is a step-by-step set of instructions that explains how to implement a policy requirement in practice. Procedures are typically maintained at the departmental or operational level and are used by staff responsible for executing day-to-day tasks. For example, a policy may state that all removable media must be encrypted before use, while the procedure specifies the exact encryption tools, approval workflows, and documentation steps involved. Together, policies and procedures ensure that security expectations are both clearly defined and operationally executable.

6.19.12 Developing and Updating Cybersecurity Plans

Developing a security plan for a healthcare organization requires more than a checklist. It requires a structured, adaptable framework that reflects the organization's risk profile, regulatory environment, and operational needs. A healthcare cybersecurity plan must address technical controls. It should also integrate governance, privacy, and cross-functional dependencies.

The structure, implementation, and focus areas of an organization's security plan vary depending on its size, resources, legal obligations, contractual requirements, and technology footprint. Security plans should be treated as living documents. They should be regularly reviewed, updated, and validated through testing and feedback. *The following are examples of areas to consider.*

6.19.12.1 Governance and Organizational Roles

Effective governance begins with clearly defined responsibilities distributed across formal leadership structures and operational teams.

6.19.12.2 Cybersecurity Risk Steering Committee

The cybersecurity risk steering committee provides strategic oversight and sets cybersecurity priorities. The committee ensures that business and clinical objectives align with the organization's cybersecurity risk tolerance, including decisions involving the adoption of emerging technologies such as AI.

6.19.12.3 Information Security Leadership Team

The information security leadership team executes cybersecurity strategy under CISO leadership. It ensures accountability for control implementation, program roadmap development, and risk tracking.

6.19.12.4 Governance, Risk, and Compliance (GRC) Team

The governance, risk, and compliance (GRC) team manages the organization's internal policies. It oversees legal, regulatory, and contractual compliance obligations. The team maintains audit readiness and updates and tracks the enterprise risk register. It also governs third-party security and compliance activities.

6.19.12.5 Privacy and Data Protection Team

The privacy and data protection team ensures compliance with the HIPAA Privacy Rule and other applicable privacy and data protection laws, regulations, and contractual requirements. The team manages the organization's privacy incident response process. It oversees de-identification and re-identification safeguards and implements data minimization practices across the enterprise.

6.19.12.6 Security Engineering Team

The security engineering team is responsible for designing, implementing, and maintaining the organization's security technology architecture. This team builds and supports the technical controls that protect systems, networks, applications, and data across the enterprise.

6.19.12.7 Security Operations Center (SOC)

The security operations center (SOC) conducts continuous monitoring, log and telemetry analysis, alert triage, and incident escalation using SIEM and Security Orchestration, Automation, and Response (SOAR) platforms; endpoint detection and response (EDR) platforms; and other monitoring tools to identify and respond to security events.

6.19.12.8 Incident Response and Threat Hunting Team

The incident response and threat hunting team conducts forensic investigations, contains active security incidents, performs root cause analysis, and carries out adversary hunting activities to identify undetected malicious activity across systems, networks, hosts, and endpoints.

6.19.12.9 Identity and Access Management (IAM) Team

The identity and access management (IAM) team oversees the full life cycle of digital identities and access rights across the organization. The team manages identity governance. It enforces strong authentication methods including MFA and passwordless authentication such as FIDO2. The team also administers privileged access management (PAM) controls for high-risk accounts. It conducts routine access reviews and ensures timely provisioning and deprovisioning of user accounts. The team also implements just-in-time (JIT) access to minimize standing privileges and reduce overall access-related risk.

6.19.12.10 Third Party Risk and C-SCRM Team

The third-party risk and C-SCRM team evaluates and monitors the security posture of vendors, partners, and other external entities that support the organization. The team manages third party cybersecurity and privacy requirements; it ensures that contractual obligations are aligned with organization's risk expectations with input from procurement, legal, compliance, and business owners.

6.19.12.11 Insider Threat Management Team

The insider threat management team is responsible for detecting, assessing, and responding to risks posed by workforce members, contractors, vendors, and others with trusted access or knowledge. The team uses behavioral analytics, user activity monitoring, and contextual risk indicators to detect unusual or policy violating activity. It conducts investigations with human resources, legal, privacy, compliance, and information security to ensure that actions are handled consistently in accordance with the organization's policies and applicable requirements.

6.19.12.12 Cross-Functional Dependencies

Security teams need to collaborate with liaisons in other departments since other functions are involved in activities that impact the organization's security posture. These functions help prevent incidents when they occur and include HR, Legal, IT, Operations, Governance, and Compliance. HR and Legal support insider threat handling. IT supports patching, system hardening, network segmentation, and secure deployment practices. Clinical leadership should participate in decisions where security controls may impact patient safety. Legal and compliance teams should advise on emerging obligations, breach response, and risk acceptance.

6.19.12.13 Asset Scope and Risk Management

This security plan applies to all assets across the organization, including information technology (IT) systems (e.g., EHR platforms, servers, and applications) and operational technology (OT) systems (e.g., biomedical devices, building controls, and facility networks). Each asset should be inventoried, classified, and evaluated for security risk. OT assets require tailored controls because they rely on legacy systems, have strict uptime needs, and use proprietary protocols.

Risk must be identified and assessed using structured methods. Control options must be aligned with business requirements. Risk acceptance decisions must be documented and revisited regularly. Incidents, near-misses, and deviations must be reported, analyzed, and used to strengthen overall response readiness. Security is not static. It is continuously tested by real-world conditions.

6.19.12.14 Technical Controls

Technical controls must be implemented across the enterprise. Network segmentation must separate critical systems from general access networks. Data must be encrypted at rest and in transit. Endpoint protection must be enforced. Configuration baselines must be maintained. Applications must follow secure development practices. Third party software must be vetted before deployment. Physical controls must limit access to workstations, servers, and sensitive facilities.

Cloud adoption introduces specific risks. Cloud-hosted infrastructure must be governed by well-defined configuration, access control, and visibility standards. Contracts must clarify data handling, breach reporting, and shared responsibility. Continuous monitoring is required to maintain visibility into workloads and prevent drift from secure baselines. Cloud storage buckets should also be properly configured.

Emerging technologies such as quantum computing will eventually challenge existing encryption methods. Organizations should track cryptographic standards, vendor readiness, and transition strategies to maintain long-term confidentiality and system integrity.

6.19.12.15 Privacy and Security Awareness Training and AI Literacy

All personnel including clinical staff, administrative staff, contractors, executives, and vendors must receive regular, role-appropriate privacy and security awareness training. This includes topics such as phishing resistance, secure use of mobile and remote systems, appropriate data handling, and reporting suspicious activity. Security awareness is not optional; it is foundational.

In addition, personnel must be trained in the responsible use of AI and data-driven technologies. This includes understanding how AI systems process data, what risks are introduced, and how to identify inappropriate or risky use. AI literacy must extend beyond technical teams. Anyone involved in evaluating, procuring, or using AI-enabled tools must understand the privacy and security implications of those systems.

Training programs must be tracked, regularly updated, and reinforced through testing and realistic simulations.

6.19.12.16 Operations and Preparedness

Healthcare organizations should maintain operational resilience. Remote access, patch management, and secure endpoint configuration are required. Vulnerability scans should be conducted regularly, and patches prioritized by criticality and exposure. Security awareness training should be required and reinforced through simulated attacks and education. Penetration testing should be regularly conducted.

6.19.12.17 Continuity, Crisis, and Resilience

Disaster recovery and business continuity plans should be in writing and regularly tested. Exercises should include key decision-makers, simulate realistic conditions, and validate recovery time and RPOs. Crisis communication procedures should include clear thresholds for escalation and communication responsibilities.

Resilience is demonstrated through recovery capability, adaptation to disruption, and incorporation of lessons learned. Post-event reviews and testing outcomes should be used to refine controls, procedures, and risk assumptions.

6.19.13 Change Management

A cybersecurity program should be capable of adapting to change. New technologies, modified workflows, business model changes, regulatory shifts, and organizational events such as mergers or restructurings can all introduce risk if not addressed through structured change management.

A change management framework such as ADKAR (Awareness, Desire, Knowledge, Ability, and Reinforcement) can support the successful adoption of security-related changes. This includes the rollout of new security controls, updates to policies or procedures, the deployment of new platforms, or shifts in access control models.

Organizational changes such as mergers, acquisitions, integrations, or internal restructuring create differences in access models and system baselines. A structured transition process is needed to maintain alignment with governance and control requirements.

6.19.14 Security Plan Review and Revision

The security plan should be aligned with the current environment and risk landscape. The following is a non-exhaustive list of when the security plan may be reviewed and potentially revised, in whole or in part:

- Introduction of new clinical or operational workflows
- Adoption of new technologies such as AI systems, cloud platforms, and medical IoT
- Architectural changes to infrastructure or identity models
- New or revised legal, regulatory, or contractual obligations
- Audit findings; recurring control exceptions
- Security incidents or patterns observed through monitoring or threat intelligence
- Organizational changes such as mergers and acquisitions, divestitures, or internal restructuring
- Shifts in the organization's business model, delivery model, or patient engagement strategies
- Plan maintenance and review

A regular review cadence should be established for the security plan. Any triggering event should initiate an out-of-cycle review. The review process should include representatives from information security, IT, clinical operations, legal, privacy, compliance, data governance, and executive leadership.

The purpose of the review is to determine whether the current plan still reflects operational realities, risk exposure, and regulatory expectations. If revisions are required, changes should be formally documented, version-controlled, approved by governance leadership, and communicated to affected stakeholders. Where changes affect how individuals perform their roles, training and reinforcement should follow. Documenting the review process ensures accountability and supports regulatory and audit requirements.

A maintained and actively governed cybersecurity plan is essential to remaining effective, credible, and responsive to risk. It should be treated not as a static policy document, but as a dynamic instrument of organizational resilience.

6.20 Summary—Governance

The governance of privacy and cybersecurity is shaped by technology, the legal and regulatory environment, and guidance from frameworks and standards. The U.S. Department of Health and

Human Services Office for Civil Rights (HHS OCR) enforces HIPAA, with authority to impose CMPs and enter into RAs for violations. The HIPAA Privacy Rule, Security Rule, and Breach Notification Rule establish safeguards that protect the confidentiality, integrity, and availability of health information. RSPs, including those aligned with the NIST CSF and the HICP, provide structured methods for implementing privacy and security controls.

Privacy and cybersecurity teams should operate in alignment. Each brings a distinct perspective, but they share the responsibility to protect patient data and patient safety. Strong governance depends on regularly updated policies, procedures, and cybersecurity plans that reinforce accountability, resilience, and trust.

Security plan review and revision should occur on a defined schedule and whenever events or conditions indicate that the plan is no longer aligned with current practices or risk exposure.

Notes

1 U.S. Department of Health and Human Services—Assistant Secretary for Planning and Evaluation (ASPE). *Health Insurance Portability and Accountability Act of 1996.* https://aspe.hhs.gov/reports/health-insurance-portability-accountability-act-1996.

2 HHS. *HIPAA for Professionals.* https://www.hhs.gov/hipaa/for-professionals/index.html.

3 HHS. *HIPAA for Professionals.* https://www.hhs.gov/hipaa/for-professionals/index.html.

4 The National Law Review. *HIPAA Omnibus Final Rule Highlights for Business Associates.* https://natlawreview.com/article/hipaa-omnibus-final-rule-highlights-business-associates.

5 A model business associate agreement may be found at: https://www.hhs.gov/hipaa/for-professionals/covered-entities/sample-business-associate-agreement-provisions/index.html..

However, one should consult with in-house counsel or retained outside counsel to ensure that the business associate agreement is sufficient for the intended purpose and complies with applicable laws and regulations.

6 HHS. *HIPAA and Reproductive Health.* https://www.hhs.gov/hipaa/for-professionals/special-topics/reproductive-health/index.html.

7 See also The Freedom of Access to Clinic Entrances (FACE) Act, 18 U.S.C. § 248 (2025) (a federal law protecting access to reproductive healthcare facilities and providers).

8 HHS. *Summary of the HIPAA Privacy Rule.* https://www.hhs.gov/hipaa/for-professionals/privacy/laws-regulations/index.html.

9 HHS. *The Security Rule.* https://www.hhs.gov/hipaa/for-professionals/security/index.html.

10 HHS. *Breach Notification Rule.* https://www.hhs.gov/hipaa/for-professionals/breach-notification/index.html.

11 HHS. *Office for Civil Rights (OCR).* https://www.hhs.gov/ocr/index.html.

12 45 C.F.R. §§ 160.400-160.426 (2025) (imposition of civil money penalties).

13 HHS. *Covered Entities and Business Associates.* https://www.hhs.gov/hipaa/for-professionals/covered-entities/index.html.

14 HHS. *Covered Entities and Business Associates.* https://www.hhs.gov/hipaa/for-professionals/covered-entities/index.html.

15 HHS. *Covered Entities and Business Associates.* https://www.hhs.gov/hipaa/for-professionals/covered-entities/index.html.

16 HHS. *Covered Entities and Business Associates.* https://www.hhs.gov/hipaa/for-professionals/covered-entities/index.html.

17 HHS. *Covered Entities and Business Associates.* https://www.hhs.gov/hipaa/for-professionals/covered-entities/index.html.

18 HHS. *Covered Entities and Business Associates.* https://www.hhs.gov/hipaa/for-professionals/covered-entities/index.html.

19 HHS. *Covered Entities and Business Associates.* https://www.hhs.gov/hipaa/for-professionals/covered-entities/index.html.

See also 45 C.F.R. § 164.308(b)(1) (2025) ("A covered entity is not required to obtain such satisfactory assurances from a business associate that is a subcontractor.").

20 HHS. *Covered Entities and Business Associates.* https://www.hhs.gov/hipaa/for-professionals/covered-entities/index.html.

21 To date, there have been no (publicly reported) enforcement actions on shadow AI. However, the use of shadow AI could potentially violate HIPAA if appropriate safeguards and assurances are not in place.

22 HIPAA Journal. *The 10 Most Common HIPAA Violations You Should Avoid.* https://www.hipaajournal.com/common-hipaa-violations/.

23 Federal Register. *Medicare Program: Modernizing and Clarifying the Physician Self-Referral Regulations.* https://www.federalregister.gov/documents/2020/12/02/2020-26140/medicare-program-modernizing-and-clarifying-the-physician-self-referral-regulations.

24 Federal Register. *Medicare and State Health Care Programs: Fraud and Abuse; Revisions to Safe Harbors under the Anti-Kickback Statute, and Civil Monetary Penalty Rules Regarding Beneficiary Inducements.* https://www.federalregister.gov/documents/2020/12/02/2020-26072/medicare-and-state-health-care-programs-fraud-and-abuse-revisions-to-safe-harbors-under-the.

25 U.S. Congress. *Public Law 116–321: Recognition of Security Practices (H.R. 7898),* 116th Cong., 2d sess. (January 5, 2021), 134 Stat. 5072, codified at 42 U.S.C. § 17941 (2025). https://www.congress.gov/116/plaws/publ321/PLAW-116publ321.pdf.

26 U.S. Congress. *Public Law 116–321: Recognition of Security Practices (H.R. 7898),* 116th Cong., 2d sess. (January 5, 2021), 134 Stat. 5072, codified at 42 U.S.C. § 17941 (2025). https://www.congress.gov/116/plaws/publ321/PLAW-116publ321.pdf.

27 U.S. Congress. *Public Law 116–321: Recognition of Security Practices (H.R. 7898),* 116th Cong., 2d sess. (January 5, 2021), 134 Stat. 5072, codified at 42 U.S.C. § 17941 (2025).

28 BankInfoSecurity. *How "Recognized Security Practices" Fit with HIPAA Actions.* https://www.bankinfosecurity.com/hhs-ocr-guidance-a-20395.

29 YouTube. *OCR Recognized Security Practices Video Presentation.* https://www.youtube.com/watch?v=e2wG7jUiRjE.

See also HHS. *Security Guidance Material.* https://www.hhs.gov/hipaa/for-professionals/security/guidance/index.html.

30 YouTube. *OCR Recognized Security Practices Video Presentation* https://www.youtube.com/watch?v=e2wG7jUiRjE.

See also HHS. *Security Guidance Material.* https://www.hhs.gov/hipaa/for-professionals/security/guidance/index.html.

31 YouTube. *OCR Recognized Security Practices Video Presentation.* https://www.youtube.com/watch?v=e2wG7jUiRjE.

See also HHS. *Security Guidance Material.* https://www.hhs.gov/hipaa/for-professionals/security/guidance/index.html.

32 YouTube. *OCR Recognized Security Practices Video Presentation.* https://www.youtube.com/watch?v=e2wG7jUiRjE.

See also HHS. *Security Guidance Material.* https://www.hhs.gov/hipaa/for-professionals/security/guidance/index.html.

33 YouTube. *OCR Recognized Security Practices Video Presentation.* https://www.youtube.com/watch?v=e2wG7jUiRjE.

See also HHS. *Security Guidance Material.* https://www.hhs.gov/hipaa/for-professionals/security/guidance/index.html.

See also BankInfoSecurity. *How "Recognized Security Practices" Fit with HIPAA Actions.* https://www.bankinfosecurity.com/hhs-ocr-guidance-a-20395.

34 HHS. *Guidance Regarding Methods for De-identification of Protected Health Information in Accordance with the Health Insurance Portability and Accountability Act (HIPAA) Privacy Rule.* https://www.hhs.gov/hipaa/for-professionals/special-topics/de-identification/index.html.

35 HHS. *Guidance Regarding Methods for De-identification of Protected Health Information in Accordance with the Health Insurance Portability and Accountability Act (HIPAA) Privacy Rule.* https://www.hhs.gov/hipaa/for-professionals/special-topics/de-identification/index.html.
36 HHS. *Guidance Regarding Methods for De-identification of Protected Health Information in Accordance with the Health Insurance Portability and Accountability Act (HIPAA) Privacy Rule.* https://www.hhs.gov/hipaa/for-professionals/special-topics/de-identification/index.html.
37 45 C.F.R. § 164.501 (2025).
38 45 C.F.R. § 164.501 (2025).
39 45 C.F.R. § 164.501 (2025).
40 HHS. *Authorizations.* https://www.hhs.gov/hipaa/for-professionals/faq/authorizations/index.html.
41 HHS. *Individuals' Right under HIPAA to Access Their Health Information.* 45 C.F.R. § 164.524. https://www.hhs.gov/hipaa/for-professionals/privacy/guidance/access/index.html.
42 HHS. *Right to an Accounting of Disclosures.* https://www.hhs.gov/hipaa/for-professionals/faq/right-to-an-accounting-of-disclosures/index.html.
43 HHS. *Summary of the HIPAA Privacy Rule.* https://www.hhs.gov/hipaa/for-professionals/privacy/laws-regulations/index.html.
44 HHS. *Right to Request a Restriction.* https://www.hhs.gov/hipaa/for-professionals/faq/right-to-request-a-restriction/index.html.
45 HHS. *Right to Request a Restriction.* https://www.hhs.gov/hipaa/for-professionals/faq/right-to-request-a-restriction/index.html.
46 HHS. *Individuals' Right under HIPAA to Access their Health Information 45 C.F.R. § 164.524.* https://www.hhs.gov/hipaa/for-professionals/privacy/guidance/access/index.html.
47 HHS. *The Security Rule.* https://www.hhs.gov/hipaa/for-professionals/security/index.html.
48 HHS. *The Security Rule.* https://www.hhs.gov/hipaa/for-professionals/security/index.html.
49 HHS. *The Security Rule.* https://www.hhs.gov/hipaa/for-professionals/security/index.html.
50 HHS. *The Security Rule.* https://www.hhs.gov/hipaa/for-professionals/security/index.html.
51 HHS. *The Security Rule.* https://www.hhs.gov/hipaa/for-professionals/security/index.html.
52 HHS. *The Security Rule.* https://www.hhs.gov/hipaa/for-professionals/security/index.html.
53 45 C.F.R. § 164.308 (2025).
54 HHS. *The Security Rule.* https://www.hhs.gov/hipaa/for-professionals/security/index.html.
55 45 C.F.R. § 164.308 (2025).
56 HHS. *The Security Rule.* https://www.hhs.gov/hipaa/for-professionals/security/index.html.
57 A model business associate agreement may be found at: https://www.hhs.gov/hipaa/for-professionals/covered-entities/sample-business-associate-agreement-provisions/index.html.

However, one should consult with in-house counsel or retained outside counsel to ensure that the business associate agreement is sufficient for the intended purpose and complies with applicable laws and regulations.

58 This refers to adequate separation between the group health plan and the plan sponsor including the separation of functions and personnel between the group health plan and the plan sponsor. The goal is to prevent unauthorized or improper use of health information by entities that are not directly involved in administering the group health plan. *Cf.*, HHS. *HIPAA Privacy and Security and Workplace Wellness Programs.* www.hhs.gov/hipaa/for-professionals/privacy/workplace-wellness/index.html.
59 45 C.F.R. § 164.316 (Policies and Procedures and Documentation Requirements).
60 HHS. *The Security Rule.* https://www.hhs.gov/hipaa/for-professionals/security/index.html.
61 U.S. Congress. *Public Law 116–321: Recognition of Security Practices (H.R. 7898)*, 116th Cong., 2d sess. (January 5, 2021), 134 Stat. 5072, codified at 42 U.S.C. § 17941 (2025). https://www.congress.gov/116/plaws/publ321/PLAW-116publ321.pdf.
62 HHS 405(d) Program. *Health Industry Cybersecurity Practices.* https://405d.hhs.gov/cornerstone/hicp.
63 U.S. Congress. *Cybersecurity Information Sharing Act of 2015*, Pub. L. No. 114-113 (Dec. 18, 2015), is codified at 6 U.S.C. § 1501 *et seq.* (2025). Section 405 of the Cybersecurity Act of 2015 ("Improving cybersecurity in the health care industry") is dedicated to healthcare cybersecurity and was codified at 6 U.S.C. § 1533 (2025).

See also H.R. 5371 § 149 (2025). *Continuing Appropriations, Agriculture, Legislative Branch, Military Construction and Veterans Affairs, and Extensions Act, 2026*, 119th Cong.

64 HIPAA Journal. *OCR Explains HITECH Recognized Security Practices and How to Demonstrate They are in Place.* https://www.hipaajournal.com/ocr-hitech-recognized-security-practices/.

65 HIPAA Journal. *OCR Explains HITECH Recognized Security Practices and How to Demonstrate They are in Place.* https://www.hipaajournal.com/ocr-hitech-recognized-security-practices/.

66 As required by section 13402(e)(4) of the HITECH Act, the Secretary of Health and Human Services must post a list of breaches of unsecured protected health information affecting 500 or more individuals. This list, including currently investigated breaches reported within the past 24 months, is available at: https://ocrportal.hhs.gov/ocr/breach/breach_report.jsf.

67 HHS. *Breach Notification Rule.* https://www.hhs.gov/hipaa/for-professionals/breach-notification/index.html.
See also 45 C.F.R. §§ 164.400–164.414 (2025) (HIPAA breach notification rule).

68 HHS. *Breach Notification Rule.* https://www.hhs.gov/hipaa/for-professionals/breach-notification/index.html.
See also 45 C.F.R. §§ 164.400–164.414 (2025) (HIPAA breach notification rule).

69 HHS. *Breach Notification Rule.* https://www.hhs.gov/hipaa/for-professionals/breach-notification/index.html.
See also 45 C.F.R. §§ 164.400–164.414 (2025) (HIPAA breach notification rule).

70 HHS. Guidance Specifying the Technologies and Methodologies That Render Protected *Health Information Unusable, Unreadable, or Indecipherable to Unauthorized Individuals.* 74 Fed. Reg. 19006 (April 27, 2009).
See also 45 C.F.R. 164.402 ("unsecured protected health information").
See also HITECH Act 13402(h).

71 HHS. *Breach Notification Rule.* https://www.hhs.gov/hipaa/for-professionals/breach-notification/index.html.
See also 45 C.F.R. §§ 164.400–164.414 (2025) (HIPAA breach notification rule).

72 HHS. *Breach Notification Rule.* https://www.hhs.gov/hipaa/for-professionals/breach-notification/index.html.
See also 45 C.F.R. §§ 164.400–164.414 (2025) (HIPAA breach notification rule).

73 HHS. *Breach Notification Rule.* https://www.hhs.gov/hipaa/for-professionals/breach-notification/index.html.
See also 45 C.F.R. §§ 164.400–164.414 (2025) (HIPAA breach notification rule).

74 HHS. *Breach Notification Rule.* https://www.hhs.gov/hipaa/for-professionals/breach-notification/index.html.
See also 45 C.F.R. §§ 164.400–164.414 (2025) (HIPAA breach notification rule).

75 HHS. *Breach Notification Rule.* https://www.hhs.gov/hipaa/for-professionals/breach-notification/index.html.
See also 45 C.F.R. §§ 164.400–164.414 (2025) (HIPAA breach notification rule).

76 A Caesar cipher is an ancient form of cryptography that Julius Caesar is said to have used. ScienceDirect. *Caesar Cipher.* https://www.sciencedirect.com/topics/computer-science/caesar-cipher.
Note: ROT +3 means shifting each letter in the plaintext three positions forward in the alphabet. The Caesar cipher is commonly used to explain in simple terms the foundation of cryptography. It is not secure by modern standards, but it serves as an example of how plaintext can be transformed into ciphertext through a consistent substitution method.

77 Cryptii. *Caesar Cipher: Encode and Decode Online.* https://cryptii.com/pipes/caesar-cipher.
See also *Caesar Cipher Wheel Template.* https://news.library.mcgill.ca/wp-content/uploads/2023/01/Cipher-Wheel-Template.pdf.

78 NIST. *NIST SP 800-57 Part 1 Rev. 5: Recommendation for Key Management: Part 1—General.* https://csrc.nist.gov/pubs/sp/800/57/pt1/r5/final.

79 For example, state data breach notification laws, the European Union's General Data Protection Regulation (GDPR), and the Federal Trade Commission's Health Breach Notification Rule, each impose distinct requirements. These requirements include whether notification is required, who must

be notified, the applicable timelines, and what information must be provided. In-house counsel, and outside legal counsel when needed, can help determine whether notification is required, when it must occur, and in which context.

State breach notification laws may be found here: https://www.ncsl.org/technology-and-communication/security-breach-notification-laws.

Information on breach notification guidelines may be found here: https://www.edps.europa.eu/data-protection/our-role-supervisor/personal-data-breach_en. Information on the FTC Health Breach Notification Rule can be found here: https://www.ftc.gov/legal-library/browse/rules/health-breach-notification-rule.

80 For example, *see* California Confidentiality of Medical Information Act (CMIA), Cal. Civ. Code §§ 56–56.37 (2025).

See also Texas Medical Privacy Act, Tex. Health & Safety Code §§ 181.001 *et seq.* (Texas Medical Privacy Act); *see also* Texas State Law Library. *Privacy and Personal Information—Medical Records.* https://guides.sll.texas.gov/privacy-and-personal-information/medical-records.

See also Wash. Rev. Code §§ 19.373.005 *et seq.* (Washington My Health My Data Act); Washington State Bar News. *The Washington My Health My Data Act: Complying With New and Novel Protection for Health-Related Data.* https://wabarnews.org/2024/04/09/the-washington-my-health-my-data-act/.

81 NIST. *Privacy Framework.* https://www.nist.gov/privacy-framework.

82 NIST. *Privacy Framework.* https://www.nist.gov/privacy-framework.

83 NIST. *Privacy Framework.* https://www.nist.gov/privacy-framework.

84 NIST. *Privacy Framework.* https://www.nist.gov/privacy-framework.

85 NIST. *Privacy Framework.* https://www.nist.gov/privacy-framework.

86 NIST. *Privacy Framework.* https://www.nist.gov/privacy-framework.

87 NIST. *Privacy Framework.* https://www.nist.gov/privacy-framework.

88 NIST. *Privacy Framework.* https://www.nist.gov/privacy-framework.

89 NIST. *Privacy Framework.* https://www.nist.gov/privacy-framework.

90 NIST. *Privacy Framework.* https://www.nist.gov/privacy-framework.

91 Federal Information Security Modernization Act of 2014, Pub. L. No. 113-283 (codified as amended at 44 U.S.C. §§ 3551 *et seq.*).

See also CISA. *Federal Information Security Modernization Act.* https://www.cisa.gov/topics/cyber-threats-and-advisories/federal-information-security-modernization-act.

92 NIST. *Journey to the NIST Cybersecurity Framework (CSF) 2.0—Workshop #3.* https://www.nist.gov/news-events/events/2023/09/journey-nist-cybersecurity-framework-csf-20-workshop-3.

93 NIST. *NIST Releases Cybersecurity Framework Version 1.0* https://www.nist.gov/news-events/news/2014/02/nist-releases-cybersecurity-framework-version-10.

94 NIST. *History and Creation of the CSF 1.1.* https://www.nist.gov/cyberframework/history-and-creation-framework.

95 NIST. *NIST Releases Version 1.1 of Its Popular Cybersecurity Framework.* https://www.nist.gov/news-events/news/2018/04/nist-releases-version-11-its-popular-cybersecurity-framework.

96 NIST. *The NIST Cybersecurity Framework (CSF) 2.0. Fig. 2.* https://nvlpubs.nist.gov/nistpubs/CSWP/NIST.CSWP.29.pdf.

97 NIST. *NIST SP 800-160, Vol. 1, Rev. 1: Engineering Trustworthy Secure Systems.* https://csrc.nist.gov/pubs/sp/800/160/v1/r1/final.

98 NIST. *Developing Cyber-Resilient Systems: A Systems Security Engineering Approach (SP 800-160, Vol. 2, Rev. 1).* https://csrc.nist.gov/pubs/sp/800/160/v2/r1/final.

99 Please see generally NIST. *The NIST Cybersecurity Framework (CSF) 2.0.* https://nvlpubs.nist.gov/nistpubs/CSWP/NIST.CSWP.29.pdf.

See also NIST. *NIST Cybersecurity Framework 2.0: Small Business Quick Start Guide (SP 1300).* https://csrc.nist.gov/pubs/sp/1300/final.

See also NIST. NIST CSF 2.0 Implementation Examples. https://www.nist.gov/document/csf-20-implementations-pdf.

100 NIST. *NIST Cybersecurity Framework 2.0: Quick-Start Guide for Cybersecurity Supply Chain Risk Management (C-SCRM).* https://www.nist.gov/publications/nist-cybersecurity-framework-20-quick-start-guide-cybersecurity-supply-chain-risk.

101 NIST. *NIST Cybersecurity Framework 2.0: Cybersecurity, Enterprise Risk Management, and Workforce Management Quick Start Guide (SP 1308—second public draft).* https://csrc.nist.gov/pubs/sp/1308/2pd.

102 NIST. *NIST SP 1303:* Cybersecurity Framework 2.0: *Enterprise Risk Management Quick Start Guide.* https://csrc.nist.gov/pubs/sp/1303/final.

103 NIST. *NIST SP 1303:* Cybersecurity Framework 2.0: *Enterprise Risk Management Quick Start Guide.* https://csrc.nist.gov/pubs/sp/1303/final.

104 NIST. *NIST SP 800-88 Rev. 1: Guidelines for Media Sanitization.* https://www.nist.gov/publications/nist-special-publication-800-88-revision-1-guidelines-media-sanitization.

105 Federal Information Security Modernization Act of 2014, Pub. L. No. 113-283 (codified as amended at 44 U.S.C. §§ 3551 *et seq.*). https://www.cisa.gov/topics/cyber-threats-and-advisories/federal-information-security-modernization-act

See also Cybersecurity and Infrastructure Security Agency (CISA). *Federal Information Security Modernization Act.* https://www.cisa.gov/topics/cyber-threats-and-advisories/federal-information-security-modernization-act.

106 National Institute of Standards and Technology (NIST*). Journey to the NIST Cybersecurity Framework (CSF) 2.0—Workshop #3.* https://www.nist.gov/news-events/events/2023/09/journey-nist-cybersecurity-framework-csf-20-workshop-3

107 NIST. *NIST SP 800-30 Rev. 1: Guide for Conducting Risk Assessments.* https://csrc.nist.gov/pubs/sp/800/30/r1/final.

108 FAIR Institute. *How to Use FAIR to Mature Your Cyber Risk Management Program with NIST CSF 2.0: A Practical Guide.* https://www.fairinstitute.org/hubfs/FAIR%20Institute%20--%20Use%20FAIR%20to%20Mature%20Your%20Cyber%20Risk%20Management%20Program%20(March%202025).pdf.

See also AUJAS Cybersecurity. *Introduction to Information Security Risk Assessment Using FAIR (Factor Analysis of Information Risk).* https://cdn2.hubspot.net/hubfs/2139287/Introduction-to-Information-Security-Risk-Assessment-using-FAIR.pdf.

109 NIST. *The NIST Cybersecurity Framework (CSF) 2.0.* https://nvlpubs.nist.gov/nistpubs/CSWP/NIST.CSWP.29.pdf.

110 A widely used change management model is the Prosci ADKAR® model, which stands for Awareness, Desire, Knowledge, Ability, and Reinforcement. ADKAR is a registered service mark of Prosci, Inc. https://www.prosci.com/methodology/adkar.

111 NIST. *The NIST Cybersecurity Framework (CSF) 2.0.* https://nvlpubs.nist.gov/nistpubs/CSWP/NIST.CSWP.29.pdf.

112 HHS HC3. *Living off the Land (LOTL).* https://www.hhs.gov/sites/default/files/living-off-land-attacks-tlpclear.pdf.

113 International Medical Device Regulators Forum. *Principles and Practices for the Cybersecurity of Legacy Medical Devices.* https://www.imdrf.org/documents/principles-and-practices-cybersecurity-legacy-medical-devices.

114 NIST. *The NIST Cybersecurity Framework (CSF) 2.0.* https://nvlpubs.nist.gov/nistpubs/CSWP/NIST.CSWP.29.pdf.

115 InfraGard is one example of a vetted community that shares information. InfraGard. *Partnership for Protection.* https://www.infragard.org/.

116 Atlassian. *Escalation Path Template.* https://www.atlassian.com/incident-management/on-call/escalation-path-template#what-is-an-escalation-path-template.

117 According to NIST Special Publication 800-53 Rev. 5, reimaging is one method of restoring system components to a known, operational state as part of system recovery and reconstitution.

National Institute of Standards and Technology. *NIST SP 800-53, Rev. 5: Security and Privacy Controls for Information Systems and Organizations. Control CP-10, System Recovery and Reconstitution.* https://nvlpubs.nist.gov/nistpubs/SpecialPublications/NIST.SP.800-53r5.pdf.

118 NIST. *Guide to Intrusion Detection and Prevention Systems (IDPS) (SP 800-94).* https://csrc.nist.gov/pubs/sp/800/94/final.

119 DMARC.org. *Overview.* https://dmarc.org/overview/.

120 DOJ. *International Kill Chain Process*. https://www.justice.gov/elderjustice/media/1364056/dl. See also Europol. *Guide: Take Control of Your Digital Life. Don't Be a Victim of Cyber Scams! 7 Most Common Financial Scams & How to Avoid Them*. https://www.europol.europa.eu/cyberscams.

121 The Wall Street Journal. *Fraudsters Used AI to Mimic CEO's Voice in Unusual Cybercrime Case: Scams Using Artificial Intelligence Are a New Challenge for Companies*. https://www.wsj.com/articles/fraudsters-use-ai-to-mimic-ceos-voice-in-unusual-cybercrime-case-11567157402.

122 U.S. Department of Health and Human Services—Healthcare Cybersecurity Coordination Center (HC3). *Social Engineering Attacks Targeting the HPH Sector*. https://www.hhs.gov/sites/default/files/social-engineering-targeting-the-hph-sector-tlpclear.pdf.

123 NIST. *Implementing a Zero Trust Architecture: High-Level Document (SP 1800-35)*. https://csrc.nist.gov/pubs/sp/1800/35/final.

Chapter 7

Board of Directors

Cybersecurity has become a core enterprise risk management issue that demands informed oversight from boards of directors, particularly in sectors such as healthcare, where the implications of a cyberattack can include financial losses, disruptions to patient care, and violations of public trust. The board plays an important role in ensuring that cybersecurity is integrated across organizational priorities and decision-making.[1]

7.1 Cybersecurity as an Enterprise Risk

Cybersecurity supports the continued operation of systems and ensures that information and assets are properly protected according to three core principles: confidentiality, integrity, and availability. These foundational principles support the delivery of patient care and help maintain the quality and reliability of healthcare services. The threat landscape continues to evolve, as ransomware attacks targeting electronic health records, vulnerabilities in connected medical devices, insider threats, and supply chain compromises are all on the rise. In light of this, boards should approach cybersecurity with the same level of seriousness as financial, legal, operational, and reputational risks.

The board sets the direction and expectations for the organization's cybersecurity posture. This includes overseeing cybersecurity risk governance, ensuring the allocation of appropriate resources, and holding leadership accountable for protecting the organization's digital and physical infrastructure. Board engagement should not be occasional or reactive. Instead, cybersecurity oversight should be a consistent and structured part of board governance, aligned with the organization's strategic priorities and an ever-changing regulatory and threat environment.[2]

7.2 The Role of Boards in Addressing Cybersecurity Risk

Boards are fiduciaries responsible for overseeing the organization—this necessarily includes oversight of risks and cybersecurity risks in particular. Cybersecurity has become a significant business risk for healthcare organizations and their third party vendors. Healthcare organizations rely heavily on third party vendors, making supply chain cybersecurity an essential area of concern.

Boards may wish to evaluate cybersecurity governance structures, oversee incident response capabilities, assess the protection of critical assets, and confirm alignment with recognized

DOI: 10.4324/9781003366560-7

frameworks such as the NIST Cybersecurity Framework. Cybersecurity oversight should help support risk mitigation and also encourage innovation, preparedness, and resilience.

7.3 Embedding Cybersecurity Expertise at the Board Level

Boards should embed cybersecurity expertise into the governance structure.[3] This can be achieved by appointing directors with cybersecurity backgrounds, leveraging independent advisors, or establishing dedicated risk or technology committees. Boards should not assume that every director must be a technical expert; instead, they should ensure the board collectively possesses adequate understanding to evaluate cybersecurity issues within a business context.

Training and periodic briefings should be provided to maintain literacy and to allow the board to ask informed questions. Independent experts can also be invited to provide external perspectives, support objectivity, and serve as resources during major decisions or crisis events.

7.4 Addressing Cybersecurity as a Recurring Board Agenda Item

Cybersecurity oversight should be addressed as a recurring agenda item in board meetings. Regular updates provide directors with the visibility needed to understand emerging threats, track the effectiveness of mitigation strategies, and assess alignment with business objectives.

Briefings may include summaries of incident trends, regulatory updates, risk assessments, third-party vulnerabilities, and progress on strategic initiatives. Metrics may include detection and response times, audit scores, employee security awareness training results, and implementation status of major security projects. Above all, it is important to tell the story in an accurate, precise, and understandable manner to the board.

By keeping cybersecurity on the board agenda, the board reinforces the message that it is a priority and an integral part of organizational governance. This cadence also allows directors to identify patterns (e.g., recurring challenges that the board might be able to help solve), ask questions about preparedness or incidents, and support continuous improvement.

7.5 Aligning Strategic Decisions with Cybersecurity Risk

Boards should request a cybersecurity assessment before the organization proceeds with any significant initiative that could change the organization's security posture. Transitions in security leadership, augmentation of security functions, organizational restructurings, divestitures, and mergers or acquisitions are all examples of strategic actions that can directly impact the effectiveness and stability of the cybersecurity program.

Integrating cybersecurity considerations into strategic decision-making helps the organization reduce unnecessary exposure and improve its ability to carry out initiatives in a secure and resilient manner.

7.6 Cybersecurity as a Business Enabler

Boards should encourage executive leadership and management to view cybersecurity as a business enabler.[4] Strong cybersecurity supports safe digital transformation, protects patient data, ensures continuity of operations, and builds stakeholder trust.

Healthcare organizations are increasingly reliant on digital systems. These technologies provide value only if they are secure, reliable, and trustworthy. A strong security posture allows the organization to scale innovation confidently, attract partnerships, and differentiate itself in the market.

7.7 Best Practices for Directors

Under normal conditions, boards may establish a regular cadence for cybersecurity discussions, review dashboards and key performance indicators, and challenge leadership to demonstrate progress in improving resilience. Directors may participate in tabletop exercises and remain current through briefings or independent learning.

During active incidents, boards of directors should be kept informed on a timely basis about the cybersecurity incident's scope, impact, and response. In the case of significant security incidents, the board may be involved in assessing whether a cybersecurity incident is material.[5] They may also be involved in decisions related to external communications to regulators, shareholders, the public, or others. Many healthcare organizations have board oversight over cybersecurity risks.[6]

7.8 Board Communications

Three categories of board communication, including routine briefings, crisis briefings, and educational sessions help ensure that directors are well-informed, engaged, and prepared to exercise their responsibilities in all conditions. Communication with the board should be intentional and strategic. By equipping directors with the right information at the right time and in the right format, organizational leaders strengthen governance, resilience, and trust.

The board of directors plays a foundational role in building and sustaining cybersecurity maturity across the healthcare enterprise. Through informed oversight and decision-making, embedded cybersecurity expertise on the board (if feasible), and strategic alignment, boards ensure that cybersecurity is a priority for the organization. Those who report to the board should provide concise, relevant, and timely information that supports oversight and decision-making, as appropriate, in normal circumstances and during active incidents.

7.9 Presenting to the Board of Directors

Reporting to the board of directors requires a tailored approach that reflects the board's strategic role and the gravity of cybersecurity as an enterprise risk. Effective communication depends on context, whether the briefing is routine, incident-driven, or educational in nature.

During normal operations, cybersecurity briefings may provide a structured overview of the organization's current risk posture, incident trends, and strategic alignment. Metrics may be used to tell a story. The overview may include key performance indicators regarding security incidents, audits, compliance with applicable laws and regulations, and ongoing risk mitigation efforts. Presenters may cover what has changed since the last report, what progress has been made, and what emerging risks are on the horizon. Presenters may use visual dashboards and focus on how cybersecurity impacts operations, finances, legal exposure, and patient trust. Such briefings may occur quarterly or in conjunction with specific risk events, such as annual audit cycles or budget planning.

7.9.1 Active Cyber Incidents

During an active cyber incident, the objective is to help the board have oversight over the situation and support time-sensitive decision-making. Presentations to the board may include the following information: cybersecurity incident overview, operational impacts, clinical, legal, regulatory, and contractual considerations, mitigation actions underway, and anticipated developments. It is important to be clear, direct, and accurate. Technical jargon should be avoided unless absolutely necessary, and any such technical jargon should be precisely defined in a manner that can be understood by the board of directors. While some boards of directors have at least one director with cybersecurity expertise, this is not always the case.

7.9.2 Regular Education

Board members should periodically receive cybersecurity education. The goal of educating the board on cybersecurity is to build a foundational understanding so that directors can provide informed oversight and so that board decisions are better informed as well. Educational sessions should be concise, interactive, and focused on realistic scenarios. Topics may include evolving ransomware tactics, third-party risk, cloud security, deepfakes, and the current risk landscape. Common questions may include "How are we doing compared to our peers? What else is going on in the industry?"

Case studies from within the industry help ground these sessions in practical implications. Educational briefings should also include simulated tabletop exercises where directors participate in cyber incident scenarios. These exercises strengthen preparedness and clarify roles during crises. Training should be conducted regularly to ensure that board members are up-to-date with their knowledge and understanding of cybersecurity matters.

7.10 Beyond the Board—Building a Culture of Cybersecurity

Cybersecurity culture is shaped by leaders across the organization. Leaders should enable a culture of cybersecurity within their domains and also consider cybersecurity matters when working with their peers in the organization.

For example, the general counsel is a respected decision-maker within the organization. Some organizations ensure that the cybersecurity team works with legal counsel that is familiar with cybersecurity-related matters. Some organizations embed a cybersecurity attorney within the cybersecurity team to support day-to-day needs. This helps to ensure that cybersecurity enables the business and the business enables cybersecurity.

The work of privacy teams also frequently intersects with cybersecurity. Cybersecurity incidents often have privacy implications such as data breaches or exposures of confidential, protected, proprietary, or sensitive information. Therefore, privacy teams can help support the cybersecurity team by lending their privacy expertise to incidents.

Clinical teams, and the professionals who support them including clinical engineers, are focused on patient safety. In many hospitals, up to fifty percent of network-connected devices are medical devices. There are also electronic health records and other systems that create, receive, store, or transmit patient data. These systems affect care delivery and the coordination of care. Clinicians and staff rely on the confidentiality, integrity, and availability of this information. Cybersecurity is vital to patient safety.[7]

Cybersecurity teams can design the technical architecture, implement controls, and monitor for threats. They can build the foundation. But sustaining a strong security posture depends on leadership. Leaders and those who report to them carry the responsibility of reinforcing safe and secure practices, making risk-informed decisions, and ensuring that cybersecurity considerations are integrated into everyday operations. Culture is shaped by what leaders prioritize, how they allocate resources, and the example they set in their own practices.

7.11 Summary—Board of Directors

Cybersecurity risk requires active oversight at the board level. This can be facilitated by ensuring appropriate cybersecurity expertise is represented at the board level. Cybersecurity matters should also be a recurring agenda item for the board of directors.

Directors benefit from timely reporting on emerging risks, significant incidents, and security posture. During active cyber incidents, boards should be briefed promptly to support informed decision-making and oversight of response activities. In normal times, the board of directors should be educated on emerging and current cybersecurity threats and mitigations.

Beyond the boardroom, leadership at all levels contributes to a culture of cybersecurity. Executives and managers are responsible for reinforcing security priorities through policies, training, and accountability measures. When boards and leadership operate in alignment, healthcare organizations are better positioned to protect sensitive information, respond effectively to incidents, and maintain trust in a digital healthcare ecosystem.

Notes

1 U.S. Securities and Exchange Commission. *SEC Adopts Rules on Cybersecurity Risk Management, Strategy, Governance, and Incident Disclosure by Public Companies.* https://www.sec.gov/newsroom/press-releases/2023-139.

2 National Association of Corporate Directors. *NACD Director's Handbook on Cyber-Risk Oversight.* https://www.nacdonline.org/all-governance/governance-resources/governance-research/director-handbooks/nacd-directors-handbook-on-cyber-risk-oversight/.

3 CSO Online. *How Much Cybersecurity Expertise Does a Board Need?* https://www.csoonline.com/article/656596/how-much-cybersecurity-expertise-does-a-board-need.html.

4 CISA. *CPG Cross-Sector Cybersecurity Performance Goals.* "Information security is a business enabler when applied through proper and effective management of risks to information confidentiality, integrity, and availability." https://www.cisa.gov/sites/default/files/2023-03/CISA_CPG_REPORT_v1.0.1_FINAL.pdf.

Whereas information security is about the protection of data in all forms, including physical and electronic, cybersecurity refers to the protection of electronic (digital) assets. Cybersecurity supports business objectives and enables the organization to operate securely.

5 U.S. Securities and Exchange Commission. *SEC Adopts Rules on Cybersecurity Risk Management, Strategy, Governance, and Incident Disclosure by Public Companies.* https://www.sec.gov/newsroom/press-releases/2023-139.

6 HHS ASPR. *Health Care and Public Health Sector Cybersecurity Framework Implementation Guide Version 2 March 2023.* https://aspr.hhs.gov/cip/hph-cybersecurity-framework-implementation-guide/Documents/HPH-Sector-CSF-Implementation-Guide-508.pdf.

7 HHS ASPR Technical Resources. Assistance Center, and Information Exchange (TRACIE). *Healthcare System Cybersecurity: Readiness and Response Considerations.* https://files.asprtracie.hhs.gov/documents/aspr-tracie-healthcare-system-cybersercurity-readiness-response.pdf.

Chapter 8

Social Engineering: Why, How, and What to Do

8.1 The Human Attack Surface

Social engineering represents a category of threat that circumvents technical defenses by targeting the behaviors, activities, habits, and emotions of individuals. It is a form of deception wherein attackers manipulate people into taking actions that compromise systems, such as revealing passwords, granting access, or clicking on malicious links. In contrast to brute force attacks or exploit-based intrusions, social engineering thrives in environments where human interaction and trust are paramount.

Doctors, nurses, administrators, and other workforce members work in fast-paced environments where they make rapid decisions and coordinate closely with colleagues. Patient care depends on cooperation, trust in authority, and uninterrupted clinical activity. These conditions create a reliance on quick judgment and interpersonal communication. This reliance increases exposure to psychological manipulation, as attackers design social engineering tactics to exploit routine interactions and the pressures of clinical environments.

8.2 Tactics of Social Engineering: Common Methods of Manipulation

Social engineering attacks typically involve one or more recurring tactics. Each is designed to exploit predictable behaviors or to introduce doubt, urgency, or distraction at a critical moment.

8.2.1 General Phishing and Spear-Phishing

General phishing is an untargeted form of social engineering attack in which malicious actors attempt to elicit sensitive information or money from recipients. A general phishing email may include malicious hyperlinks, attachments, or embedded code. Simply opening a phishing message may pose risk under certain conditions, particularly in environments where email clients

DOI: 10.4324/9781003366560-8

automatically render active content due to misconfiguration or outdated security controls. Clicking on a hyperlink or opening an infected attachment may install malware, redirect the user to a spoofed login page, or exfiltrate credentials. Because a general phishing message is not directed at specific individuals or groups, attackers typically cast a wide net, sending deceptive messages to large numbers of potential victims with the expectation that a small percentage will engage.[1]

In contrast, spear-phishing is a targeted form of phishing attack. It is frequently used by malicious actors as a preferred infection vector due to its specificity and effectiveness. Spear-phishing messages are tailored to the target recipient—whether an individual or group within an organization—and often include references to internal projects, policies, roles, or relationships. A significant amount of information is publicly accessible online, including organizational hierarchies, employee roles, contractor affiliations, prior initiatives, and vendor relationships. Attackers leverage this information to craft convincing and contextually relevant messages. As a result, spear-phishing emails may appear legitimate and trustworthy, increasing the likelihood that the recipient will comply with a fraudulent request.[2]

For example, an email sent to a hospital's finance department might appear to come from the Chief Financial Officer, requesting urgent wire transfer approval for a new or existing vendor. This type of targeted financial fraud is known as business email compromise (BEC). BEC is a specific form of spear-phishing in which attackers impersonate executives, vendors, or trusted partners to manipulate recipients into transferring funds, revealing payroll data, rerouting payments, or disclosing sensitive business information. The attacker may spoof an email address, compromise a legitimate account, or exploit trust in hierarchical communication.

BEC attacks are often convincing and highly effective, as they exploit human psychology, particularly factors such as perceived authority, a sense of urgency, and procedural familiarity. Attackers craft messages that appear to come from trusted figures, such as executives or senior managers, and use time-sensitive language to pressure recipients into acting quickly without verification. By leveraging these psychological triggers, BEC attacks bypass technical defenses and manipulate individuals into performing actions that compromise organizational security.

Both phishing and spear-phishing (as well as BEC) aim to convince recipients to click on links, download attachments, or disclose sensitive information (also known as elicitation).[3] The email may mimic the style and branding of trusted vendors or internal departments, complete with legitimate-looking domains and signatures. In high-volume inboxes, such emails may not appear unusual.

8.2.2 Impersonation

Attackers use voice calls or face-to-face interactions to pose as trusted individuals, including IT personnel, maintenance workers, or external partners. The impersonator may reference internal systems, drop the names of real employees, or fabricate technical issues that demand immediate resolution. The goal is to lower the target's guard by presenting a plausible identity and scenario.

Healthcare workers are accustomed to interacting with a variety of support personnel, which increases the likelihood that an impersonator will be believed. Without a formal verification process, there is little to prevent someone from gaining access to sensitive areas or systems.

Increasingly, attackers are deploying impersonation attempts using deepfake technologies.[4] Deepfakes are becoming more convincing and more difficult to discern from a real image, audio, or video and involve the use of synthetic media,[5] such as manipulated audio or video, to mimic the voice, appearance, or behavior of a real individual. For example, a deepfake voice message may imitate a hospital executive requesting immediate action on a financial transaction, or a video call may mimic the voice or appearance of the organization's IT administrator. These techniques make impersonation attacks more convincing and harder to detect, particularly in fast-paced environments where quick decisions are common. As deepfake tools become more accessible, healthcare organizations should account for this evolving threat vector in both their training and verification protocols.

8.2.3 Pretexting

Pretexting occurs when an attacker (social engineer) constructs an elaborate backstory to justify a request for information or access. The attacker's success hinges on authority and credibility. In one example, a threat actor may impersonate a HIPAA compliance officer conducting an audit. By referencing regulations, policies, and deadlines, the attacker may pressure staff into releasing confidential patient information or other information that the workforce member would not normally divulge had they known the truth.

Unlike general phishing, pretexting requires in-depth preparation. It often targets individuals with specific roles, such as billing clerks, records custodians, or department heads. The attacker exploits the target's responsibility and desire to follow protocol.

Accordingly, maintaining metrics on who is targeted, when the attempts occur, and how individuals respond can help identify patterns and inform risk-based training. Tracking repeat offenders, defined as individuals who consistently fall for phishing simulations or fail to report suspicious activity, can support targeted education and reduce overall organizational vulnerability.

8.2.4 Baiting

This tactic involves the use of a physical or digital lure. A USB drive labeled "Confidential Physician Salaries" left in a breakroom, or an email attachment promising "Updated COVID-19 Protocols," are examples. These triggers rely on curiosity, interest, or perceived value. Baiting may appear as a legitimate internal communication or event.

8.2.5 Quid Pro Quo

The attacker offers a service or benefit in return for information. Commonly, this takes the form of "IT support" offering to fix a technical issue, provided the user supplies login credentials. The exchange may seem helpful and routine.

8.2.6 Tailgating and Piggybacking

These techniques involve unauthorized individuals physically following authorized personnel into secured areas. Although the terms are related, they describe different behaviors. Tailgating occurs when an unauthorized person follows an authorized individual without the authorized individual's knowledge. Piggybacking occurs when an authorized individual provides some level of permission to enter. Tailgating or piggybacking may take place at access-controlled doors, supply rooms, or server locations. The attacker may carry items such as boxes or toolkits to appear legitimate and use polite conversation or urgent-sounding excuses to facilitate entry. Proofpoint. *Tailgating Attacks.* https://www.proofpoint.com/us/threat-reference/tailgating-attacks-cybersecurity.

8.3 The Psychology Behind Successful Attacks

Social engineering exploits psychological tendencies, particularly under conditions of stress, urgency, or ambiguity.

8.3.1 Trust

Healthcare staff operate within a hierarchical structure. They routinely take direction from physicians, managers, vendors, and auditors. Additionally, healthcare is about helping people. Thus, there is a culture of trust inherent within healthcare organizations of all sizes, types, and locations.

8.3.2 Urgency

Clinical environments require swift action. Social engineers exploit this dynamic by creating messages that imply severe consequences for delay. An email warning of an account lockout or an impending patient safety issue can provoke a quick response.

8.3.3 Fear and Consequences

Fear of non-compliance or system failure is a strong motivator. Attackers may imply that inaction will result in disciplinary measures, HIPAA violations, or loss of access to essential systems.

8.3.4 Curiosity

Baiting tactics target curiosity by offering items such as insider information or confidential documents.

8.4 Targets of Social Engineering Attacks

8.4.1 Frontline Clinical Staff

These individuals can be frequent targets due to their access to EHRs, patient portals, and routine interactions with vendors. Their need to move quickly and manage multiple tasks simultaneously increases vulnerability to well-orchestrated social engineering efforts.

8.4.2 IT Administrators

Possessing elevated system privileges, IT administrators are high-value targets. A successful attack on an IT staff member can result in full network access, disabling of access controls, or elevated privileges (privilege escalation).

8.4.3 Executives

C-suite personnel are targets for business email compromise (BEC) schemes. The attacker may impersonate the CEO or CFO, requesting approval for payments or urgent transfers. These messages often rely on the executive's authority and time constraints to bypass scrutiny.

8.4.4 Third-Party Vendors

Vendors and contractors with legitimate access to facilities or systems may ignore internal security training. Attackers may exploit these individuals directly or impersonate them to deceive hospital staff.

8.4.5 Facilities and Clinical Engineers

These roles manage access to physical systems, including HVAC controls, medical devices, and communication infrastructure. If these individuals or their access is compromised, this may result in security failures that affect physical systems within secure networks.

8.5 Emerging Threat Vectors: Mobile, Voice, and Others

As healthcare organizations expand their use of mobile devices and voice communication, attackers have shifted tactics to exploit these channels, where defenses may be less mature and verification options more limited. These emerging threat vectors take advantage of the speed and trust that characterize mobile and voice interactions, making it easier for adversaries to deceive staff and capture sensitive information.

8.5.1 Smishing

Staff members may also receive deceptive SMS messages eliciting sensitive information.[6] The link provided may appear to lead to a legitimate portal, but instead captures credentials. The growing use of AI has made these attacks more convincing, allowing attackers to generate highly tailored messages, mimic organizational tone and style, and scale smishing campaigns in ways that increase the likelihood of success.

Attackers can harvest detailed information about their targets from publicly available sources on the internet. This may include social media profiles, business directories, professional networking platforms, organizational websites, press releases, and personal web pages. Additional data can be gathered from online resumes, conference presentations, published research, and news articles. When combined, these sources allow attackers to build a comprehensive profile of an individual, covering professional roles, contact information, work schedules, affiliations, and personal interests or family details. This information enables highly convincing and targeted social engineering messages that are more likely to succeed because they appear contextually relevant and trustworthy.[7]

8.5.2 Vishing

Voice-based attacks (vishing) use spoofed caller IDs to impersonate IT, billing, or vendor support. In busy environments, staff may respond without verifying the caller's legitimacy. Recent reports from HHS HC3 note an increase in these attacks across the HPH sector. Hybrid vishing campaigns, also known as callback phishing, often begin with a deceptive email, such as a fake subscription or invoice notice, that instructs the recipient to call a phone number. The call is then answered by a threat actor who uses social engineering to elicit sensitive information or trick the victim into installing remote access software. Advanced persistent threat (APT) groups have also been observed using voice-altering software to impersonate trusted contacts, further increasing the risk of successful compromise. These tactics allow attackers to gain unauthorized access, bypass multi-factor authentication through MFA fatigue, and in some cases deliver malware or exfiltrate protected health information (PHI).[8] The use of voice cloning through audio deepfake software has made vishing attacks more convincing.[9]

8.5.3 Calendar Phishing (Calendar Fraud)

Fake meeting invitations may contain embedded links or malicious files. To increase the likelihood of acceptance, attackers often reference urgent matters such as policy reviews, compliance deadlines, or EHR outages. These invitations may appear to come from trusted colleagues, senior executives, or external partners and may include realistic details such as meeting platforms, calendar formatting, or spoofed sender addresses. When accepted, the victim may be prompted to enter credentials, download a malicious attachment, or grant access to a compromised conferencing platform, giving attackers a foothold in the organization's systems.[10]

8.5.4 Malicious Applications (Malware)

Attackers may deploy counterfeit (rogue) applications that mimic legitimate hospital tools. Once installed, these applications may request excessive permissions and can record communications, log keystrokes, or exfiltrate patient data. Distribution may take place through mobile application stores, malicious links in emails or text messages, or embedded QR codes. Because they appear legitimate, individuals may install or scan them without suspicion, particularly in fast-paced environments where time is limited. These applications can also disrupt clinical workflows, alter or delete records, or provide remote access to internal systems.[11]

8.5.5 Man-in-the-Middle (Person-in-the-Middle) Attacks

Man-in-the-Middle (MitM) attacks occur when an adversary positions malicious infrastructure between a user and a legitimate service to intercept or alter communications. A common method involves the use of rogue Wi-Fi access points with names resembling official hospital networks. Attackers may employ subtle character substitutions—such as replacing the letter "i" with the number "1"—to create deceptive network names, a tactic known as a homoglyph or homograph attack. For example, a fraudulent network labeled "hosp1tal" may appear legitimate at a glance. Once a device connects, the attacker can intercept login credentials, monitor or manipulate traffic, and inject malicious payloads into communications, placing user privacy and institutional security at risk.[12]

8.6 Anatomy of a Social Engineering Attack

Each social engineering attack unfolds in distinct phases.[13]

8.6.1 Reconnaissance

The attacker gathers publicly available data such as staff names, organizational structure, and technical systems. Social media, job listings, and press releases are primary sources.

8.6.2 Crafting the Hook

The message is tailored using known terminology and visual branding. The attacker may use spoofed domains, legitimate-looking headers, and internal jargon.

8.6.3 Delivery

Timing is critical. Emails may be sent during shift changes, weekends, or system maintenance windows to increase the chances of careless engagement.

8.6.4 Execution

The recipient clicks a link or opens a file. A fake login page captures credentials, or malware installs silently.

8.6.5 Exfiltration and Exploitation

The attacker uses access to pivot deeper into the network. Patient records may be exfiltrated, ransomware deployed, or lateral movement initiated to gain access to other systems.

8.7 Modern Social Engineering Attacks

Social engineering tactics have evolved beyond traditional phishing emails to exploit new channels and changing circumstances. Attackers increasingly design lures that align with current events, workplace dynamics, and the technologies healthcare staff use every day. These methods are often more subtle and harder to detect, relying on context, urgency, and trust to bypass traditional safeguards.

8.7.1 Business Email Compromise

Executive impersonation is a common form of business email compromise (BEC) and may lead to fraudulent wire transfers or unauthorized release of sensitive documents. These messages often reference prior communications or ongoing projects to appear credible. They may mimic urgent requests for payments to vendors, procurement of medical supplies, or expedited approval of contracts.[14]

8.7.2 Pandemic-Themed Phishing

Attackers exploit the urgency of global health crises with lures about vaccines, testing, and new procedures. Such messages continue to appear during public health emergencies, drawing on concerns regarding safety and compliance. They may include attachments labeled as new clinical guidelines or links to purported health authority portals.[15]

8.7.3 QR Code Phishing (Quishing)

Malicious QR codes that may be placed on posters, flyers, or digital documents can redirect users to attacker-controlled phishing pages. Individuals may unknowingly scan these malicious QR codes using their mobile devices. Attackers may design these codes to appear linked to legitimate services, such as patient portals, EHR access, or scheduling systems. In the case of physical QR codes, attackers may place a malicious sticker directly over a legitimate one, causing users to unknowingly scan a code that redirects them to an attacker-controlled site.[16]

8.8 Spotlight on Mobile Phishing

8.8.1 Mobile Phone Phishing: Threats, Tactics, and Considerations

As mobile phones continue to serve as primary devices for work, personal communication, and access to critical systems, they have also become a growing target for cybercriminals. Mobile phone phishing involves the use of deceptive messages, apps, calls, or services designed to trick users into revealing sensitive information, installing malicious software, or interacting with attacker-controlled systems. These attacks often target login credentials, financial information, or protected health data, and may also serve as an initial step in broader campaigns against healthcare organizations.

One of the most prominent forms of mobile phishing is smishing, or SMS-based phishing. In a typical smishing attack, a user receives a text message that appears to come from a trusted entity, such as a healthcare provider, a bank, or a delivery service. The message may include a link or file that, once clicked, leads to a credential-harvesting site or installs malware on the device. Smishing gained traction as early as 2014, particularly in financial cybercrime, and has since become a widely used tactic. The Federal Communications Commission (FCC) has reported a continued rise in smishing attacks, noting that people are more likely to open text messages than emails from unknown senders. Federal Communications Commission. *FCC Fact Sheet: Targeting and Eliminating Unlawful Text Messages. Rules and Regulations Implementing the Telephone Consumer Protection Act of 1991.* https://docs.fcc.gov/public/attachments/DOC-391239A1.pdf. This behavioral pattern, combined with the reduced ability to easily inspect links or sender information on mobile devices, makes smishing especially effective.

Social media phishing is another mobile-centric tactic. On platforms such as Facebook, Instagram, or LinkedIn, threat actors may impersonate a known contact or create fake profiles to build trust. Messages may contain shortened links, obscuring the true destination and increasing the risk of engagement. Phishing via social media is particularly dangerous on mobile devices, where visual cues are limited and users may respond quickly without validating the source.

Email-based phishing is a common threat, even on mobile platforms. However, mobile email clients often hide the full email address of the sender and limit the user's ability to verify hyperlinks. Unlike desktop environments, mobile interfaces do not allow users to hover over a link to inspect the URL. This limitation makes it easier for threat actors to disguise malicious links and redirect users to spoofed login pages or malware-hosting sites.

Calendar invite phishing represents another method of mobile-targeted social engineering. In these cases, the attacker sends a fake meeting invitation that may contain a malicious link or file. If accepted, the invitation may trigger further compromise, such as credential harvesting, spyware installation, or malware delivery, especially in environments where users frequently engage with automated calendar systems.

Rogue or malicious mobile applications are also a significant concern. Attackers may publish apps that mimic legitimate software to capture login credentials, access communications, or monitor device activity. These apps may be distributed through unofficial app stores or sideloaded onto devices, particularly in bring-your-own-device (BYOD) environments. Some may request excessive permissions, such as access to messages, contacts, or microphones, under the guise of delivering functionality.

Man-in-the-middle attacks targeting mobile users are often facilitated through rogue wireless access points or fake virtual private network (VPN) applications. In public or semi-secure environments, attackers may configure a Wi-Fi network with a name resembling a legitimate provider. Some VPN apps posing as legitimate applications may collect network data or intercept user credentials.

Voice phishing, or vishing, is also frequently used against mobile phone users. Due to limited caller ID information on mobile screens, individuals may be more likely to answer calls from unfamiliar numbers. Threat actors commonly spoof the phone numbers of banks, government agencies, or healthcare providers to increase credibility. These calls often convey a sense of urgency, claiming that the recipient's account has been compromised or that a payment is overdue, prompting individuals to reveal sensitive information.

Messaging platforms such as WhatsApp are also frequently exploited for phishing and social engineering. In many regions, these platforms serve as a primary communication channel, which makes them attractive to attackers. A message appearing to come from a known contact or a group member may contain malicious links or attachments, often disguised as routine correspondence.

These tactics are effective due to a combination of behavioral and technical factors. Recipients often expect messages or calls from unknown numbers and are accustomed to acting quickly on mobile devices, which reduces scrutiny. The limited screen size, lack of hover functionality, and partial display of sender or link details all contribute to reduced scrutiny. Attackers often exploit urgency, familiarity, or authority, such as impersonating a senior executive (whaling), sending a fake delivery notification, or claiming to be from human resources or a healthcare insurer.

In educational or organizational testing environments, simulated scenarios may be used to measure awareness and identify areas of vulnerability. These can include fake SMS messages about unpaid tolls or HR-related notices, emails from supposed IT administrators requesting login credentials, fraudulent voice calls from "fraud departments," rogue Wi-Fi access points to monitor unauthorized connections, and fake calendar invites with embedded phishing links.

8.9 Mitigation of Social Engineering Attacks through Culture, Controls, and Training

Mitigation of social engineering attacks requires coordination between training, policies, technical safeguards, and organizational culture.

8.9.1 Security Awareness Training

Individuals benefit from regular, interactive, and role-specific training. Frequent simulated phishing campaigns that reflect current threats strengthen awareness, while post-training debriefs reinforce key lessons.

8.9.2 Policies and Procedures

Policies should clearly outline verification steps for sensitive requests and establish role-based access controls to reduce the impact of compromised accounts. Credential sharing should be prohibited. Organizations should establish procedures to ensure consistent compliance.

8.9.3 Technical Controls

Foundational technical controls include email filtering, activity monitoring, and multi-factor authentication. Alerts that identify unusual login activity, unauthorized data transfers, or device anomalies support early detection and response.

8.9.4 Organizational Culture

Cybersecurity is a shared responsibility. Recognizing individuals who report phishing attempts or demonstrate vigilance reinforces positive behaviors. Embedding security champions within departments fosters sustained engagement and accountability.

8.9.5 Incident Reporting Protocols

Nonpunitive reporting mechanisms encourage individuals to disclose suspected attempts without fear of reprisal. Security teams should respond promptly, investigate incidents, and apply lessons learned to strengthen defenses.

8.10 Summary—Social Engineering

The threat of social engineering will persist as long as there are people. Human vulnerabilities—and the risk of individuals falling prey to manipulation—should be addressed through training, awareness, and organizational culture. Technical defenses alone cannot compensate for lapses in human judgment. Protection requires a comprehensive approach that integrates behavior-focused education with operational safeguards.

Social engineering exploits the human attack surface through tactics that manipulate trust, urgency, and authority. Understanding the psychology behind these attacks is as important as deploying technical defenses. Attackers increasingly adapt their methods to target mobile and voice channels, using sophisticated lures such as fake meeting invitations, QR code phishing, and pandemic-themed messages. The anatomy of a social engineering attack shows how reconnaissance, tailored hooks, delivery, execution, and exploitation converge to compromise individuals and institutions.

Every individual, regardless of role or seniority, should be equipped to recognize deception, question unusual requests, and report suspicious activity without hesitation. Awareness training should explain key concepts and promote critical thinking.

Notes

1 Public-Private Analytic Exchange Program. *Phishing: Don't Be Phooled*! Homeland Security Digital Library. https://www.hsdl.org/c/view?docid=820189.

2 Public-Private Analytic Exchange Program. *Phishing: Don't Be Phooled*! Homeland Security Digital Library. https://www.hsdl.org/c/view?docid=820189.

3 Federal Bureau of Investigation (FBI). *Eliciting Corporate Information*. https://www.fbi.gov/file-repository/private-sector-partnerships/elicit_corp-508.pdf.

4 Internet Crime Complaint Center (IC3). *Deepfake Media Scams*. https://www.ic3.gov/Outreach/Brochures/2025-ABA-Foundation-Deep-Fake-Infographic.pdf.

5 The Digital Speaker. *What Is Synthetic Media? The Ultimate Guide.* https://www.thedigitalspeaker.com/what-is-synthetic-media-ultimate-guide/.
6 Federal Communications Commission (FCC). *FCC Fact Sheet: Targeting and Eliminating Unlawful Text Messages, Rules and Regulations Implementing the Telephone Consumer Protection Act of 1991.* https://docs.fcc.gov/public/attachments/DOC-391239A1.pdf.
7 IBM. *What Is Open Source Intelligence (OSINT)?* https://www.ibm.com/think/topics/osint.
8 FCC. *FCC Fact Sheet: Targeting and Eliminating Unlawful Text Messages, Rules and Regulations Implementing the Telephone Consumer Protection Act of 1991.* https://docs.fcc.gov/public/attachments/DOC-391239A1.pdf.
9 FBI—Internet Crime Complaint Center (IC3). *Senior U.S. Officials Impersonated in Malicious Messaging Campaign.* https://www.ic3.gov/PSA/2025/PSA250515.
10 FBI—Portland Field Office. *Oregon FBI Tech Tuesday: Building a Digital Defense Against Calendar Fraud.* https://www.fbi.gov/contact-us/field-offices/portland/news/press-releases/oregon-fbi-tech-tuesday-building-a-digital-defense-against-calendar-fraud.
11 CISA. *Malware, Phishing, and Ransomware.* https://www.cisa.gov/topics/cyber-threats-and-advisories/malware-phishing-and-ransomware.
12 *Types of Threat Actors That Threaten the Healthcare Sector.* https://www.hhs.gov/sites/default/files/types-threat-actors-threaten-healthcare.pdf.
13 Public-Private Analytic Exchange Program. *Phishing: Don't Be Phooled*! Homeland Security Digital Library. https://www.hsdl.org/c/view?docid=820189. (The phases of a social engineering attack as noted in the text are adapted from the Public-Private Analytic Exchange Programs paper.)
14 FBI. *Business Email Compromise.* https://www.fbi.gov/how-we-can-help-you/scams-and-safety/common-frauds-and-scams/business-email-compromise.
15 U.S. Department of Health and Human Services—Office of Inspector General. Fraud Alert: COVID-19 Scams. https://oig.hhs.gov/fraud/consumer-alerts/fraud-alert-covid-19-scams/.
See also HHS HC3. *COVID-19 Vaccine Themed Phishing Emails (Sector Alert).* https://www.hhs.gov/sites/default/files/sector-alert-covid-phishing-tlp-white.pdf.
16 HHS HC3. *QR Code-Based Phishing (Quishing) as a Threat to the Health Sector.* https://www.hhs.gov/sites/default/files/qr-codes-and-phishing-as-a-threat-to-the-hph-white-paper.pdf.

Chapter 9

Information Sharing

9.1 The Imperative of Information Sharing

In the rapidly evolving landscape of healthcare, the protection of sensitive patient information and the integrity of medical systems are major priorities. Cybersecurity threats have become increasingly sophisticated, targeting vulnerabilities within healthcare organizations that may lead to significant disruptions in patient care and financial losses. Information sharing emerges as a key strategy in combating these threats, enabling organizations to collectively enhance their security posture.

Information sharing involves the deliberate exchange of data, insights, and intelligence related to cybersecurity threats, vulnerabilities, and best practices among various stakeholders. This collaborative approach fosters a unified defense against cyber adversaries, allowing healthcare entities to anticipate, identify, and mitigate potential risks more effectively.

By participating in information sharing initiatives, organizations gain access to a broader spectrum of threat intelligence, enabling them to stay ahead of emerging threats. Moreover, collaborative efforts contribute to the development of industry-wide best practices and standards that help increase the overall resilience of the HPH sector.

9.2 Understanding Information Sharing

9.2.1 Definition and Scope

Information sharing, in the context of cybersecurity, refers to the systematic exchange of data, threat intelligence, vulnerabilities, and best practices among organizations and stakeholders. This exchange aims to enhance collective security measures, enabling entities to better anticipate, identify, and respond to cyber threats.

The scope of information sharing encompasses various forms of data. This may involve threat indicators such as IP addresses, malware signatures, and phishing email characteristics; vulnerabilities affecting systems, devices, or software; incident reports describing security breaches or attempted attacks; and mitigation strategies outlining recommended responses and best practices.

DOI: 10.4324/9781003366560-9

9.2.2 Importance in Healthcare

The HPH sector is a prime target for cybercriminals due to the wealth of sensitive information it holds and the critical nature of its services. A successful cyberattack can disrupt patient care, compromise PHI, and lead to financial and reputational harm.

Information sharing helps healthcare organizations maintain situational awareness. It keeps them informed about current threats and vulnerabilities. Lessons learned from peers strengthen preventative and mitigation measures. Collective participation in information sharing efforts supports a unified defense across the HPH sector.

9.3 The Role of Internal Information Sharing

9.3.1 Enhancing Organizational Resilience

Internal information sharing involves the dissemination of cybersecurity-related information within an organization. This practice is crucial for building a cohesive defense strategy, as it ensures that all departments and personnel are aligned in their understanding of potential threats and the measures in place to address them.

Effective internal information sharing leads to improved communication between IT security teams and other departments, coordinated response during incidents, and proactive risk management by empowering staff to identify and report security issues.

9.3.2 Mechanisms for Internal Sharing

To establish robust internal information sharing practices, healthcare organizations can implement regular training sessions focused on cybersecurity awareness, distribute internal newsletters and bulletins with updates on trends and incidents, utilize incident reporting systems that are user-friendly and accessible, conduct cross-departmental meetings to discuss security matters, and maintain centralized information repositories with relevant cybersecurity resources.

9.4 The Role of External Information Sharing

9.4.1 Building a Collective Defense

External information sharing involves exchanging cybersecurity information with entities outside the organization, such as other healthcare providers, government agencies, industry groups, trusted peers, and validated threat intelligence vendors. Peer-to-peer exchanges should be conducted in accordance with applicable law. This collaborative approach is vital for developing a collective defense against cyber threats.

The Cybersecurity Information Sharing Act of 2015 (CISA 2015) reinforced the importance of information sharing by providing a framework that encourages private sector organizations to exchange cybersecurity threat indicators and defensive measures with each other and with the federal government. CISA 2015 established liability protections for entities that share information in good faith through designated channels, reducing concerns about legal or regulatory exposure.

The benefits of external information sharing include access to broader threat intelligence, use of shared resources and expertise, and coordination of sector-wide preparedness to address systemic vulnerabilities.

9.4.2 Cybersecurity Act of 2015

Section 405 of the Cybersecurity Act of 2015 (6 U.S.C. § 1533) is specific to healthcare and emphasizes the need for sector-wide coordination on cybersecurity practices. For the HPH sector, this provision supports collaboration with organizations such as the Health-ISAC, the Cybersecurity and Infrastructure Security Agency (CISA), and the U.S. Department of Health and Human Services (HHS) HC3. Section 405(d) of the Cybersecurity Act of 2015 established the HHS 405(d) Program.[1] By fostering collaboration and the development of common cybersecurity practices, Section 405 of the Cybersecurity Act of 2015 helps healthcare organizations strengthen resilience against adversaries.

9.5 Addressing Legal Concerns: The Role of Lawyers

9.5.1 Overcoming Barriers to Sharing

Overcoming barriers to information sharing can require direct involvement from legal teams. Sharing information externally (i.e., outside the organization) can be facilitated by reviewing all information before it is shared. Any personal information about a specific individual or information that identifies a specific individual must be removed when it is not directly related to a cybersecurity threat. The entity should also remove any personal information it knows at the time of sharing unless that information is directly related to the cybersecurity threat, in accordance with the Cybersecurity Information Sharing Act of 2015.

Clear parameters for what can be disclosed should also be established. Non-Disclosure Agreements (NDAs) and participation agreements can define the type of data being shared, the authorized recipients, and the security measures that should be applied—treating the data as confidential information and specifying lawful restrictions on its use and redisclosure.

Liability protections under the Cybersecurity Information Sharing Act of 2015 apply when cyber threat indicators or defensive measures are shared in good faith for a cybersecurity purpose, after required review and removal of personal information not directly related to the threat, and through a sharing mechanism designated by the Federal Government for receipt of such information.

U.S. Department of Homeland Security and U.S. Department of Justice. *Guidance to Assist Non-Federal Entities to Share Cyber Threat Indicators and Defensive Measures with Federal Entities under the Cybersecurity Information Sharing Act of 2015.* https://www.cisa.gov/sites/default/files/2025-11/NonFederal-Entity-Sharing-Guidance-Nov-2025-Update.pdf.

9.6 Best Practices for Information Sharing

Information sharing in healthcare cybersecurity needs to rely on trusted, legally supported, and technically secure mechanisms. Organizations should use vetted channels such as ISACs and ISAOs, direct peer-to-peer exchanges conducted in accordance with the Cybersecurity Information Sharing Act of 2015, and validated threat-intelligence provider feeds. External sharing should follow applicable guidance and include removing any personal information about a specific individual or information that identifies a specific individual not directly related to a cybersecurity threat. When appropriate, organizations may share cyber threat indicators or defensive measures with the federal government through a mechanism designated for the receipt of such information, in accordance with the Cybersecurity Information Sharing Act of 2015 or successor legislation.

Data elements should be limited to what is necessary for cybersecurity purposes, and sharing parameters should be documented. Regular evaluation of information sharing practices helps ensure accuracy, compliance, and ongoing effectiveness.

U.S. Department of Homeland Security and U.S. Department of Justice. *Guidance to Assist Non-Federal Entities to Share Cyber Threat Indicators and Defensive Measures with Federal Entities under the Cybersecurity Information Sharing Act of 2015*. https://www.cisa.gov/sites/default/files/2025-11/NonFederal-Entity-Sharing-Guidance-Nov-2025-Update.pdf.

9.6.1 Collaboration

Information sharing is a core component of effective collaboration. Strengthening internal communication, cultivating external partnerships, and addressing legal hurdles are essential steps to improving collective cybersecurity resilience.

9.6.2 Practical Realities of Information Sharing

Information sharing must be a functional, daily practice within healthcare operations. Organizations must move beyond intent and ensure that processes, platforms, and personnel are equipped to facilitate effective communication. This includes building trusted relationships, using secure communication tools, and training staff to apply shared intelligence.

9.6.3 Practical Examples

9.6.3.1 Internal Information Sharing: Strengthening Communication within a Hospital

A mid-sized hospital experiences a surge in phishing emails that mimic IT department messages. The cybersecurity team identifies these attempts through monitoring tools and begins disseminating threat information internally. They analyze the emails, extract sender domains and subject line patterns, and develop a bulletin outlining these indicators. This bulletin is distributed via email, posted on the intranet, and presented at staff meetings. Targeted training is conducted for vulnerable departments. Staff reports enable stronger technical defenses. The campaign is neutralized before significant harm occurs.

9.6.3.2 Peer-to-Peer Information Sharing: Responding to Ransomware in a Regional Network

A ransomware attack cripples a regional hospital's electronic health records. Recognizing the threat, the hospital shares a detailed incident report with peer institutions, including the ransomware variant, IOCs, and attack timeline. Peer hospitals scan their networks and identify and isolate threats. A follow-up meeting is held to discuss best practices. The collaboration prevents spread and strengthens regional preparedness.

9.6.3.3 External Information Sharing: Proactive Defense

A healthcare organization discovers malware on a network-connected radiology imaging modality, raising concerns about a broader campaign targeting connected medical devices. The incident is promptly reported to a trusted investigative partner that specializes in analyzing cyber threats across multiple sectors and which has supported prior coordinated operations to disrupt organized cybercrime activity. The organization provides technical details, including file hashes, suspicious domains, and information on affected device models. The partner conducts an analysis and correlates the activity with similar reports from other organizations and issues a sector-wide alert with recommended mitigation steps. Law enforcement, including the Federal Bureau of Investigation (FBI), is informed, leading to a broader advisory being shared with healthcare providers and medical device manufacturers. The organization collaborates with the medical device manufacturer to apply necessary patches. The shared indicators contribute to a coordinated law enforcement operation that dismantles a cybercrime ring responsible for related intrusions across multiple sectors, demonstrating the value of timely and accurate information sharing.

9.6.4 Setting Up a Tabletop Exercise for Information Sharing

Objectives of a tabletop exercise include evaluating internal and external communication during incidents, identifying bottlenecks, improving collaboration, and building organizational confidence.

Steps to conduct an effective tabletop exercise begin with defining the scope. Scenarios might include phishing, ransomware, or insider threats. Assemble a team that includes IT, clinical, legal, compliance, communications, and executive leadership. Develop a realistic scenario. Facilitate the exercise by walking through the scenario and asking participants to respond. Document strengths, weaknesses, and recommended actions. Share findings with leadership and update procedures accordingly. Plan follow-up exercises.

9.7 Spotlight on Tabletop Exercises for Information Sharing Purposes

To build and test effective information sharing capabilities, healthcare organizations can conduct tabletop exercises. A tabletop exercise is a discussion-based session that simulates a (preferably realistic) cybersecurity incident. It brings together stakeholders from across the organization to walk through a hypothetical scenario and evaluate how they would respond. The purpose is to assess how well information is collected, analyzed, and shared internally and externally during a cyber event. The exercise also identifies communication breakdowns, procedural gaps, and coordination challenges.

The goals of a tabletop exercise include testing the organization's ability to share actionable intelligence, evaluating internal and external communication protocols, identifying bottlenecks in information flow, improving coordination among key departments, and strengthening team readiness for future incidents. Most importantly, these exercises promote a shared understanding of cybersecurity responsibilities across clinical, technical, and administrative roles.

For the exercise to be effective, it should include a broad and representative group of participants. A recent analysis of tabletop exercise participants in healthcare settings demonstrates that organizations most commonly involve IT staff, cybersecurity staff, senior management, and executives. However, participation should extend well beyond these groups to reflect the operational reality of a healthcare organization.

Key participants may include the following, depending on the area of focus:

- IT staff and cybersecurity staff who manage and monitor security controls
- Senior management and executives who make policy and resource decisions
- Compliance personnel responsible for regulatory adherence
- Clinical staff such as nurses, physicians, and medical assistants who rely on systems to deliver care
- Informatics professionals who bridge clinical workflows and technical systems
- Human resources and legal staff who manage insider threats, personnel policy, and liability
- Accounting and finance departments that oversee payment systems and financial transactions
- The legal department to guide communication boundaries and data-sharing policies
- Vendors and contractors who support critical third-party services
- The board of directors and communications/public relations teams responsible for external messaging

Even groups that have historically had lower participation—such as board members, contractors, or vendor representatives—should be included when applicable, as their roles during incident response can be significant. Inclusion of these groups reflects a whole-organization approach to cybersecurity readiness.

Organizers of the tabletop exercise should first define its scope and objectives. The scenario should be specific, such as a phishing campaign that targets hospital staff, a ransomware event that disables electronic health records, or an insider threat that results in unauthorized access to patient data. The scenario should escalate over time to mimic how real incidents evolve, creating natural inflection points where information should be shared or decisions should be made.

Organizers should then assemble participants, ensuring representation from the appropriate stakeholders. The scenario should clearly define the triggering event, escalation path, and moments requiring internal and external information sharing. Participants will be asked to describe their roles and decisions at each stage. Facilitators should prompt them with questions such as "Who should be notified?," "What type of information should be shared?" "How will it be communicated?," and "What challenges could delay or disrupt information flow?"

Throughout the exercise, the emphasis should be on communication dynamics, timing, clarity, and decision-making processes. Participants should consider how sensitive data will be handled and what legal or compliance considerations should be factored in.

After completing the scenario walkthrough, organizers should document key findings. This includes strengths, breakdowns, and specific action items. Gaps might be identified in communication protocols, technology limitations, or a lack of clarity around roles. These insights should be summarized in a report shared with organizational leadership and translated into changes in policy, training, and systems.

Tabletop exercises should not be treated as one-time events. Regular simulations should be conducted, and each should include clinical and nonclinical participants from across the organizational structure. The insights gained from repeated exercises help institutionalize a culture of preparedness and ensure that when a real incident occurs, information sharing will be timely, effective, and collaborative across all levels of the organization.

Research from other critical infrastructure sectors highlights several additional considerations for effective information sharing tabletop exercises. Exercises should evaluate the timeliness, accuracy, and completeness of information shared between departments and external partners, as delays or inconsistent reporting can impede coordinated response. They should also reflect the interdependent nature of healthcare operations by incorporating scenario elements involving external stakeholders such as vendors, peer organizations, or information sharing partners. Exercises should test the organization's ability to operate in a degraded state, including reliance on manual or fallback workflows when digital systems are disrupted. Clear role expectations should be validated to reduce ambiguity during high-stress incidents, and participants should practice reconciling and confirming information before it is shared externally. Finally, repeated exercises should track whether previously identified communication bottlenecks and information-flow challenges have been corrected over time, reinforcing a sustained culture of preparedness. Public-Private Analytic Exchange Program. *Shoring Up Maritime Cybersecurity—Enhancing Cybersecurity and Resilience.* https://www.dhs.gov/sites/default/files/2024-09/2024aepphasellusmaritimetradeandportcybersecurity.pdf.

9.8 Summary—Information Sharing

9.8.1 Realizing the Benefits of Information Sharing

Regular and structured information sharing strengthens healthcare cybersecurity by enabling earlier detection of threats, faster response times, and improved sector resilience. Organizations that actively participate in trusted exchanges build confidence with partners, enhance their own defenses, and support the continuity and integrity of patient care across the healthcare ecosystem.

9.8.2 Turning Information Into Action

Information sharing is not a one-time activity but an ongoing commitment that requires trust, clarity, and disciplined execution. Healthcare organizations cannot operate in isolation against cybersecurity threats that routinely target multiple entities across the sector. Legal counsel plays a critical role in addressing barriers by ensuring HIPAA compliance, drafting agreements, and mitigating liability.

Best practices—such as structured reporting, participation in public–private partnerships, and incorporating lessons from tabletop exercises—help transform shared information into actionable defense. Real world examples show that when organizations exchange threat indicators, share mitigation strategies, and learn from peers, they improve preparedness and reduce risk. A culture of collaboration ensures that information sharing is a strategic capability that enables healthcare organizations to defend against evolving cyber threats.

Note

1 HHS 405(d) Program. *About Us; Our History.* https://405d.hhs.gov/about.

Chapter 10

Artificial Intelligence

10.1 An Explanation of AI

AI refers to the ability of machines and systems to perform tasks that would normally require human intelligence. These tasks include learning from data, reasoning through complex situations, making decisions, and adapting over time. AI is not a single technology. It is a collection of methods, tools, and systems that enable machines to operate in ways that mimic or support human cognition.

There are three general categories of AI. The first is narrow AI, which refers to systems that are designed to accomplish specific tasks such as recognizing faces in images, translating languages, or recommending treatment options. The second category is artificial general intelligence, which refers to systems that could perform any intellectual task that a human being can perform. The third category is super-intelligent AI, which refers to machines that surpass human intelligence across all areas, including reasoning, creativity, and emotional intelligence.[1]

10.2 Key Components of AI

AI systems are built using combinations of software algorithms, training data, and hardware infrastructure.

One core component is machine learning, which involves training systems to identify patterns and make predictions based on data. Instead of being explicitly programmed for every decision, machine learning systems improve over time as they are exposed to more examples.

Another core component is natural language processing, which enables systems to understand, interpret, and generate human language. This allows computers to engage in dialogue, summarize documents, and convert speech to text.

Computer vision enables AI systems to analyze and understand visual data such as photographs, scans, or real-time video. Computer vision is used to detect abnormalities in X-rays or analyze pathology slides. Robotics combines AI with mechanical systems, enabling machines to perform physical tasks such as surgical procedures, patient transport, or rehabilitation exercises.

All these systems depend on large volumes of data, high-speed computing capabilities, and sophisticated algorithms to deliver accurate and meaningful results.

DOI: 10.4324/9781003366560-10

10.3 History of AI in Healthcare

AI has had a long and evolving history in healthcare. Early developments in the 1970s focused on rule-based systems known as expert systems, which used predefined rules to simulate clinical decision-making. One of the earliest and most notable examples was MYCIN, developed at Stanford University circa 1976 and first presented circa 1977. Designed to assist physicians in identifying bacterial infections and recommending appropriate antibiotics, MYCIN demonstrated the potential of AI to support medical diagnosis and treatment. However, it was never deployed in clinical practice due to concerns about reliability and limited computing power.[2]

In the 1990s and early 2000s, advances in machine learning led to new applications in healthcare. Unlike rule-based systems, machine learning models learned from data and improved over time. These systems began to analyze diagnostic images such as X-rays, CT (computed tomography) scans, and MRIs (magnetic resonance imaging) to detect abnormalities like tumors or fractures.[3] At the same time, the digitization of patient records created large data sets that could be analyzed to identify trends, predict outcomes, and improve administrative efficiency.

In the 2010s, the availability of large data sets and advances in deep learning fueled a new era of AI in healthcare. Convolutional neural networks (CNNs) became widely used to interpret complex medical images.[4] The digitization of healthcare records also enabled predictive analytics and operational efficiencies across large populations.

More recently, natural language processing has enabled virtual assistants to assist patients with scheduling, symptom checking, and medication management.[5] During the COVID-19 pandemic, AI was leveraged to model disease spread, support resource allocation, and accelerate vaccine development.[6]

10.4 The Impact of AI in Modern Society

AI is transforming nearly every sector by automating routine tasks, supporting complex decision-making, and generating insights from vast amounts of data. AI supports more accurate diagnoses, enhances personalized treatment plans, and improves operational efficiency in hospitals. AI systems can identify anomalies in medical images. This assists radiologists in detecting conditions such as cancer or pneumonia at earlier stages. AI also plays a role in managing hospital logistics, forecasting patient admissions, and monitoring supply chains.

The adoption of AI can introduce risks. Systems trained on biased data may contribute to existing disparities, including within healthcare settings. Privacy concerns can also arise because AI may require access to confidential, protected, proprietary, or sensitive information.

10.5 Ethical Considerations in AI Development

Ethical considerations play an important role in guiding the responsible design and use of AI systems. First, it is essential to avoid bias by ensuring that training data sets include diverse and representative populations. Failing to do so may result in AI systems that make inaccurate or unfair decisions.[7] Second, privacy should be protected by building safeguards into every stage of the system's design and deployment. This includes encrypting sensitive data, limiting access, and adhering to data protection regulations.[8]

Transparency is another key requirement. Users should be able to understand how decisions are made by AI systems, especially when those decisions have direct consequences for individuals' lives. Accountability should also be defined. Organizations need to establish policies to determine who is responsible when an AI system fails, causes harm, or produces inaccurate results.

10.6 AI in Practice

AI is in use across a wide range of applications. Generative AI tools can help with drafting reports, translating languages, summarizing documents, and assisting in research.[9] Predictive models analyze patient histories to identify individuals at higher risk for chronic diseases or complications.[10] AI-assisted robotic surgeons perform precise movements in minimally invasive procedures.[11] AI also supports administrative tasks such as scheduling, billing, and responding to patient inquiries through virtual assistants and chatbots.[12]

It is important to implement enterprise-grade AI solutions that incorporate strong safeguards to protect the privacy, security, and integrity of information. Selecting systems that align with organizational policies and regulatory requirements helps ensure that sensitive data is managed responsibly.

But the use of *shadow AI* tools outside official channels may introduce significant risk. These unapproved tools operate outside established governance processes. This means that they may lack transparency, accountability, and adequate protections for privacy and security. Confidential, protected, proprietary, or sensitive information may be exposed if shared with shadow AI tools.[13]

10.7 Types of AI in Healthcare

AI in healthcare includes systems that support diagnostic, clinical, administrative, and research activities. Diagnostic and predictive analytics help identify patterns in clinical data to detect diseases and predict outcomes. For example, machine learning algorithms can analyze mammograms to detect signs of breast cancer or evaluate retinal images for signs of diabetic retinopathy. Predictive models also help healthcare providers anticipate patient outcomes, such as the likelihood of readmission or the progression of chronic illnesses.

Natural language processing is used to process unstructured data such as physician notes and clinical narratives. These tools convert spoken language into text, summarize medical histories, and generate reports. They also allow healthcare professionals to interact with electronic health record systems using voice commands.[14]

Robotics plays a significant role in both clinical and nonclinical applications. AI-assisted surgical robots help perform complex procedures with greater precision and smaller incisions. Rehabilitation robots adjust exercises based on a patient's progress, while service robots deliver medications and supplies within hospitals.[15]

Computer vision is critical in radiology and pathology, where it assists in interpreting visual data such as scans and microscope slides. This technology helps to reduce the risk of human error and can speed up diagnosis.[16]

Generative AI tools assist healthcare workers by drafting emails, summarizing journal articles, and creating synthetic data for training or research purposes.[17]

AI can be used to accelerate drug discovery and vaccine development. AI, when applied within the field of computational chemistry, accelerates the identification of potential therapeutic compounds and reduces the time and cost traditionally associated with laboratory screening. AI can analyze large data sets of molecular structures, chemical properties, and biological interactions.[18]

Wearable devices and Internet of Things (IoT) technologies collect continuous data on vital signs such as heart rate, oxygen saturation, and blood pressure. This data can be analyzed in real-time to detect early signs of health problems and alert healthcare providers, aided by AI-based wearable sensors.[19]

AI is used to support clinical decision-making. For example, decision support systems assist oncologists in selecting treatment protocols based on patient data and medical guidelines.

AI improves hospital operations by forecasting patient admission rates, optimizing staff schedules, and managing inventory.

Patient engagement is enhanced through AI-powered virtual assistants that answer questions, remind patients about medications, and offer guidance on managing chronic diseases.[20]

10.8 Safe and Ethical Use of AI

To realize the benefits of AI, healthcare organizations should ensure that systems are used ethically and safely. Embedding ethical principles into the development process is essential. AI systems should be fair and equitable, trained on diverse data sets, and tested for unintended consequences. Transparency is critical so that patients and clinicians understand how AI decisions are made. Accountability should be clearly established to determine who is responsible when AI systems cause harm or make errors.

Privacy and security should be protected by design (i.e., privacy by design and security by design). AI systems should include built-in safeguards to prevent data breaches and ensure compliance with regulations such as HIPAA. Building trust in AI systems also requires clear communication with patients and staff. Regular audits and third party evaluations can also support oversight of AI systems.[21]

AI models should be continuously monitored for performance. Issues such as model drift or declining accuracy should be addressed promptly.[22] Updates should reflect new medical knowledge and changing clinical standards. It is also important to engage a multidisciplinary team that includes healthcare professionals, ethicists, technologists, and legal experts—to ensure that AI systems are designed and used appropriately.

10.9 Frameworks and Guidelines for Safe and Ethical AI

Several frameworks and principles guide the responsible use of AI. The NIST AI Risk Management Framework Playbook (AI RME) provides a roadmap for managing AI-related risks, and the NIST AI Risk Management Playbook provides practical perspectives.[23] The *HPH Cybersecurity Performance Goals*[24] help healthcare organizations prioritize and implement foundational cybersecurity practices that reduce risk, support cybersecurity preparedness, response, and resilience.[25] The principle of *privacy by design* emphasizes embedding privacy principles into every phase of system design, development, and implementation.[26] The principle of *security by design* emphasizes embedding security principles and controls into every stage of system design, development, and implementation.[27]

10.10 AI in Healthcare—Looking to the Future

Understanding the foundations of AI and its key components provides context for its impact on modern society and its expanding role in healthcare. The history of AI in healthcare demonstrates a steady progression from early expert systems to advanced deep learning applications, with growing use in areas such as medical imaging, precision medicine, and clinical decision support.

The safe and ethical use of AI in healthcare depends on adherence to principles of fairness, transparency, and accountability. Guidance such as the NIST AI Risk Management Framework (AI RMF) and the NIST AI RMF Playbook provides healthcare organizations with structured guidance for managing risks while fostering trust. NIST. *AI Risk Management Framework.* https://www.nist.gov/itl/ai-risk-management-framework. See also NIST. *AI RMF Playbook.* https://www.nist.gov/itl/ai-risk-management-framework/nist-ai-rmf-playbook.

When ethical considerations and governance are integrated into AI development and deployment, healthcare organizations can improve outcomes, strengthen resilience, and maintain public confidence in healthcare technology innovation.

Notes

1 IBM. *Understanding the Different Types of Artificial Intelligence.* https://www.ibm.com/think/topics/artificial-intelligence-types.

See also IBM. *What is Artificial Superintelligence?* https://www.ibm.com/think/topics/artificial-superintelligence.

2 National Library of Medicine—PubMed Central. *Informatics in Radiology: Mycin: A Knowledge-Based Computer Program Applied to Infectious Diseases.* https://pmc.ncbi.nlm.nih.gov/articles/PMC2464549.

3 One example—the first computer-assisted system to read mammograms for clinical use. University of Chicago Medicine. *Computer-aided Mammography Arrives.* https://www.uchicagomedicine.org/forefront/news/computer-aided-mammography.

See also National Library of Medicine—PubMed Central. Anniversary Paper: History and status of CAD and quantitative image analysis: *The role of Medical Physics and AAPM.* https://pmc.ncbi.nlm.nih.gov/articles/PMC2673617/.

4 STM Journals. *Detection and Classification of Diabetic Retinopathy Using Deep Learning Techniques.* https://journals.stmjournals.com/rrjomst/article%3D2024/view%3D166313.

5 National Library of Medicine—PubMed Central. Artificial Intelligence Solutions to Increase Medication Adherence in Patients With Non-communicable Diseases. https://pmc.ncbi.nlm.nih.gov/articles/PMC8521858.

See also Notable Health. *AI and Patient Scheduling Software: Addressing Common Misconceptions.* https://www.notablehealth.com/blog/patient-scheduling-software.

6 National Library of Medicine—PubMed Central. *Application of Artificial Intelligence in COVID-19 Medical Area: A Systematic Review.* https://pmc.ncbi.nlm.nih.gov/articles/PMC8743418/.

See also Vaccines Work. *Using AI from Lab to Jab: How Did Artificial Intelligence Help Us Develop and Deliver COVID-19 Vaccines?* https://www.gavi.org/vaccineswork/using-ai-lab-jab-how-did-artificial-intelligence-help-us-develop-and-deliver-covid.

7 ScienceDirect. *Ethical and Bias Considerations in Artificial Intelligence/Machine Learning.* https://www.sciencedirect.com/science/article/pii/S0893395224002667.

8 CGI. *Privacy by Design: Integrating Data Protection Best Practices in AI Solutions Development.* https://www.cgi.com/en/blog/artificial-intelligence/integrating-data-protection-best-practices-in-ai-solutions-development.

9 IBM Research. *What Is Generative AI?* https://research.ibm.com/blog/what-is-generative-AI.

10 National Library of Medicine—PubMed Central. *Unveiling the Influence of AI Predictive Analytics on Patient Outcomes: A Comprehensive Narrative Review.* https://pmc.ncbi.nlm.nih.gov/articles/PMC11161909.

11 National Library of Medicine—PubMed Central. *Clinical Applications of Artificial Intelligence in Robotic Surgery.* https://pmc.ncbi.nlm.nih.gov/articles/PMC10907451.

12 thoughtful.ai. *Scheduling, Billing, and Beyond: AI's Comprehensive Role in Clinic Management.* https://www.thoughtful.ai/blog/scheduling-billing-and-beyond-ais-comprehensive-role-in-clinic-management.

13 Becker's Hospital Review. *How Health Systems Are Tackling the Rise of "Shadow AI."* https://www.beckershospitalreview.com/healthcare-information-technology/ai/how-health-systems-are-tackling-the-rise-of-shadow-ai/

14 Foresee Medical. *Natural Language Processing in Healthcare.* https://www.foreseemed.com/natural-language-processing-in-healthcare.

15 National Library of Medicine—PubMed Central. *Clinical Applications of Artificial Intelligence in Robotic Surgery.* https://pmc.ncbi.nlm.nih.gov/articles/PMC10907451/.

16 National Library of Medicine—PubMed Central. *Applied Artificial Intelligence in Healthcare: A Review of Computer Vision Technology Application in Hospital Settings.* https://pmc.ncbi.nlm.nih.gov/articles/PMC11050909/.

17 The University of Texas at San Antonio. *How AI is Transforming the Role of Medical Administrative Assistants.* https://www.utsa.edu/pace/news/ai-medical-administrative-assistant-roles.html.

18 National Library of Medicine—PubMed Central. *The Role of AI in Drug Discovery: Challenges, Opportunities, and Strategies.* https://pmc.ncbi.nlm.nih.gov/articles/PMC10302890/.

19 National Library of Medicine—PubMed Central. *The Emergence of AI-Based Wearable Sensors for Digital Health Technology: A Review.* https://pmc.ncbi.nlm.nih.gov/articles/PMC10708748/

20 National Library of Medicine—PubMed Central. *AI-Driven Clinical Decision Support Systems: An Ongoing Pursuit of Potential.* https://pmc.ncbi.nlm.nih.gov/articles/PMC11073764/.

21 CISA. *Software Must Be Secure by Design, and Artificial Intelligence Is No Exception.* https://www.cisa.gov/news-events/news/software-must-be-secure-design-and-artificial-intelligence-no-exception.

22 IBM. *What is Model Drift?* https://www.ibm.com/think/topics/model-drift.

23 NIST. *AI Risk Management Framework.* https://www.nist.gov/itl/ai-risk-management-framework.
See also NIST. *AI RMF Playbook.* https://www.nist.gov/itl/ai-risk-management-framework/nist-ai-rmf-playbook.

24 HHS. *HHS Cyber Gateway.* https://hhscyber.hhs.gov/.

25 HHS. *Healthcare and Public Health Sector Cybersecurity Performance Goals (HPH CPGs).* https://hhscyber.hhs.gov/performance-goals.html.

26 Agencia Española de Protección de Datos. *A Guide to Privacy by Design.* https://www.aepd.es/guides/guide-to-privacy-by-design.pdf.

27 Cybersecurity Infrastructure and Security Agency. *Secure by Design. Shifting the Balance of Cybersecurity Risk: Principles and Approaches for Secure by Design Software.* https://www.cisa.gov/sites/default/files/2023-10/SecureByDesign_1025_508c.pdf.

Chapter 11

Emerging Technologies and Innovation

11.1 The Challenge

In the dynamically evolving landscape of healthcare cybersecurity, organizations are confronting unprecedented challenges. Cyber adversaries are becoming increasingly sophisticated, leveraging automation, machine learning, and AI to target the HPH sector with precision and persistence. As healthcare systems integrate complex digital platforms that span legacy infrastructure to Internet of Things (IoT) medical devices, and cloud-based electronic health records (EHRs), the attack surface expands significantly.

Modern cybersecurity, privacy, and data protection frameworks, automated detection tools, and forward-looking governance strategies offer healthcare entities a pathway to resilience. Organizations that make cybersecurity, privacy, and data protection an enterprise-wide priority are better equipped to address evolving risks. This approach improves patient safety, strengthens data integrity, supports operational continuity, and enhances resilience.

11.2 Barriers to Progress

Healthcare organizations face several challenges in strengthening their healthcare cybersecurity programs. The following are common examples:

- Budgetary constraints are frequently cited as a reason for cybersecurity deficiencies.[1] However, the underlying issue is often the absence of prioritization of cybersecurity as a business issue rather than the availability of funding. Leadership should recognize that cybersecurity is not a discretionary spend but a critical investment in organizational continuity and patient trust. Underinvestment today may result in significant costs tomorrow, including unexpected system downtime, fines, and reputational harm.
- Many healthcare systems operate with a patchwork of outdated technologies that lack modern security controls. Legacy medical equipment, in particular, was not designed with cybersecurity in mind and is often incompatible with modern security patches or monitoring

DOI: 10.4324/9781003366560-11

tools. These devices represent a significant risk, particularly when connected to broader hospital networks.[2]

- Maintaining an inventory of assets that include systems, devices, applications, and data remains a significant challenge for healthcare organizations.[3]

11.3 Shifting Culture, Governance, and Economics

Healthcare organizations should cultivate a culture where cybersecurity is seen as a shared responsibility. Cybersecurity should be embedded into daily operations, not treated as an obstacle to care delivery. Leadership should actively support and advocate for security initiatives.

Governance structures should provide defined roles, responsibilities, and accountability. Cybersecurity goals should be aligned with broader enterprise risk objectives. Boards of directors and senior executives should be regularly briefed on the cybersecurity program. The NIST Cybersecurity Framework provides the CSF Tiers and Organizational Profiles (as well as Community profiles) to help organizations assess maturity and establish clear objectives.

The economics of cybersecurity improve when an organization recognizes at the enterprise level that cybersecurity is a core business priority. As healthcare operations, administrative functions, and clinical care become more dependent on digital systems, investing in safety, security, and reliability is reasonable and necessary.

11.4 AI: Capabilities and Risks

AI enhances cybersecurity through behavioral analytics, predictive threat intelligence, and automated incident response. AI systems can continuously monitor user activity, network traffic, and system processes, to detect deviations that may signal emerging threats. By learning from historical data, these systems can anticipate potential attack vectors before they are exploited.

AI-driven intrusion detection and prevention systems can isolate compromised assets, block malicious traffic, and initiate containment procedures without waiting for human intervention. This accelerates response time and limits harm. In healthcare environments, where medical devices are increasingly interconnected, AI supports network segmentation and device monitoring to prevent lateral movement of threats.

At the same time, AI introduces new risks. Adversaries use AI to craft highly convincing phishing lures designed to bypass traditional defenses. AI-generated deepfakes can impersonate clinicians or executives to authorize fraudulent transactions or manipulate patients and staff. AI-enabled malware can alter its observable activity in real time.

Healthcare organizations should address these risks by training individuals to recognize indicators of AI-enabled social engineering, including unusually persuasive communications, unexpected voice or video messages, or requests that appear urgent but do not align with established protocols.

11.5 Quantum Ready

Patient records, medical device communications, and system configurations protected by encryption may be at risk from future quantum-enabled decryption attacks. Certain widely deployed public-key cryptographic algorithms, such as Rivest–Shamir–Adleman (RSA) and Elliptic Curve Cryptography (ECC), may be vulnerable to future quantum attacks.

Preparation begins with evaluating quantum-resistant encryption algorithms. NIST has released its first post-quantum cryptographic standards, designed to replace vulnerable methods in the years ahead. NIST. *NIST Releases First 3 Finalized Post-Quantum Encryption Standards.* https://www.nist.gov/news-events/news/2024/08/nist-releases-first-3-finalized-post-quantum-encryption-standards. See also NIST. *Quantum Information Science.* https://www.nist.gov/quantum-information-science.

Healthcare organizations should inventory cryptographic assets, analyze dependencies on algorithms that could be broken by large-scale quantum computers (including widely used public key algorithms such as Rivest–Shamir–Adleman (RSA) and Elliptic Curve Cryptography (ECC)), and initiate migration planning as part of a broader post-quantum transition strategy.

Healthcare entities should assess their quantum readiness now to ensure the confidentiality, integrity, and availability of sensitive health data in a post-quantum era. This includes discussions and planning with vendors and other suppliers to ensure that they are also prepared for a quantum transition.

11.6 Mobile Device Security

Clinicians rely on mobile devices to access EHRs, communicate with care teams, review lab results, and manage schedules. Whether owned by the organization or individual employees, mobile devices may introduce cybersecurity and compliance risks if not properly secured.

Mobile devices can be lost or stolen, connect over public or unsecured networks, and run unauthorized third-party applications (often referred to as shadow IT or shadow AI). Bring Your Own Device (BYOD) arrangements add further complexity because personal devices often store both personal and work data, which creates blurred lines around ownership, monitoring, and control.

Clear, enforceable mobile device security policies are essential. Individuals should read and understand these policies, participate in training, and seek clarification when needed.

Company-Owned Devices: Organization-issued devices offer the greatest security and control. The organization retains ownership and can centrally enforce settings such as encryption, remote wipe, mobile device management (MDM), app restrictions, and usage monitoring. This standardization improves security, supports compliance, and reduces the attack surface.

BYOD Devices: BYOD introduces a higher risk. While convenient, these devices may not necessarily meet organizational security standards. A formal BYOD policy is required to govern their use, supported by legal review to ensure compliance with applicable regulations.

Mobile devices pose a risk in either scenario. Unauthorized access to a lost or stolen device containing PHI can result in a reportable breach. Training is critical to ensure individuals know what is permitted, what is required, and what is prohibited.

11.7 Cloud Computing

Cloud computing offers the scalability, accessibility, and flexibility required by modern healthcare systems. When properly configured, cloud computing enables secure data sharing across organizations, supports telehealth delivery, and facilitates real-time clinical decision-making. Cloud-based backups support disaster recovery and business continuity, but they must be verified and tested to ensure that data can be restored reliably during an actual incident.

The benefits of cloud computing, however, are accompanied by significant risks. Data breaches due to misconfigured storage, weak or inconsistent access controls, and insufficient vendor oversight are common.

Cloud accessibility also amplifies insider threats, whether caused by negligence or malicious intent. Misconfigured permissions, insecure APIs, and inadequate monitoring increase the likelihood of exposure. In addition, the growing use of third-party services and integrations expands the attack surface.

Not all cloud service providers are the same. Organizations should conduct appropriate due diligence on prospective providers, evaluating business, technical, and legal considerations. If contractors or subcontractors are involved, their roles, responsibilities, and compliance obligations must also be assessed to ensure that all parties meet the required security and regulatory standards.

Tabletop exercises focused on cloud-specific threats, such as data exfiltration, service outages, or vendor compromise, should be conducted regularly. These exercises test readiness, clarify roles under the shared responsibility model, and help identify areas for improvement before an incident occurs.[4]

To stay secure, healthcare organizations should ensure that only authorized individuals can access data, that data is encrypted, and that cloud service providers meet applicable requirements under regulations, laws, and contracts. Cloud security is generally a shared responsibility: the provider secures the infrastructure, while the healthcare organization protects its own data, applications, and user access. (Specific responsibilities and requirements may be negotiated between the provider and the organization.) Best practices for cloud security include those published by the Cloud Security Alliance (CSA). In addition, the Cybersecurity and Infrastructure Security Agency (CISA) and the National Security Agency (NSA) have issued cloud security best practice sheets that provide further guidance.[5]

11.8 Summary—A Vision for the Future

Robust healthcare cybersecurity needs a strong foundation of governance, culture, and collaboration. Frameworks such as NIST CSF 2.0 and future successor frameworks offer structured and scalable approaches to risk management. When cybersecurity is integrated into into clinical operations and enterprise governance, healthcare organizations can shift from reactive defense to proactive resilience, ensuring both patient safety and organizational continuity.

AI and quantum computing are transformative technologies that bring both significant risks and new opportunities. Preparing now for their impact, including the transition to post-quantum cryptography and the responsible use of AI, will position healthcare organizations to navigate the threats of tomorrow with greater confidence.

At its core, cybersecurity is about trust. Patients, clinicians, and stakeholders should be able to trust that systems will function reliably; that sensitive data will remain protected; and that leadership will anticipate and address evolving threats. Through continuous investment, strategic alignment, and cultural transformation, healthcare organizations can preserve that trust while advancing the state of healthcare cybersecurity across the sector.

Notes

1 Klas Research. *US Healthcare Cyber Resilience Survey: Why Elevating Cybersecurity to A Strategic Priority Can Drive Transformation.* https://klasresearch.com/report/us-healthcare-cyber-resilience-survey-why-elevating-cybersecurity-to-a-strategic-priority-can-drive-transformation/3941.

2 HIPAA Journal. *House Committee Hears New Concerns About Legacy Medical Device Cybersecurity.* https://www.hipaajournal.com/house-committee-concerns-legacy-medical-device-cybersecurity/.

3 Blumira. *Navigating Healthcare Security Challenges: Essential Enablers.* https://www.blumira.com/blog/healthcare-security.

4 Informative resources on cloud security include those by Cloud Security Alliance. https://cloudsecurityalliance.org/.

5 CISA. *CISA and NSA Release Cybersecurity Information Sheets on Cloud Security Best Practices.* https://www.cisa.gov/news-events/alerts/2024/03/07/cisa-and-nsa-release-cybersecurity-information-sheets-cloud-security-best-practices.

Index

Note: Page numbers in *italics* indicate a figure and page numbers in **bold** indicate a table on the corresponding page.

J

K

L

M

T

U

V

W

Z